Richard Marsh

The Great Temptation

e-artnow 2020

Richard Marsh
The Great Temptation

Crime & Mystery Thriller

e-artnow, 2020
Contact: info@e-artnow.org

ISBN 978-80-273-0510-0

Contents

BOOK I	13
CHAPTER I THE PONY-SKIN COAT	13
CHAPTER II IMPRISONED	19
CHAPTER III CRASH! CAME THE KNOCKER	21
CHAPTER IV UNDERSTANDING	25
CHAPTER V THE PILL	27
CHAPTER VI TO NEW YORK FOR £500	33
CHAPTER VII AT THE RISK OF HIS LIFE	36
CHAPTER VIII GROVE GARDENS	39
CHAPTER IX CATHERINE	41
CHAPTER X THE OWNER OF THE COAT	45
CHAPTER XI CATHERINE'S IDEA	50
CHAPTER XII TWENTY-TWO	54
BOOK II	59
CHAPTER XIII THE FIRST STAGE OF THE JOURNEY	59
CHAPTER XIV ABEDNEGO P. THOMPSON	61
CHAPTER XV HUGH'S NOTE	68
CHAPTER XVI A MEMORY OF MOSCOW	72
CHAPTER XVII MR. TROUNCER'S STORY	76
CHAPTER XVIII CATHERINE'S TROUBLE	81
CHAPTER XIX CHANGED	85
CHAPTER XX AN UNSOLICITED INTRODUCTION	89
CHAPTER XXI TWENTY-FIVE THOUSAND DOLLARS	94
CHAPTER XXII THE FIRST NIGHT	99
CHAPTER XXIII "DEVIL OF A WOMAN!"	101
CHAPTER XXIV ALMOST WITHIN SIGHT OF LAND	103
BOOK III	107
CHAPTER XXV THE PATIENT	107
CHAPTER XXVI TWO FRIENDS	110
CHAPTER XXVII CALLERS	115
CHAPTER XXVIII NURSE ADA	120
CHAPTER XXIX PARKER VAN GROOT	123
CHAPTER XXX AN UNEXPECTED VISITOR	128
CHAPTER XXXI EXERCISING PRESSURE	133
CHAPTER XXXII MR. BENNINGTON'S OPINION	137
CHAPTER XXXIII POSTE RESTANTE	140
CHAPTER XXXIV HUGH'S PORTRAIT	142
CHAPTER XXXV THE GREAT TEMPTATION	146

CHAPTER XXXVI PRINCESS KITTY	152
CHAPTER XXXVII MRS. VAN GROOT DISCLAIMS RESPONSIBILITY	155
CHAPTER XXXVIII HIS FIRST APPEARANCE	157
CHAPTER XXXIX "THE JOYOUS BRIDE"	163
CHAPTER XL THE MOST EXPENSIVE HAT IN THE WORLD	166
CHAPTER XLI THE "MAISON CATHERINE"	170

BOOK I

THE PONY-SKIN COAT

CHAPTER I
THE PONY-SKIN COAT

It came smash on to my hat, slipped off the brim on to my shoulder, then fell to the pavement. I did not know what had happened. I took off my black felt hat and looked at it. There was a great dent in the crown; if it had not been for my hat something would have happened to my head. And my shoulder hurt. Then I looked at the pavement. At my feet was what seemed to be some sort of canvas bag. I picked it up. It was made of coarse brown canvas, perhaps five inches square, and was stuffed full of what felt to be some sort of metal. It was heavy, weighing perhaps a pound. No wonder it had dented my hat made my shoulder smart. Where could the thing have come from?

As I was wondering I became conscious that a man was moving towards me from the other side of the road moving rapidly. I had been vaguely aware as I came striding along that there was someone on the other side of the road. Now he was positively rushing at me was within a foot before I realised that he was making for me. He said something in some guttural foreign tongue I supposed it to be a foreign tongue, although, so far as I knew, I had never heard it spoken before and made a grab at the bag which had struck me. I put it behind my back in my left hand; my right I placed against his chest and pushed.

"What are you up to?" I inquired.

The inquiry was foolish; it was pretty plain what he was up to he was after that bag. The effect on him was curious. He was so slight and apparently weak that though I had used scarcely any force at all he staggered backwards across the pavement into the road. When I looked at him he raised his arms above his head as if to ward off a blow. He struck me as a man who might be recovering from a severe illness. His hairless face was white and drawn, thin to the verge of emaciation. He wore an old, soft black felt hat which was certainly not English. The whole man was un-English his oddly shaped, long, black frock-coat, so old and shabby that, so to speak, only the threads of the original material seemed to be left; the ancient trousers, so tight and narrow that only thin legs could have got into them; the unblacked, elastic-sided boots everything about him suggested something with which I was unfamiliar.

If he startled me, I seemed to terrify him. When, as it seemed, he realised what kind of man I was to look at no one can say there is anything alarming in my appearance he swung round and tore off down the street as if flying for his life. I stared after him.

"You're a curiosity," I told myself. "What's the meaning of this, I wonder."

I looked at the brown canvas bag, then had another look at my hat. It was badly dented. Whoever was responsible for the damage would have to buy me a new one. I could not walk about with my hat in that condition; at that moment I could not afford to spend money on a substitute. Who was responsible for the damage? I looked about me at the house I was passing up at the windows. I was just in time to catch a glimpse of a head protruding from a window on the top floor. It was only a glimpse I caught; it was withdrawn the moment I looked up. An impression was left upon my mind of a beard and long black hair. No doubt the owner of the head was looking to see what had happened to the canvas bag which he had dropped from the window. A nice, careless sort of person he was, not to take the trouble, in the first instance, to find out who or what was beneath. That wretched bag of his might have killed me. Then, after seeing what had happened, instead of expressing contrition, to snatch back his head as if he wished me to suppose that he had seen nothing! I called out to him:

13

"Hi! You up there!"

He took not the slightest notice of my call, but I felt sure he had heard. I did not want his canvas bag; I did want a new hat so I knocked at the door of the house. That door had been originally stained to imitate oak, but the stain had peeled off in patches, so that you could see the deal beneath. The instant I touched it with the knocker the door flew open; it opened so rapidly that it is no exaggeration to say that it flew. The moment it opened someone came through the door, took me by the shoulders, drew me into the house unexpectedly, before I could offer the least resistance and shut the door with a bang. So soon as the door was banged the same person continued to grip my shoulders with what seemed to me to be actual ferocity, hauled me along a narrow, darkened passage into a room which was at the end. To say that I was taken by surprise would be inadequately to describe my feelings. I was amazed, astounded, confused, bewildered. Some person or persons I was aware that in that darkened passage there were more persons than one had been guilty of an outrage. A liberty had been taken with me which was without the slightest justification.

"What on earth," I demanded, as soon as I was in the room and had regained a little of my breath, "is the meaning of this? Who are you, sir, that you should handle me as though I were a carcase of beef?"

I put my question to a huge man, well over six feet, broader than he was tall, with a big head and dark, square-jowled face. He had dark hair, which was longer than we wear it in England, and a long frock-coat, fashioned somewhat like that worn by the man on the other side of the road, only not so shabby. Altogether he gave me the idea that he was a giant, in stature and in strength.

It seemed that my words had affected him in a way I had not intended; he glowered at me in a manner to which I objected on every possible ground. Stretching out his immense arm he again grabbed my shoulder with the immense hand at the end of it, and without speaking a word drew me towards him as if I were a puppet which he could handle as he liked. It was no use my attempting to offer resistance. Shaken, disconcerted, confused, I really was like a puppet in his grip. He caused me actual pain. I have a notion that, without intending it, I called out "Don't! you hurt!" Whereupon he hurt me more than before, as if he understood, though, judging by what followed, I doubt if he did. With his face within a foot of mine, he glared; I have seldom felt more uncomfortable.

I was aware that the others were glaring also; there were five other men in the room. My words seemed to have affected them all. They were all glaring; more unprepossessing-looking men I do not remember to have seen.

Close by me on my right was a little man, so short as to be almost a dwarf. Behind him was a big, fat, fair fellow, with an untidy fair beard which seemed to be growing all over his face. Then there was a dark, thin man; something had happened to his nose it was not only broken, it looked as if it had been cut right in two, a long time ago, and never properly joined. Then there was a man who might have been an Englishman; he was well-dressed, properly barbered, red-faced. English or not, there was something sensual about the man which I instinctively disliked. At sight of him I had a ridiculous feeling that he was of the sort of stuff of which murderers are made.

From the spectacular point of view, the fifth man was the most remarkable of the lot. He seemed to be crooked, as if something had twisted his body so that he could not hold himself straight. He had a very long, thin face, with small, reddish-looking eyes which matched his reddish hair. His mouth was a little open, as if he found it difficult to keep it closed; he had a trick of putting the first finger of his right hand between his yellow teeth and gnawing at the tip. Not one of the men in that room was good to look at; but he, I think, was the worst of them all. If these were not undesirable aliens, then their appearance belied them. I wondered what foreign land had been relieved of their presence.

The room itself was not a pleasant one. It was not clean; I doubt if it had known any sort of cleansing process for goodness knows how long. The ceiling was black, the walls grimy, the floor suggestive of undesirable things, the one window obscured by dust and dirt. There was scarcely any furniture an old deal table which looked as if it had had pieces cut out of it, five or six wooden chairs of various patterns, a rickety couch covered with horse-hair, with flock coming out of a hole in the middle, a little painted cupboard in a corner, with glasses, bottles, and plates on the top, no carpet to hide the filthy boards. The most prominent object in the room was what looked to me like a pile of clothing which was heaped on the couch. A less attractive apartment one could scarcely imagine.

The company matched the room. It struck me that that was the kind of apartment to which they had been accustomed all their lives; they seemed so ill-clothed, unkempt, badly washed. Even the man who looked like an Englishman I felt sure was not fond of soap and water. They stared at me with such unfriendly eyes, as if each in his heart would like to murder me. What I had done to cause them annoyance I could not imagine, yet it was sufficiently obvious that they were seriously angry with me about something.

They were silent for some moments, then broke into a babel of speech. The huge man spoke first. They did not wait for him to finish whatever it was he wished to say; directly he opened his mouth they all began to talk together. I know French when I hear it, I know German, and Dutch; I believe, also, that I know the sound of Spanish and Italian. What language they were talking I had not the faintest notion. I had never heard such sounds before; they seemed to me like guttural grunts. They gesticulated, shaking their fists, extending their hands towards me in a way I did not like at all. They seemed to be quarrelling expressing opinions about me which it was perhaps as well I did not understand.

Then, when I was wondering what the talk was all about, the huge man suddenly put out his arm and snatched the canvas bag, which I was still holding, from my hand. When he held it up in the air they simply yelled. In an instant, to my discomfort, each man had a weapon in his hand. The little man near me, and the red-headed man, had each a long, thin knife dreadful-looking weapons. The others had revolvers. They made a general move in my direction; I really thought for a moment that they were going to kill me in cold blood for some offence of which I had not been guilty, but the huge man extended his great left arm, holding it rigid as if it were a bar of iron, and held them back. Then the talk began again. I am aware that when people talk in a language of which you know nothing it often sounds as if they were quarrelling when they are doing nothing of the kind. About the anger of those five men there could be no shadow of doubt. I half expected to see them vent it on each other if they could not get at me. There were, for me, some moments of uncomfortable tension.

Then the decently dressed man said something which induced the giant to hand him over the canvas bag. They all gathered round to look at it, poking at it with their unpleasant fingers. Presently there was an interval of comparative silence; then the decently dressed man said to me, addressing me in English:

"Who are you?"

"I am an inoffensive stranger," I told him.

"What is your name?"

"Hugh Beckwith." I felt it the part of wisdom to answer his questions as briefly and clearly as I could.

"What are you doing with this?" He held out the bag.

Then I did become a little voluble.

"Someone dropped it out of the window of a room upstairs. It fell on my head and smashed my hat just look at that!" I held out the hat for him to look at. "If it hadn't been for my hat it might have killed me. I knocked at the door first of all to return the bag, which is no property of mine, and then to point out that whoever dropped it from the window must buy me a new hat."

The red-faced man looked at me for some seconds, as if he were trying to make up his mind how much of what I said was true. Then he said something in that guttural tongue. In an instant they rained on him what I had no doubt was a torrent of questions. He explained, telling them, probably, what it was I had said. They regarded me with suspicious eyes, as if they did not believe a word of it. Then the red-faced man returned to English.

"What are you?"

"I am a clerk."

"What kind of a clerk?"

"I am a clerk in a dried-fruit firm at least I was until a couple of hours ago. This morning they dismissed me."

"Dismissed you why? What had you been doing?"

"Nothing absolutely nothing! One of the partners was in a bad temper, and let it loose on me. Because I asked him what I had done he paid me a week's wages and told me to leave at once. The injustice of it made me so mad that I have been walking about the streets ever since. Now this happens! What I have done to you to cause you to behave to me like this is beyond me altogether."

"You are very talkative, full of explanations plausible. I wonder if, by any chance, you are connected with the police an artist in your own line. You are playing the part very well if you are."

I stared at him. "I'm no more connected with the police than you are."

"Than I am!" He laughed, oddly. "That's an unfortunate remark. I have been connected with the police a good deal in my time, as it is possible you know."

"I know nothing of the sort! I know nothing about you of any kind. Who are you?"

He spoke with marked deliberation, a pause between each word.

"I am who I am; we all of us are who we are. If you are trying to trick us we'll tear your tongue out by the roots. In spite of what you say you probably know that we should make nothing of a little jest like that."

"I declare to you I don't know why you doubt me I have no thought of trickery. If you will come with me to where I live I will prove that what I said is true."

"No, thank you; I would rather not come with you to where you live. We would rather keep you here."

There was an ominous something in the tone in which he said this which grated on my nerves. The huge man said something, as if he were impatient at being kept in ignorance of what it was that we were saying. The red-faced man replied to him. The clamour was renewed. So angry were their voices, so excited their gestures, that I felt as if every moment I was going in peril of my life. Then the red-faced man asked another question.

"What proof can you give us here that what you say is true? We should like to search your pockets."

They did not wait for my permission; before I could speak the big man took me in some deft way by the scruff of the neck and literally tore my coat off my back. Before I could even expostulate he had turned the pockets inside out. There were two letters in the inside pocket in their original envelopes, my name and address on each. As if he could not make much of them, he passed them to the red-faced man. In the right-hand outside pocket there were a pipe and tobacco and a box of matches, which he threw upon the table. In the left-hand pocket was my handkerchief, which he stretched out and examined. My name was on it in ink "H. Beckwith." There was nothing else in the pockets of my coat; having satisfied himself on that point, he dropped it on to the table.

I supposed that they had taken liberties enough with my attire; there was proof on the envelopes and in the letters they contained that I was who I claimed to be, which must have been plain to the red-faced man. But I was mistaken in imagining that they had subjected me to enough indignity. Before I had even guessed his intention, the huge fellow had even stripped me of my waistcoat, amid what were clearly the jeers of his companions. They regarded the way in which I was being treated as a joke. The big man turned out my waistcoat pockets my watch and chain, pen-knife, pencil-case, the little bone instrument with which I manicured my finger nails. The others snatched up each of the articles as he put it down. I saw that the red-headed man had taken off his filthy coat and was trying on my jacket. I did remonstrate then.

"It is no use, I suppose," I said to the English-speaking person, "to point out that you are treating me in a way for which you have no excuse; at least, you have in your hands proof of the truth of what I said; and, anyhow, I shall be obliged if you would ask your friend behind you not to put himself into my jacket."

I believe that until I called his attention to the fact he did not notice what the other was doing; then, glancing round, he said something to him in his guttural lingo. The fellow answered. What he said I had no notion; it was clearly something which those who understood found amusing. The little fellow by me shrieked with laughter, as if in the enjoyment of some tremendous joke. The fat, fair fellow pressed his hands to his sides as if he feared he might be tickled to the bursting-point. The red-haired man stood as straight as his twisted body permitted, stretching out his arms, as if asking the others to observe the fit of my jacket on his crooked form. As they all shouted and laughed he put his hand on the English-speaking person's shoulder and said something to him in a peremptory insistent tone, as if he were issuing an order. When the other seemed reluctant to do as he was told to do, they pressed round him, repeating, so I took it, in a sort of chorus, what the red-haired man had said. As if he found them difficult to resist, he said something to the giant. In an instant the monster, putting his arms about my neck, began to unbutton my braces. It was useless for me to resist; his strength was so much more than mine that I was helpless. To render me more helpless still the others gave him their assistance. They tore my trousers off, my boots, my shirt they stripped me to the skin, hooting with laughter all the while.

The red-haired man, who had been disrobing while they stripped me, put on my garments as they tore them off. Presently he was arrayed from head to foot in my clothes: I am bound to say he presented a much more pleasant appearance than in his own. They fitted him better than might have been expected. I was about his height, and slim they might almost have been made for him. He was enraptured, gesticulating, exclaiming, capering. I was afraid that they would suggest that I should don his filthy rags in place of my own. I should not have been able to resist if they had. But all at once the little fellow gave a sort of screech, pointing to the couch. What he was after I could not guess but they knew. The fat man caught up what seemed to be the heap which I had noticed.

It resolved itself into garments. An old fur coat of a fashion which I had never seen before: baggy breeches, enormous boots, a tall, round, brimless something, covered with some mangy black skin, which I took to be a hat. Left on the couch, when the garments had been removed, was a large piece of coarse brown paper, on which were half a dozen labels, which I took to be the wrapper in which the garments had come to the house.

The fat man held up the garments one after the other, displaying them to the best advantage; they shouted at the sight of each. When they had seen them all they yelled in chorus. The red-faced man said to me:

"You cannot go about naked; as a respectable clerk it is impossible. Here are two suits you can have your choice. Will you have the one which our friend is willing to offer you in exchange for your own, or will you have the other? This is the uniform of a drosky driver of St. Petersburg. The drosky is the Russian cab; the drosky driver is a splendid fellow; he is perhaps a little given to drink, but still a splendid fellow. This uniform, which has come to us this morning God knows from whom or why it has been sent is not so gay as some of them, and is perhaps a little worn. Now, quick; which do you choose this or the other?"

He professed to give me my choice, but I did not have it really. The huge man, assisted by his friends, put me in that drosky driver's uniform. There were no braces for the breeches; they fastened them on to me with a strap, drawing it so tight that I could scarcely breathe. The top boots came above my knees; they were so large that I could have kicked them off. In the coat, made, I fancy, of some sort of pony skin, there was room enough for another as well as for me. The coarse hair with which it was covered had come off it in a dozen places; it must have been very many years old. An unpleasant odour from it assailed my nostrils. As if to crown the insults which they were piling on me, they placed upon my head the tall, black, brimless thing which I had rightly supposed to be a hat. Like the other things it was much too large for me. The monster corrected that defect by clapping it with his huge palm upon the top with such force that he drove it down right over my eyes. I raised my hands to free myself I could see nothing. While I was still struggling my head had got fixed in the thing I heard the door open and the sound of a woman's voice. NEW PAGE

CHAPTER II
IMPRISONED

When I had got my head sufficiently out of the ridiculous, heavy structure they had given me to serve as a hat the room was in confusion; I mean in even greater confusion than it had been. The six men were grouped about a girl, their eyes fixed on her. I felt that she regarded them as if they were so much dirt. She was a dainty example of her sex short, slender, well set up, carrying her head in a fashion which suggested that she looked upon the world with scorn. She was quite young; I doubt if she was more than twenty. She had an abundance of fair hair, which she wore gathered in a knot and parted on one side. Her attire was simple and in exquisite taste, and, I had a notion, cost money. She looked as if she had just stepped out of a drawing-room, wearing neither hat nor jacket. That there was a decent apartment, suitable for a lady's use, in that house, I could not imagine. In her elegant simplicity she looked singularly out of place in that company, in that unclean room. I had a notion that she might be thinking the same of me. Her big oval eyes were fixed upon my form as if she were wondering what I was doing there. She was addressing the others in the dissonant, guttural tongue, in which she seemed to be as much at home as they were somehow, coming from her lips, it sounded a little more musical. Obviously she was asking questions about who I was and how I came to be there. When she had obtained their answers she seemed suddenly to become possessed with excitement, which she seemed to impart to them. They glared at me in the unpromising fashion they had done at first. Certainly something like murder was in their eyes. Surely this slip of a girl could not be inciting them to commit further acts of violence. I appealed to her, taking advantage of a pause in her speech.

"You speak English?" She answered neither yes nor no; but just stood with her head thrown back and looked at me. I felt sure she understood that she did speak English. "I appeal to you," I went on, "for protection. I have done nothing to incur the resentment of your" I hesitated, changing from one form of words to another "of these gentlemen. I merely knocked at the door to return something which had fallen on to my head from a window above. The instant I knocked they assailed me, dragged me in here, subjected me to all sorts of indignities, and now they have deprived me of my clothing and forced me to wear these disgusting things. I beg you to explain to them that I am an innocent and peaceable stranger, and that I desire to quarrel with no one. All I want them to do is to give me back my own clothes and let me go."

"All you want them to do is to give you back your own clothes and let you go."

The echo came from the red-faced man, who, leaning upon the table, kept his eyes fixed on my face. There was an ominous something about everything he said. Perhaps it was my imagination to me his simplest words seemed to convey a threat. I hated the man! English though he might be, I feared and disliked him more than any of the others. What seemed to be his sneering echo of my remark, whether she understood it or not, seemed to have upon the girl anything but a pacific effect. She said something in short, quick tones which seemed to move the men to anger. They moved towards me with in their hands the weapons which had appeared before. The short man had a knife whose blade, I should think, was sixteen or eighteen inches long an evil-looking thing. He raised it as if to strike at me. I thought he would strike. Such a blade would go right through me, spitting me like a lark on a skewer. I did not propose to let him do that if I could help it. I stepped back, picked up an old wooden chair, swung it over my shoulders, and brought it down upon that small gentleman. It was the only weapon of defence I could find. The tumult which ensued! I doubt if I did the little scoundrel with his horrible knife much harm he moved aside so swiftly that the side of the chair but grazed his shoulder. Judging by the behaviour of his friends and companions one might have thought that I had killed him, without the slightest provocation. They rushed at me with uplifted knives and pointed revolvers. The girl shouted half-a-dozen words which undoubtedly conveyed a command. Knives and revolvers were lowered in an instant. I still held the chair, prepared to defend myself with it somehow. Before I guessed his intention, the huge man wrenched it away, gripping my wrists in his two great hands. In spite of me he drew them behind my back and held them there. The fat fellow with a beard produced from somewhere what looked to me like a piece of clothes-line. While the monster squeezed my elbows so cruelly with his iron fingers all the sense seemed to go out of my arms with the clothesline his colleague tied my wrists together, so that I stood before them with my hands pinioned behind my back. It was nothing short of a cowardly outrage. I started to tell them so. I did not fear them; I began with the most perfect frankness to let them know it; but I had not uttered a dozen syllables before again the girl said something. The big man clapped his filthy hand across my mouth. The little man left the room, returning almost instantly with what looked to me like a dirty duster. He tore a strip off one side. Although I shouted and raved and did my best to stop them they forced the foul rag into my mouth and kept it in its place by passing the strip of material across the gag and tying it at the back of my head.

Just as the knot was tied the door was opened and still another man came in an elderly man with a long black beard, and coarse black hair, which he wore in greasy ringlets. I had a feeling that his was the head of which I had caught a glimpse as it was being drawn back through the window of the upper room that probably he was the man who had dropped the canvas bag. The instant he entered he broke into what seemed to me to be noisy ejaculations. I had not a notion what he was talking about, but whatever it was its utterance seemed to fill his listeners with what looked very like panic fear. I thought that they were going to make a general stampede, but the girl stopped them. Acting, as I took it, upon her instructions, the big man and the fat man seized me on either side and ran me from the room, almost pitching me down a narrow, rickety flight of stairs, and pushed me through a door into pitch black darkness. I heard the door locked and bolted on the other side, and knew that in the very heart of London, for no reason at all that I could understand, I was a prisoner indeed. NEW PAGE

CHAPTER III
CRASH! CAME THE KNOCKER

I do not know how long it was before I realised, even in the faintest degree, what had happened; they had thrust me through the door with such unnecessary violence that, stumbling over some unseen obstacle, I had fallen flat on my face. The fall shook me. It was some moments before I was sufficiently recovered to endeavour to raise myself from where I had fallen. Then, gagged and pinioned as I was, I got on to my feet. Let a person unaccustomed to such exercises lie flat on his stomach and raise himself without the use of his hands; it will quickly be found that the thing is not to be done in an instant. I first of all rolled over on my back doing that with difficulty; then, after a series of jerks, I raised myself to a sitting posture; then, with a lop-sided, crab-like motion, on to my knees: finally, somehow, I gained my feet.

When I had done that I was no better off. My turnings and twistings had taught me not only that the ground was uneven, but also that there were objects on it of all sorts and shapes and sizes, which, in the darkness, it was not easy to avoid. For instance, I sat upon what I believed to be a broken bottle; possibly only the thickness of the skin coat I was wearing prevented its doing me an injury. I had no wish to stumble over something which I could not see, and possibly fall on something worse than a broken bottle.

My sensations during the first few minutes which I passed in that gloomy place I am not able to describe. I think what I felt chiefly was anger; I was half beside myself with rage. My inclination was to seek for something anything which would explain what had occurred. Who were the people who occupied the house? What had I done, or what did they imagine I had done, which had caused them to subject me to such treatment? That they were afraid of something was obvious but what? I realised before I had been in that filthy room a couple of minutes that they were all in what struck me as a state of almost panic terror. Their nerves were all on end: they were suffering from what, when I was a youngster, we used to call the "jumps." They were afraid of everything.

Who did they suppose had knocked at the door? They were afraid of him, whoever it was; but they feared still more when they saw it was not the person they expected. In their terror they would have murdered me. The English-speaking ruffian's inquiry as to whether I was connected with the police suggested a possible explanation. Probably the occupants of the house were criminals, hiding from justice, in continual alarm that vengeance was upon them. Of what crime had they been guilty? They were not Englishmen. Since I was wearing the costume of the St. Petersburg equivalent to our cab-drivers, possibly they were Russian.

I had no personal knowledge of Russia or the Russians, but I had read things which caused me to feel that in that part of the world people were constantly guilty of all sorts of crimes of violence. Those men had been guilty of some dreadful deed in their own country; to avoid the consequences they had fled for their lives; so conscious were they that the pursuit was probably still hot-foot after them that every trivial event put them in a tremor of fear that the avenger of blood was upon them.

Lately ill-luck seemed to have dogged my footsteps. That morning, at a moment's notice, I had lost a situation which I had held for nearly four years, I vow and protest for no fault of my own. Messrs. Hunter & Barnett, of Commercial Buildings, Southwark, had presented me with the key of the street for no other reason than that the junior partner had probably had a row with his wife I believe he was always having them and wanted to get even with someone. So he fired me. Hunter was away; possibly when he returned he would ask Barnett a question or two. But he would not return for two or three weeks, and meanwhile what redress had I? There had been talk of my marrying Catherine in three or four months. It looked like it! situations are easier to lose than find. On the top of that trouble had come this! I had been robbed of my clothes, put into filthy garments which had once adorned a cab-driver; and now, gagged and pinioned, I was locked up in some sort of cellar in which the darkness was Egyptian. Heaven only knew how long I should be kept there. And it had all come upon me because I had had the ill-luck to be passing along the pavement in an unknown street at a moment when someone had chanced to be dropping something from a window which had fallen upon my hat and broken it, and I had knocked at the door of the house to return the something to its proper owner.

In other words, I had done nothing to deserve the plight which I was in. Had I had the dimmest suspicion what the occupants of the house were like I would have walked miles and miles to avoid the street which it was in. What made me so mad was the consciousness that all those things had come upon me because, with the best intentions in the world, I had raised a knocker.

But while I raged I knew that anger would not mend the situation. What I wanted was a cool head and a clear one; presence of mind; to make the best use of such wits as I had. Frenzy was no use I was not going to get through the door that way.

When I had realised that much I began to grow calmer. After what seemed to me to be a long interval of waiting I moved gingerly in the direction in which I believed the door was to be brought up suddenly by a wall; whether it was of brick or stone I could not tell. When I fell I lost all sense of direction before I gained my feet; I groped my way along that wall for quite a distance before I came upon the door. It was not at all where I had supposed it to be.

When I had satisfied myself that it was the door I stood still and listened. I could hear nothing; possibly sounds from above did not penetrate to that underground pit. Although I strained my ears to listen not a sound came to me.

What was I do? Every sense I had revolted at the idea that I should do nothing; that I should just stay there, helpless as a trussed fowl, waiting for someone to come and let me out. No one might ever come; at least until too late for their coming to be of use to me. At that moment the house might be empty; those guilty wretches might have fled for their lives. The bearded man had brought them agitating news of some sort. Conceivably he had come to tell them that the officers of the law were on their track; in which case, unless I misjudged them, they certainly would not stand upon the order of their going. With all possible haste they might have rushed from the place, never to return. In that case what would become of me? With that disgusting rag in my mouth, which felt each second as if it would choke me, I could not utter a sound. Suppose someone did come to the house the police, for instance; I could not hear them. Possibly they might not discover the presence of a cellar at the foot of those mean, rotten stairs. What could I do?

I suppose I stayed in that condition of helpless inaction for five or six hours, wandering, to the best of my ability, all over the cellar. I could not be sure that I did not traverse the same piece of ground twice, but I did my best to learn with my feet what kind of place it was. I walked from wall to wall, counting my steps as I went by which I judged it to be about sixteen feet across in one direction and fifteen in the other. What it had been used for I could not make out possibly as some sort of lumber room. There seemed to be all sorts of queer things upon the floor whose nature I could not ascertain. I should have liked to be able to strike a match, and see what some of them were.

As time went on I became both hungry and tired. I had been a little late that morning; there had only been time for me to scamp my breakfast. I had had no dinner, which I always had at the Borough Restaurant as near as possible to one o'clock, and which was to me the meal of the day. I began to feel the want of it. It is odd how hungry one can get if one knows it is impossible to get anything to eat and thirsty.

I do not know how long I had been there when it first began to dawn upon me that my hands were not so tightly tied as they had been. I had become weary of standing, and found that leaning against the wall afforded a little rest. I was unwilling to sit down; one experience of the difficulty of rising from a sitting posture with my hands tied behind was enough. My hands and arms and wrists were growing more and more painful; they were in an unnatural position. If I could only loosen my wrists a little I might be eased. With this idea I gave my wrists a little tug, and found that they were looser than I had supposed; they had been tight enough when that fat man tied them the cord had cut into my skin and galled me terribly; but

I take it that unconsciously I had been continuously fidgeting, with the result that my bonds had gradually slackened.

I was startled to find how slack they actually were. By opening my left hand so as to make it as thin as possible I managed, after one or two tugs and twists, to withdraw it from the slackened noose and both hands were free. The relief it was I

The first use I made of my freedom was to relieve myself of the horrid rag which they had stuffed into my mouth. What a comfort it was to be able to open one's mouth wide, and to breathe as one chose. I was all at once a much better man than I had been. In my sudden exhilaration I jumped to the conclusion that now I could use my hands I could be through that door in less than no time. But I was wrong. I picked up all sorts of things from the floor bricks, bottles, and all sorts of odds and ends and brought them to bear against the door which shut me in.

It resisted them all. So far as I could judge I made no impression on it of any kind. It was a pretty solid piece of work I had learnt that already. Nothing I could get hold of availed to force it open.

The disappointment was acute; I had been so sure. When I recognised that I was beaten I just sank down on the ground and stopped there. I was no longer afraid of being unable to raise myself, but I was worn and weary, hungry and thirsty, uncomfortable in my ill-fitting attire, conscious of grime and dirt I would have given a good deal for a wash sick at heart. I had never pretended to be a hero; I felt singularly unheroic then. If I could only have been at home in my room, just about to sit down to supper, with the prospect of a comfortable bed to follow, what a happy man I should have been. How many men who work in the city clerking for forty or fifty shillings a week are prepared to face what I had gone through then? How many of them, after my experiences, would have been fit and cheerful? I admit that I was not; I was in a state of abject misery.

All at once what seemed to me to be the dreadful silence was broken by the barking of a dog. I sat up straighter and listened. Was the animal in the house? Had it just come in? With whom? It barked once, a short, sharp bark, and then no more. Silence again. Then after what appeared to me to be a prolonged interval, another bark; a single note, as it were, of exclamation. All through the night the dog kept barking. I arrived at the conclusion by degrees that the noise it made was proof that the house was empty. The inmates were gone; the dog, shut in one of the upstairs rooms, had been forgotten; possibly it had been asleep. Waking at last, it had possibly waited to be released, When no one came it expostulated, and continued, as I have said, to expostulate all through the night. Sometimes it would give a series of yaps spreading over a long period; then, as if tiring, it would cease and possibly snatch another snooze; after an interval it would begin again, now and then bursting into a series of explosive cries as if to show its anger at the way it was being neglected. Probably, too, it was hungry, and that was its way of calling attention to the fact.

I doubt if it was as hungry as I was; I feel sure it had more sleep.

I altered my position, sitting close to the wall, so that I had it to rest my back against. I will not say I did not close my eyes because I did, again and again, to shut out the darkness. But I did not sleep a wink. And when my eyes were closed the darkness became more visible; I fancied I could see things which I knew perfectly well were not there; yet I had to open them again to make sure. Then that dog would bark; I was conscious of what seemed to be the ridiculous desire to get within reach of him and to comfort him.

I know now that I was in that cellar for close on four-and-twenty hours. They thrust me in about noon on the one day; I was out of it about noon on the next. They were interminable hours. I should have suffered more than I did had it not been for a queer little thing. It is curious what a trifle can divert a man when, for want of occupation and all the comforts of life, he feels that he is going mad.

What happened to me was this. There were two big pockets in that drosky driver's coat, one on either side. I thrust my hands deep down in them for the sake of whatever solace they could afford. Fidgeting about with my fingers I gradually became aware that in the lining of the one on the right-hand side there seemed to be something of the nature of a pea, or a small round bullet. It might either have lost its way through a hole which I could not find, or been sewn in. It was, as I have said, a trifle, but it occupied me at intervals through that dreary night to try to work it loose to ascertain what the thing might be.

It was on one side of the pocket, in the seam. I actually searched for a piece of broken glass, or something of the kind, and had to grope about all over the floor to find it. There was a box of matches in the pocket of the coat of which they had deprived me If I had only had it then! The story of that night would have been altogether different and the story, I think I may say, of all that followed.

I found a piece of glass at last; with its sharpest edge I dug at the seam of the pocket. It was sharp enough to cut me I was conscious that the blood was flowing from a gash which it made on my finger; it was not sharp enough to cut that tough material. With my finger nails and the glass together I did loosen some of the stitches, enough of them to thrust a finger through the opening. But even then I could not reach the thing I was after. It seems absurd when one looks back, but I daresay I spent two or three of those dragging hours in trying to get at it without success. I could feel it on both sides of the material. The pocket was lined; the thing was sewn, or fastened somehow, between the lining and the stuff of which the pocket was made. I decided that after all it was nothing but a pea or a large round shot; yet I had an idea that when I pressed it hard it yielded which neither a pea nor a shot would do. It was preposterous how annoyed I became at not being able to work it loose. Of such folly can an ordinary, level-headed man be capable.

I was still trying to work the thing loose when the events happened which resulted in my release if release it could be called. The first unusual incident of which I became aware was the barking of the dog. It had been silent for some time when, all at once, it broke out into what sounded very like a paroxysm of barking not the yaps in which it had been occasionally indulging, but a sustained volley of full-lunged, open-mouthed, frenzied barking.

Something, I told myself, had happened to excite that dog.

I listened to learn if I could discover any reason. Presently, while the dog still barked, there was a knocking, as I judged, at the front door; not one modest knock, but a peal of loud, insistent assaults with the knocker. I got up from where I was sitting and groped my way to the cellar door.

"Who's that?" I asked myself, as I stood with my face close to the woodwork. "That sounds as if someone were in a hurry to get in who does not mean to be denied."

Crash! crash! crash! came the knocker. Then a tearing noise which at first I could not understand; then footsteps were heard.

"They've forced the door open, that's what it is they've not waited for an invitation. Who are they? what do they want? Had I better call their attention to my presence?"

I hesitated a moment, then yelled with the full force of my lungs; almost regretting having done so the second after. I could not tell if anyone had heard. The point was, Were those above the sort of persons I would like to have hear me? After all, I might pass from the frying-pan into the fire. Clearly, whoever had come into the house were men of violence; if they were more violent than those whose acquaintance I had already made it might fare ill with me.
NEW PAGE

CHAPTER IV
UNDERSTANDING

While I stood against the door, still in two minds, a hubbub arose, a pistol shot was fired, then another; there were shouts, angry voices somewhere a struggle was taking place. Above the din there was the barking of the dog. It was an agreeable uproar at least to have to listen to, after having been locked up for more than four-and-twenty hours, without light, or food, or drink, or sleep, or even a stool to sit upon. Eager though I was to be out of my prison, I did not feel moved to call the attention of people who seemed to be fighting for their lives to the fact that I was there. Almost better stay where I was than fall into the hands of ruffians, who in my weakened, helpless condition, would make nothing of slitting my throat.

Yet they found me. Suddenly I heard steps descending what I knew were the stairs leading to my cellar. A dog came with them the barking dog. Was the creature leading them to me? I picked up from the floor two bottles; with one held in either hand I awaited their coming. At least I would break one on someone's head before they had me I cared not whose the head might be. The footsteps paused just outside the cellar door. Voices muttered sinister voices they sounded to me. The key was turned in the lock, bolts were drawn, the door flung open, and the same instant I dashed through it.

Two men stood just outside it; I did not stop to see what kind of men they were; I struck at each with my bottles. I struck both, with what result I did not wait to learn. I know that one of them struck at me with some bright thing which he had in his hand, which I took to be a knife, and missed. I imagined I kicked the dog; I was not conscious of its presence, but a dog yelped as if it had been badly hurt. I supposed that it was hurt by me, though willingly I would not hurt a living thing.

I reached the top of the stairs before anyone could touch me. A man was waiting there for my arrival; I fancy the rapidity of my movements, my agility, took him by surprise. I still had my two bottles; I struck at him first with one and then with the other; one of them shivered into splinters as if it had come into contact with something metallic. The man dropped down. I turned to the left to find myself in the filthy room whose acquaintance I had already made. Someone was after me I fancied more than one. The window was open; I made for it. Without hesitation I screwed myself through it the window was small, my coat was huge it had to be a squeeze. Without looking what was below I let myself drop. But I did not drop. The skirt of my preposterous coat caught on a nail in the wall, or on something of the kind. I turned upside down. For some seconds I was suspended in that position between heaven and earth. I kept my senses enough to see that the ground was not very far beneath me. I gave myself a sort of jerk I fancy the nail gave way I went toppling to earth.

I do not think I fell more than three or four feet. Luckily I alighted on my hands, still in the possession of my senses. Scrambling to my feet I saw that a man was leaning through the window above with what looked like a revolver in his hand. I did not wait for him to fire; I rushed across the yard to a door which I had become aware was in the corner. The yard was but a tiny one; three or four steps took me to the door; I was through it with another and then that fellow fired. I heard the bullet strike the door behind me; it did not touch me. I tore straight on, through what seemed to be a narrow entry running by another house, into a street beyond. Then I paused, dazed, wondering where I had got to, where I was next to go. The moment I paused I reeled; if it had not been for a friendly railing I should have tumbled. I had taken more out of myself than I had supposed. Feet were coming after me I should be taken after all! I had lost my bottles; I had nothing with which to offer even a show of resistance. Just as I was trying to reconcile myself to the fact that all was over, I became conscious that a motor car was standing by the pavement, that the door opened, that someone came out of it someone who took me by the arm and led me to the car; someone, moreover, who, when in my state of haziness I found the car a little difficult to enter, gave me at a judicious moment a dexterous boost from behind which not only induced me to enter the car, but also landed me on the seat to my left. The moment I was on my feet my assistant followed, the door was banged, and the car was off. I daresay the whole thing was done inside five seconds.

I think I must have fainted, or done something equally grotesque, because when I again became conscious of my surroundings I knew that the car was passing through a wide street, in which there were many vehicles as well as people, and that by my side was a woman. I did not turn to look at her; I knew she was there without turning. I was content to sit right back and drink in the clean, strong air which the movement of the car drove against my face. I had no notion whose the car was or where we were going, or who the woman might be. In a dozy, hazy state of mind and body, all I wanted was to drink in the air, enjoy the movement of the car, and keep quite still.

It was a shock to me when the car all at once came to a stop. The woman at my side, leaning towards me, placed her hand upon my arm and said something which I did not understand. When she shook me slightly I sat up, and glancing round realised that the car was standing in front of a house, the front door of which was approached by a flight of steps. The woman spoke to me again. I still did not understand what she said. When the chauffeur got off his seat, and the door was opened, and she descended, I did understand that I was invited to follow. With uncertain legs and tottery feet I got on to the pavement. The chauffeur lent me the support of his arm. The woman had mounted the steps I believe she opened the door with a key. At any rate the chauffeur helped me up the steps, and when we reached the top the door was open. Having a vague recollection of my previous experience of entering a strange house, I was feebly inclined to ask what it was that they proposed to do with me. But I was too feeble to get the words out. I know I entered the house with the assistance of the chauffeur and the woman, was helped along a passage, and was presently deposited in an easy-chair in some sort of sitting-room. In that easy-chair I leaned back and, I fancy, was instantly asleep.

How long I slept I cannot say. Only, I imagine, a few minutes. I was roused by someone taking me by the shoulders and treating me to a shaking. I awoke to find a man standing by my side and bending down to look at me.

He was a biggish man, with a clean-shaven, pleasant face not at all the type of face I had seen in that filthy room. Even in my then soporific condition I should have said that this man was a gentleman. From the first moment I saw him with my sleep-laden eyes he inspired me with confidence. I knew that his was the face not only of an intelligent, but also of a clever and resourceful man. I don't know how I knew it, but I did. When he saw that I was awake he said something to me in an unknown tongue; then he laughed I fancied at the puzzlement which was in my eyes.

Then he spoke to someone who was not me.

"Poor devil! He looks as if he had been scared half out of his life, and lost his wits for keeps. He's not the sort assassins ought to be made of. Gentlemen who have been engaged on jobs like his ought to be made of tougher stuff. He's just a babe."

Then I knew that the woman was in the room and that he spoke to her. She answered.

"Men who, as you put it, are engaged on jobs like his are not chosen for their fitness, but by the hazard of the lot they draw for the honour."

"My word! the honour! that's a pretty word."

"Self-sacrifice has been held to be honourable. When a man does what he has done he sacrifices all."

"He does not look as if he ever had much to sacrifice."

"That is not a fault to reproach him with. When a man gives all that he hath he cannot give more."

"True; that's a pretty plain proposition I'm not out to deny it. You speak to him; perhaps he'll understand you better than he seems to do me."

"Pardon me I understand you perfectly." I was in a state in which my perceptions were not keen, yet I was conscious that those two persons started as if I had said the one thing for which they were unprepared. NEW PAGE

CHAPTER V
THE PILL

They stared at me. The man drew a little away from my chair and stood inspecting me as if I were a singular specimen of he knew not what. The woman placed herself right in front of me and frankly stared. I became aware that she herself was worth looking at. I had a vague idea as I dozed beside her in the car that she was a woman of mature age. Now I perceived that she was little more than a girl, tall and slender, big-eyed, oval-faced, with a mouth which was at once strong and tender, and an abundance of light brown hair framing her brow in a mass of little curls. She wore some sort of motoring costume which I cannot describe, but I know that she had on a little grey fur cap which became her well. Something about her air, her carriage, her attire I know not what, but it was there suggested the caste of Vere de Vere, aristocrat to the finger-tips. And withal so sweet, so sympathetic, so gentle. The way she was gazing down at me proved that.

"You speak English?" She asked the simple question in a voice which fell like music on my ears. I had had no notion that the human voice was capable of such delicate modulation. Something in her words, her voice, her look, served to stiffen my backbone, to rouse me from my state of semi-stupor.

"I not only speak English," I told her, "but I am English." I sat more upright in my chair.

"English? You are English? How can that be?"

"Since my father and mother were English, and I was born in England, I do not see how it can help but be."

"You have lived in Russia?"

"Never in my life."

"But you speak Russian?"

"Not a word."

She was silent, as if what I had said had deprived her, at least for the moment, of the power of speech. She continued to gaze at me, then turned her head a little round and gazed at the man. He said to her:

"Where in the name of all that's great did you get him from?"

"He came out of the house the police were there you see how he is dressed." Then she added something in a language which I did not know. I gathered from what she had just been saying that it might be Russian. He replied to her in the same tongue, and they exchanged half a dozen animated sentences. Then the man said to me, speaking so that I was not certain if he was in jest or earnest.

"Hark here, young fellow my lad. There seems to be something here which wants a little bit of straightening out. This lady took you to be one person, but it appears that you're another. As she brought you here at some risk and considerable inconvenience to herself, in my motor car, taking it for granted that you were the person she supposed you to be, it looks as if you were here under a sort of false pretence: so perhaps before the sitting continues any longer you'll kindly explain to us just who you are."

I told him as plainly as I could as I told those ragamuffins who had treated me so scurvily.

"I am Hugh Beckwith, a clerk in the dried fruit trade, until recently in the employ of Messrs. Hunter and Barnett, of Commercial Buildings, Southwark."

I had a notion that those two persons were round-eyed with wonder.

"What does he say?" the lady asked. "What does he mean?"

I had supposed what I said and what I meant were clear enough; but it seemed that the man thought otherwise.

"The great Panjandrum only knows! This does beat anything! I've been in some queer situations, but it looks as if I were in the queerest now. You've made a pretty hash of things."

"Hash! what do you mean by hash? How am I to blame? See how he is dressed!"

"Yes, there I'll give you best he does look the part. Perhaps you'll explain, Mr. Hugh Beckwith, clerk in the dried fruit trade, how you come to be in that rig-out, and in the house you were in?"

I did explain. It took me a considerable time they kept interrupting asking questions which I did not always find it easy to answer. My story seemed to amuse the man; he began laughing before I had gone very far, and kept on laughing all the while, as if what I had suffered struck him as funny. He laughed when I told him about the canvas bag which had fallen on my head, about my dented hat, about my reception when I knocked at the door, about the way those scoundrels treated me. When I told of the sandy-haired creature who had put himself into my clothes, and of how I had been forced into the ridiculous garments which I had on instead, he dropped on to a chair, stretched out his legs in front of him, and laughed as if I were the funniest fellow he had ever encountered. I have heard that one man's misfortunes are another man's jest, but I had never appreciated the fact before.

The lady was not quite so amused, though she also occasionally smiled, and when I was nearly at the end of my narrative she observed:

"You did look so funny as you came running towards me; if I had not been so concerned for you I should have smiled."

She smiled then but I forgave her, for her smile added to her charm.

"I suppose," remarked the man, "you understand all that has happened, Mr. Hugh Beckwith."

"Understand!" I shouted by that time I was fairly roused. "I understand nothing not one single thing! How can you imagine that I understand?"

"But you know for whom those gentlemen mistook you, Mr. Beckwith."

"Know!" Leaning forward I struck with my clenched fist a polished table which was in front of me. "Know! how could I know? If I'd been the greatest villain unhung they could not have treated me worse."

"I fancy, Mr. Beckwith, that they did mistake you for a person who you might hold is one of the greatest villains still unhung."

The girl spoke in that unknown language, interrupting him, as if fearing that if he was not careful he might commit himself to statements which he would rather were not made. He replied to her. There was a brisk exchange of words. Plainly a discussion was taking place in which he brought arguments to bear which presently caused her to see the matter from his point of view.

"I believe, Mr. Hugh Beckwith," she said, "that you are an honest man."

"I say nothing about that," I told her. "I am as honest as a clerk in the dried fruit trade may be."

The man roared with laughter.

"That is as well put," he declared as soon as his mirth permitted, "as you're ever likely to get it. In no line of business, nowadays, can a clerk be honest beyond a certain point."

"I am of opinion," the lady said, "that you are more honest than you care to admit. It's not a disgrace to be honest."

"Perhaps," I ventured, "you don't know very much about the dried fruit trade."

"No," she admitted, "I do not; but I think I do know an honest man when I see him, and I believe I'm looking at one now." As she was looking straight at me then the inference seemed clear; but I still felt that if she had known anything about the dried fruit trade her words would have been more guarded. "At least," she added, "I trust you. You will see how much I trust you." Then she said to the man, "You can tell him all about it."

"If you take my advice," I interjected, "you will trust no one. I would rather you told me nothing which might affect your interest if it became public."

"As for being made public, it is public enough already." Then to the man a little dictatorially, as if it were him to obey her, "Tell him."

The man got up from the chair on which he had been sitting, crossed to a brass rack for holding newspapers and returned towards me carrying two or three in his hand.

"Am I to gather," he began, "that you would rather have no explanation of the singular manner in which those gentlemen treated you, Mr. Hugh Beckwith? I take it that you at least think it possible that they had reasons for what they did."

"Infamous reasons!"

"Infamous if you like that depends on the way in which you look at it. I might prefer to describe them as sufficient. What they did to you they believed themselves to be doing in self-defence. I am not sure that they were not right."

"What had I done that they need defend themselves from me?"

"Have you seen a newspaper lately, Mr. Hugh Beck with?"

"I see two every day, one in the morning and one in the evening. I hold that it is not extravagant to spend sixpence a week on keeping yourself abreast of the news of the world."

"Soundly put I Many people would not be so ignorant of what is taking place around them if they thought what you think. Do you read either Russian or Polish?"

"Neither. I am taking lessons in the languages of the countries from which we purchase most of our dried fruits; but so far as I know we purchase nothing from either Poland or Russia."

"I daresay that is correct; so I will confine myself to what has been published in the English papers. Look at this." He held out a copy of the Daily Telegraph, open at the centre page. "See these scare lines." He read aloud. "Assassination of Russian Prefect of Police. Extraordinary Story." He looked at me. "That's who they took you for, the man who killed him. The Russian Prefect of Police has been murdered at St. Petersburg, in a public street. He was stabbed in the back with a long knife which was driven right through him. The assassin found it easier to leave it in than to take it out again. One of the Prefect's officers, who was standing at some little distance, actually saw the murder committed; but before he could reach the Prefect he was dead and the murderer was out of sight. If, as is possible because even in that most policed country in the world criminals do get away that particular murderer did escape, he may have made for London; in a certain quarter he may even have been expected."

"Do you mean to say that those fellows took me for a murderer?"

The man smiled I really did not see what there was to smile at: there was a quality in his smile which I found curious.

"The thing is conceivable."

"I really cannot agree with that. I cannot see how let the circumstances be what they may anyone is entitled to take me for a murderer."

"My dear Mr. Beckwith, perhaps I see better than you do. In all little affairs of this kind--"

"Little affair, you call it! The Chief of Police I suppose a Prefect is a Chief of Police is murdered in a public street, and you call it a little affair."

"I will speak of it as you like. I only wish to point out that in affairs of this kind there are apt to be wheels within wheels, plots within plots, mysterious complications which well, I will say, which make all things conceivable. Do you know it occurs to me, Mr. Beckwith, that you may be hungry."

The change of theme was sudden, but I was equal to the occasion.

"Considering," I told him, "that I have had nothing to eat since yesterday at breakfast you may take it for granted that I am."

He addressed the lady.

"Do you not think that we might be able to give this gentleman something to eat?"

She touched an electric bell. "I must apologise to Mr. Beckwith," she said, "for my want of consideration; I ought to have thought of it before."

A man-servant entered at least I took him for a servant: he was big and brawny, and wore a beard; he reminded me of those undesirable aliens, though I admit that he was cleaner, neater, better dressed than they were. She said something to him; he vanished, almost immediately returning with various articles upon a tray. He set these out upon the table. There was a cold chicken, bread, butter, fresh cut lettuce, a bottle of red wine. I did not need a second invitation to attack the food. While I ate they talked, asking me questions, sometimes laughing at my answers. The kind of interest they seemed to feel was beyond my comprehension. They did not seem to be the kind of people who would be mixed up even in what they might call a "political" murder. I gave frank expression to my feelings. I said to the man:

"Do you know you'll excuse my saying so but I'm beginning to wonder if you had anything to do with the awful thing which happened to this man what's his name?"

"The name of the Prefect of Police was Stepan Korsunsky."

"You talk as if you knew all about it."

The pair exchanged glances; then the man said:

"Mr. Beckwith, you are a simple-minded Englishman."

"And what are you--you're not Russian?"

"No; as it happens, I'm American. I was born in a small township in Wisconsin, which, as you may or may not be aware it is funny how much even educated Englishmen don't know about America is a state in the Upper Lake region of the greatest country on God's earth. Now and then I go to visit the place where I was raised but not too often. I am fond of motion, Mr. Hugh Beckwith, so I keep moving; there are few places on the surface of this small, round globe which I haven't moved over. I've interests business interests in quite a lot of them; and that's how I've come to have a kind of feeling in what happened to Stepan Korsunsky. I've business interests in St. Petersburg of rather a peculiar kind."

He pronounced those last words in a way I could not but feel he meant that I should notice. I did not quite like to ask what he meant by "a peculiar kind"; but, as I had made quite an inroad into that chicken, I was content to sit and stare and wonder. And as I sat I had my hands in the pocket of that nonsensical coat. Without thinking what I was doing I returned to what had occupied me in the cellar. In the centre of one side of the lining of the right-hand pocket was still that rounded something. I thrust my fingers through the place where I had torn away the stitches inside the lining. By some queer accident the hidden something wormed itself through what I felt to be a threadbare spot into my fingers. I closed them on it just in time to save it from dropping to the bottom of the coat. Gingerly I drew it out and looked at it.

I take it that there was something in my demeanour which struck them as peculiar. When they saw me staring intently at something which I held in my hand they both moved towards me as if to learn what I was staring at.

"What have you there?" asked the man. "Something worth looking at?"

"I don't know what it is," I answered; "I'm wondering. It looks to me as if it might be some sort of pill."

"Pill?" The man seemed startled; he came closer, bent down to see what I had, and almost at the same instant took me with his right hand by the throat and shouted: "You rogue! Hand that over."

I was taken by surprise when, so soon as I had knocked at the door, that huge fellow dragged me into that mysterious house; but I think I was even more surprised when that man accorded me such treatment. He had been so courteous, so pleasant, a man of peace, evidently the best type of American gentleman: that he should suddenly start strangling me was grotesquely unexpected. However, his onslaught only lasted a second. Snatching from my open palm what looked to me like a pill, he drew back, examining it closely with eager eyes.

"What is it?" the girl asked. "What have you there?"

"It's one of them." He did not speak loudly, but with a voice which seemed to be shaking with excitement.

"One of them?" She echoed not only his words but his manner of uttering them. She seemed all at once to be quivering.

"As I live and breathe, it's one of them! Of all the wonderful things! And I had given up hope."

"How did it get here?"

"How can I tell you! As if I knew! It has dropped from the skies."

"Where did it come from?"

"From--from--"He glared at me. "Mr. Hugh Beckwith, will you be so good as to tell me where it came from. None of your lies, none of your nonsense about the dried fruit trade! I felt, somehow, that you were too simple to be real. Out with it, man! You'll find that I, also, can be dangerous. Where did this come from? Tell me the truth if you want to keep your soul and body together."

I already had reason to know that by some mischance I had dropped into a region where strange things happened. I ought to have been prepared for anything; yet I was wholly unprepared for the sudden, startling, and quick change in his manner and bearing. As I looked at him I knew without his telling me that he, also, could be dangerous; that it would need very very little to induce him to treat me even worse than the others had done. What I had done to cause this amazing alteration in his demeanour was beyond my comprehension. I tried to tell him so.

"What I have done to induce you to take me by the throat, and to speak to me as if I were a dog--"

He cut me short.

"Never mind what you've done! Where did this come from?"

He held what looked like a pill in his finger and thumb.

"From the lining of this pocket."

"What do you mean?"

"What I say. I felt last night that there was something there, and I've been picking at it ever since with my fingers, trying to get it out. I've just succeeded; you saw me get it out."

"Do you mean to tell me you don't know what this is?"

"I've not a notion. If you'll permit me to look at it for a minute or two at close quarters I may be able to guess. From the glimpse I caught of it it looked to me like a pill."

He put his face quite close to mine, unpleasantly close.

"Are you acting? If you are--" He left his sentence unfinished. "Do you swear you don't know?"

"If you won't believe my simple statement you won't believe me if I swear. I tell you that I do not know."

He continued to glare at me for some instants longer, his face so close that I could feel his breath upon my cheek; and just as I was coming to the uncomfortable conclusion that he really meant to do me an injury he stood straight up, and said to the girl:

"Shall I believe him?"

Standing in front of me she regarded me with her clear, calm eyes as critically as if she were appraising some inanimate object.

"I think you may." This she said to the man; then she spoke to me. "Let us understand each other. You have already told us, but tell us again in detail how did you get that coat be very exact."

"I did not get it; they thrust me into it."

"They? Any particular person, or did they do it in a body?"

"In a body."

"Where did they get it from! Was it in the room when you saw it first, or did they bring it in?"

"It was lying with the other garments on an old horsehair couch, on the top of a brown paper wrapper which it had apparently come in."

"A wrapper? in which it had apparently come? What made you think it had come in the wrapper?"

"Something had come in it. There were labels on it marks where it had been sealed. I noticed that in more than one place there was a name and address. I noticed the name it was addressed to Isaac Rothenstein."

"Rothenstein!" The exclamation came from the man. He scared at the girl and the girl at him. Evidently something had moved them deeply.

31

"By the way," I went on, "I don't know what that pill-like object is, but I've a sort of notion that that is not the only one which is hidden in the lining of this coat. I believe there's one here I can feel it."

He pressed his finger against the spot which I was touching, then broke again into exclamations.

"Darya, I believe there is something there there is! It may be another."

"Why not?" Though she spoke more quietly than he, in her voice there was a tremor. "Suppose they are all there! They might have sent them like that; they were as safe that way as any other. They must have been sent in the wrapper Mr. Beckwith saw to Rothenstein."

"Rothenstein! Holy smoke! Dear Isaac! That would mean that he has out-generalled me; yet" He paused, as if he feared that if he continued he might say too much. Then he suddenly said to me, "Mr. Beckwith, I shall have to have that coat."

"Give me another and I shall be delighted. I shall be glad to be out of it."

"Give you another?"

She said, as he seemed to hesitate as if my suggestion had taken him by surprise:

"Nothing could be easier. Mr. Beckwith is not much smaller than you; he is not so broad, but a suit of your clothes would not fit him so badly.

Take him to your bedroom and let him change into one; he does not appear to be unwilling to let you have that coat in exchange."

"To say that I am not unwilling is to put k mildly. So long as I am out of it anyone can have it for all I care."

"Then come along we'll do a deal on the spot. Allow me to conduct you to my room we'll exchange old clothes for new." NEW PAGE

CHAPTER VI
TO NEW YORK FOR £500

Both parties to the bargain seemed to be pleased when he opened a wardrobe door, showing a number of suits hanging there, and bade me take my choice. I had a bath what a luxury that was! then arrayed myself from head to foot in his garments. I was smaller than he was; he possibly scaled a couple of stone more than I did; but as the young lady had foretold, his clothes were not so ill-fitting as they might have been. I know that, as I stood before the long glass in the wardrobe door, I could not but feel that my appearance was materially improved. Even his boots were not so bad they were better ones than I had ever been able to purchase. That remark applied to the whole rig-out; from the point of view of cost I was better dressed in his things than I ever had been in my own.

I went downstairs to the sitting-room he had told me to go when I was ready. There was no one there. Food and drink were yet on the table, so I helped myself to a little more. The bath and change had renewed my appetite. There was not much left in the way of provisions, and I was just wondering if I had not better return to Grove Gardens I wondered what Catherine and her mother were thinking had become of me; they would possibly be more than half off their heads when the door opened, and the young lady put her head in. At sight of me she smiled.

"I am glad, Mr. Beckwith, you have found something to occupy your time." She referred to my eating and drinking. "If you'll excuse my saying so, I don't think you look any worse in your new attire. I certainly should not have known you for the person who came stumbling down that entry."

"You were quite right, you see. Mr. I do not know what his name is the gentleman's clothes do not fit so badly; many a ready-made suit fits worse. I hope he has had luck, and found more of his pills."

"He has had luck; he has found well, he has found what he never hoped to find."

Apparently she also had had luck. If I had had to describe her, I should have said that she was one great beam she beamed, as it were, from top to toe. It is extraordinary how even a pretty girl is improved by a smile; I thought that she looked lovely.

"I am glad to hear it," I remarked. "In that case neither he nor you need be worried by my presence any longer. If I may I should like to take myself off at once. I have people waiting for me at home who must be very anxious. I have never before been away from them so long without letting them know where I am."

I had risen from my chair, and was about to move towards the door, when she stopped me.

"Still a few moments, Mr. Beckwith, if you don't mind. Mr.–" she hesitated, then went smilingly on: "I don't see that there's any objection to your knowing his name; you may have to know it before very long what does it matter? Mr. Stewart has something which he wishes to say to you before you leave, and which I think you may like to hear. Here he comes to tell you for himself what it is." Mr. Stewart since that seemed to be the gentleman's name came into the room. She said to him, "Paul, Mr. Beckwith wishes to go home."

The man was as radiant as the girl; I am not sure that the beam in him was not more pronounced. He paused at the door and eyed me again with keen appraisement yet all the while he smiled.

"Mr. Beckwith," he began, "I believe you have done me a service unwittingly. You could hardly have done me a better turn."

"I am glad to hear it. You have done me one. Without you and this lady I don't know where I should have been; in a pretty bad hole. Now, with your permission, I will say good-day, and thank you."

"One moment; gently! I should like to have a word with you before you go. You are, I take it, a man of affairs a busy man."

"I am sorry to say that for the moment I am not. I have lost my situation since yesterday."

"Since yesterday? Is that so? That's fortunate."

"I'm afraid I can't agree with you. It's much easier to lose a situation than to find one especially in the dried fruit trade."

"That's as may be. Suppose that I had a situation to offer you."

"You? Are you in the dried fruit trade?"

"Not exactly, but I am in trade."

"May I ask what trade?"

"Oh, I buy things and I sell them, and I buy them again and sell them again that sort of thing." His explanation of the trade he was in was not very clear, but I was not disposed to ask questions; until, as he presently did, he made a remark which startled me. "Are you a rich man, Mr. Beckwith?"

"No, Mr. Stewart, I emphatically am not. I wish I could say that I was even moderately well off, but I can't. I am poor very poor."

"Then if that really is the case, I wonder if you'd like to earn five hundred pounds."

"Would I like to earn five hundred pounds? Wouldn't I!"

I did not like to tell him that that was a sum which I had been for some time one might say dreaming of. Its possession would mean to me a great deal more than I could put into words. I thought he was joking; yet, though his shrewd eyes danced and his clever face was lighted by smiles, he seemed to be serious enough. He continued:

"Say inside a month. That is, Mr. Beckwith, would you care to give a month to earn five hundred pounds? Could you spare a month?"

I drew a long breath; something in his manner made me tingle.

I could; I could spare a month very well. "Are you a discreet man, Mr. Beckwith?"

"In business yes. Even Mr. Barnett can't say that I'm not."

"Who is Mr. Barnett?"

"He is the man who fired me; the junior partner in the firm of Messrs. Hunter & Barnett; the kind of man who acts first and thinks afterwards. I shouldn't wonder if by now he's sorry that he did fire me, and I shouldn't be surprised to find a request awaiting me to go back again."

"If you do, will you go back?"

"Not if I can help it."

"Will five hundred pounds help you to help it?"

"It would if I only had a chance of getting it." Mr. Stewart had been perching himself on a corner of the table, swinging one leg in the air; now he came and stood within a foot of where I was and observed me very attentively. His face became graver.

"I'll give you the chance to earn it if you are the kind of man I think you are."

"And also," struck in the lady, "the kind of man *I* think you are."

"I don't know," I told her, "what that is, but I'll try not to disappoint you."

"I am sure you will. I believe in you and I do not believe in a man for nothing. Although I am only a woman I'm a judge of a man."

Mr. Stewart spoke before I could.

"It's because she's a woman that she's a judge of a man. Mr. Beckwith, this lady has the profoundest faith in you: although she arrived at her conclusion a little rapidly, and by methods which I do not understand, her faith inspires me. So I am going to offer you the handling of rather a delicate piece of business."

"What is it? I should tell you that the dried fruit trade is the only branch of business I know anything about."

"Well this has not much to do with the dried fruit trade: it's just a question of a trip across the pond."

"I'm afraid I don't understand."

"The pond in this case is the Atlantic Ocean. I want you, Mr. Beckwith, to take something for me from London to New York."

I stared, again wondering if he was joking. To take something from London to New York seemed a trifle; it could not be for doing that that he was offering five hundred pounds.

"I again fear, Mr. Stewart, that I don't grasp your meaning."

"It is simple or it will be when I explain. In the first place, tell me one thing can you start tonight?"

"To-night for New York?" I found the question a trifle surprising. "That does not give me much time to prepare."

"Leave all preparations to me. Is there anything to prevent your starting?"

"So far as I am personally concerned no; I should say there wasn't."

"So far so good. Now, Mr. Beckwith, the proposition is this. If you will leave England to-night by a steamer in which a berth will be provided for you, and all your expenses paid, out and home, and deliver something which I will give you at an address in New York, on delivery five hundred pounds will be paid to you in English money. Is that good enough, and is it plain? You ought to be back in London inside three weeks, so you'll earn your money in less than a month. What do you say?"

"What is it I am to deliver? It must be something pretty remarkable."

"It is a case of pills." NEW PAGE

CHAPTER VII
AT THE RISK OF HIS LIFE

His remark was so puerile, so devoid of sense, that I hardly knew how to take it. I said so.

"I don't know if you wish me to take you seriously, Mr. Stewart: I scarcely imagine that you are proposing to pay me five hundred pounds for taking a case of pills to America."

It was a second or two before he answered, but when an answer did come it was drawled, his face being illuminated with what I will call a whimsical smile.

"Well, Mr. Beckwith, we will call them pills what's in a name? If I choose to pay you five hundred pounds to convey a case of pills or a case of poisons to the United States of North America what difference does it make to you?"

"I should be unwilling, even for the sum you name, which to me represents a fortune, to carry your poisons."

The girl spoke. "They are not poisons, Mr. Beckwith. Mr. Stewart jests; he does not always mean exactly what he says."

Mr. Stewart's smile became more whimsical.

"What this lady says is the plumb truth; I'm a humorist, Mr. Beckwith. This is what I want you to carry across the pond this and others like it." He drew from his waistcoat pocket what I took to be the small brown pellet which had been concealed in the lining of the drosky driver's coat. "It looks like a pill why shouldn't we call it a pill?"

"But it is not a pill. Have you any objection to telling me what it is?"

He and the girl looked at each other. He said to her:

"You might explain, Darya, how the matter appears to us."

She acted upon his suggestion.

"We think, Mr. Beckwith, that it is just as well you should not know. Then if anyone puts to you inquisitive questions you need not commit yourself. Your ignorance will be a defence."

"A defence? You think a defence will be needed?"

"My good Mr. Beckwith," this was the man "do you suppose that I'm willing to pay you five hundred pounds for nothing? I will tell you just how the situation lies. It is of the first importance that these pills should reach America and be delivered at an address which I will give you, before a certain date. They are, as you perceive, not large: at this moment they are all in my waistcoat pocket but they are of interest to a good many people. You know for yourself what means were used to get them to England so that they might escape notice. They might have been sent by post: it is doubtful if they would have reached their destination if they had been. A good many people are on the look-out for them: I daresay some of them suspect that they are in this house at this moment."

An exclamation came from the girl. She was standing up, looking through the window, from which she was distant perhaps six or seven feet, He, moving to her, followed the direction of her glance. I, also, turned and looked. As I did so an uncomfortable little shiver went up and down my back. In the street, on the opposite side of the road, was a man. I had only caught a glimpse of him for perhaps two or three seconds, but I knew him again it was the man who had rushed at me from across the street when the canvas bag fell on my head, and who, when I turned and saw him, fled as if for life. He was motionless, his hands in his jacket pockets, his head hunched between his shoulders a bird of ill omen.

"That," I informed them, "is the fellow for whom I believe the canvas bag which fell from the window above on to my hat was intended."

They asked me what I meant. I explained. When I had finished they exchanged glances which conveyed something which I did not understand. They spoke to each other in that guttural foreign tongue; then he said his laughter could not hide the fact that he was serious enough inside:

"You see it begins. There is a gentleman whom it appears you have met before who is, I fancy, interested in these we will call them pills. He would cut my throat for one of them if he had what he would judge to be a reasonable expectation of getting safely away with it."

"Who is the man? I don't like the look of him at all."

"Who does? My good Mr. Beckwith, ask no questions; notice nothing, if you can help it especially do not notice people like the one across the road. Will you finally yes or no for five hundred pounds take the pills to New York? starting to-night?"

"Where am I to carry them? I mean, am I to have them on my person, or where are they to be hidden if they are to be hidden."

"Oh, yes, you may take it they are to be hidden, but where is for you to say. You have a certain amount of intelligence, I presume. If you had something of your own which you wished to take to New York without letting people guess that you had it, what would be the best hiding-place you could find?" As he saw that I was about to speak he held up his hand. "I'm not asking for an answer. I don't want one. I don't wish to know where you propose to hide the pills. There are twenty-two of them. I ask you to take them with you to New York. I trust you completely. Again will you or won't you act as my messenger?"

Something in my very bones seemed to warn me to be careful before I committed myself to a definite statement. I was full of all sorts of fears and fancies lest the man might be using me as a cat's-paw in an affair from which I should derive neither advantage nor credit.

"I don't understand," I told him, "why you won't send what you call your pills by post. There is such a thing as a registered post which is used by hundreds of thousands of people every day. Surely they would be much safer with it than me."

"Sometimes, Mr. Beckwith, trifles sent by your registered post are apt to go astray; several registered packets in which I have had an interest have lately reached their destinations in America safely enough in one sense, but with the packets empty. What is the use of receiving a boxful of pills when the box is found to be empty?"

"Could not the police recover the pills?"

"They are not asked. There are pills with which one would rather the police had nothing to do even if they are lost. Better to 'bear the ills we have than fly to others that we know not of.' That is a quotation, Mr. Beckwith, of which you may have heard. But we'll leave all that alone. Now play the man speak out! Will you earn that five hundred pounds yes or no?"

I was still reluctant; I felt that I was committing myself to a business altogether out of my line and of which I knew nothing. The mention of the five hundred pounds tipped the beam. It was a sum of which I had dreamt for years. Only a few hours before I had been driven to the conclusion that it was further from me than it ever had been. Now the idea that I could win it in a month or three weeks was a temptation I could not resist. It was a chance which might never recur again; I could not afford to let it slip I would not.

"I will take your pills to New York if you will satisfy me that the five hundred pounds are sure to be mine when I get there."

"That is a point on which it will afford me the greatest possible pleasure to give you entire satisfaction, Mr. Beckwith. You see these look at them; they are genuine English bank-notes."

He produced from an inner pocket in his coat a roll of what looked like bank-notes and which were bank-notes; he placed them in my hands for examination and I proved it. They were of various denominations fives, tens, fifties, and hundreds. There must have been three or four thousand pounds worth. I won't say that I looked at each separate one, but I took careful stock of several. On their genuineness there could not be the faintest possible shadow of a shade of doubt.

The idea that he carried about with him, in such a careless fashion, such a huge sum of money impressed me almost more than anything which had gone before. The individual who would carry about a small fortune in his jacket pocket, and treat it as if it were nothing at all, must either be a very rich or a very remarkable person. I had been taught, in a hard school, to treat money with respect. How anyone could walk about the streets with thousands of pounds lying loose in his jacket pocket was beyond my comprehension. I should have rushed to the nearest bank to ensure its safety. As with his face still lighted by a smile he stood and watched I fancy he understood something of what I felt as I assured myself that those notes of his were genuine.

"If you like," he said, "I will deposit your five hundred pounds in any bank you choose to name, as the property of Hugh Beckwith, to be handed over to you on your return from New York, if you will give me a written agreement to fulfil your share of the bargain I am proposing. More, I will add this; if you fail you shall still have your five hundred pounds if you satisfy me that you have done your best to achieve success."

"I think that is only fair," said the girl, "because Mr. Beckwith may fail through what is really no fault of his."

"Exactly," returned Mr. Stewart, "that is what I had in my mind. So you perceive, Mr. Beckwith, on the lines of this lady's suggestion you stand to win five hundred pounds and to lose nothing."

"Except his life," struck in the girl. "I think it only right that he should be informed that he runs a certain risk of losing that." As she spoke she glanced through the window. "He has gone," she said to the man.

Mr. Stewart laughed, as if she had perpetrated some joke,

"Precisely just as shadows go. You talk of risk? What's risk? You risk your life when you cross the street, because you may be knocked down and killed by a runaway or a skidding motor car."

The girl, who was still looking through the window, observed, "There's a policeman come instead." NEW PAGE

CHAPTER VIII
GROVE GARDENS

Since I had left the service of Messrs. Hunter and Barnett I seemed to have tumbled into a sort of topsy-turvydom, where things happened as they had never happened before. For instance, there was the way in which I left that house. Ordinarily, as a matter of course, I should have gone through the front door, out into the street, and so home. But no, Mr. Stewart would not have it. He took me down some stairs to the basement as I descended I thought of the cellar in which I had spent the night; then through a back door which opened into a little yard.

"There are times," he explained the mode of egress needed a little explaining "when I find it advisable to have two ways in and out of a house, one behind and one in front; so I thought it well to rent the house at the back to use as a means of going' to and fro when the door in front is attracting more attention than I care for."

He led me across the yard to where a pair of steps stood against a wall, up the steps, over the wall, on to a second pair of steps which was on the other side, down them, by the side of the house to which I presume he referred, and so into the street beyond.

"I do not think," he observed, "that any of my friends have so far tumbled to this way out. Here you will not find yourself an object of attention. You see the street is empty. You had better stroll to the end; you will find a taxi-cab stand just round the corner; get into one, drive from your house, I should suggest to the City. In the City dismiss your cab and get into another; then discharge that and get into a third; then, by the time you get to your own quarters, if anyone started on your track I should fancy you will have put them off it."

I did not know what to fancy. When I left him my head was in a whirl. I had heard and read about people getting on to other people's "track" and that sort of thing, but never had I dreamed of anyone ever wanting to get on mine. It seemed incredible! Nor was I in the habit of riding in taxicabs; a clerk in the dried fruit trade, who is in receipt of fifty shillings a week, has precious little to spend on cabs. When I reached the rank of which he had spoken and got into a taxi, I felt as if this were the beginning of still another adventure. I told the driver to take me to Queen Victoria Street, then felt in my pocket to make sure that I had the money to pay him.

I knew I had; Mr. Stewart had given me ten sovereigns and some silver for what he called preliminary expenses; still I liked to make sure that I had it. It seemed so amazing that I should have all that money to do with as I liked.

I got out at the corner of King Street, looked round to see if I was being followed, then, deciding in the negative, strolled into Cheapside. There I bought a paper and hailed another cab, reading my paper as I went along. It was an early edition of an evening journal; the chief item of news immediately caught my eye. It was sufficiently boldly displayed. The "headlines" filled nearly a quarter of a column. "Police Raid on Russian Nihilists. They receive Information that the Assassin of the Prefect of Police is in London. They Attempt to Capture Him. His Dramatic Escape."

It was only when I had read a large part of the article which followed that it began to dawn on me that I was the "assassin" who had effected a "dramatic escape." When I did realise that I almost collapsed in the cab. I appeared to have made rather a muddle of things; evidently the whole thing referred to the house at which I had received such outrageous treatment. What I had taken to be those desperadoes coming back again, or what might have been even worse, their more ruthless friends, were in fact the police making a "raid" upon the house in search of what I learned were "Russian Nihilists." When they opened the cellar door and I rushed out it seemed that they had jumped to the conclusion that I was the "assassin" they were in search of. That was why they had tried to stop me. They merely wanted to hale me to a police station and charge me with doing something I had never heard of. I had balked them of that pleasure by scrambling out of the window and getting into that waiting motor car.

Probably my proceedings had left them more than ever convinced that I was the miscreant they were in search of. Which was charming for me!

39

From one point of view the position might be regarded as amusing. It was not an aspect which would appeal to me. I did not know of what offence I had been guilty; I had a hazy notion that it was an offence to resist arrest, and I certainly had knocked a policeman over. Possibly one of those constables had had a good look at me, my description might be circulated; although my return to the garb of civilisation must have made a considerable difference in my appearance, I still might be recognised; if I were, heaven only knew what might happen. As I leaned back in that taxi-cab it struck me forcibly that the sooner I was out of England the better it might be. I have always had a horror of being mixed up with the police, no matter how. It comforted me to reflect that I should be out of England in less than four-and-twenty hours. "Assassin" indeed! I did not want to have such a word associated with the name of Hugh Beckwith, even if it were only for half an hour. At the best folks might regard it as a first-rate joke, and one of which I should never hear the last for the rest of my life.

I dismissed that second cab in Highbury, strolled again, and got into a third. In that I drove home. It is a long way from Highbury New Park to Fulham Palace Road. I do not pretend to be a hero; I am merely a clerk in the dried fruit trade, who only wishes to be allowed to make an honest livelihood in peace. By the time I had reached home I had worked myself into a state of nervous agitation which I am quite willing to admit was absurd. As we passed through Walham Green I saw on the pavement or thought I saw the sandy-haired villain who had robbed me of my clothes. I confess that I nearly fainted. I dared not look out of the window to make sure for fear he should see me. The thought that after all he might be tracking me was dreadful. When we got into Grove Gardens and stopped in front of Mrs. Fraser's, I stumbled out of the vehicle, over-paid the driver I do not know how much I did pay him, but I am sure it was too much, he was so civil dashed across to the front door, fumbled with my latch-key; before I could get it home the door was opened from within and I was in Catherine's arms. NEW PAGE

CHAPTER IX
CATHERINE

Catherine is not as a rule demonstrative. Rather the other way. She is not seldom more frigid than I quite care for, but her treatment of me was warm enough then; almost too warm. She put her arms right round me and squeezed me tight she is a muscular young woman, Catherine is and exclaimed:

"Oh, Hugh, I thought you were dead. If you only knew what I have suffered because of you!"

Then she cried; which, in my then state, was to me the worst thing she could have done. I practically said as much.

"My dear Catherine,! soon shall be dead if you don't take care. I am in momentary danger of a nervous breakdown, and the slightest thing may bring it on."

I believe that something in my tone struck her as peculiar; she stopped crying on the instant. I will say this for Catherine, she has great self-control; she is always calm and collected, never seeming to lose her equilibrium. The prompt way in which her tears ceased to flow proved that she was mistress of herself even in that agitated moment. Relaxing what I should describe as her grip, she drew back half a step and looked at me. I saw that her eyes were dry. What she saw on my face I am not sure; I do know that she took me quickly by the arm and led me into the sitting-room.

"What is the matter, Hugh? What has happened?"

It was like her to jump into the middle of a subject without any sort of preface. She wastes no time in preliminaries, but gets where she wants in one. I did not give her a direct answer. I said to her:

"Look through the window, see if anyone is in the street, but don't let them see you."

Who should be in the street?" She has rather a disconcerting trick of asking what seem to me to be foolish questions. il And why should I be afraid of being seen? There is a milk cart on the other side of the road in front of Mrs. Cullen's, but there is nothing and no one else."

"Thank God! There's some brandy in my cupboard; I wish you'd give me half a wineglassful."

That time she said nothing. When she saw me sink on the armchair and gasp for breath she just did what I told her. As she was offering me the brandy her mother burst into the room.

"My dear boy, thank goodness you've returned! The sight of you is such a weight off my mind you can't think. What had become of you I could not imagine. I wanted Catherine to send for the police--"

"The idea, mother, of sending for the police! Be quiet, mother, Hugh isn't very well."

For a wonder Mrs. Fraser was quiet; her daughter has more influence over than I shall ever have. I believe she is afraid of Catherine she never will be afraid of me. Catherine went on:

"Drink this brandy, Hugh." I drank it with lamb-like docility. It took my breath away for a moment, but presently it began to do me good. My agitation lessened. She took the empty glass from me, knelt on the floor beside my chair, and put her hand upon my shoulder. "Now, dear, tell me all about it. Would you rather mother left the room?"

Mrs. Fraser remonstrated.

"Catherine, the idea! Why should I leave the room? Am I not as much interested in what has happened to Hugh as you can possibly be? What can he have to say to you which I ought not to hear?"

As it chanced I had something to say which it was necessary that she should hear.

"Catherine, before I speak of anything else I ought first of all to tell you that I am leaving for America to-night."

Mother and daughter both started. I fancy Mrs. Fraser gave a little shriek; Catherine cried: "Hugh!" Then she added, "Leaving for America! My dear Hugh, what do you mean? Tell me what has happened."

"My dear Catherine, a great many things have happened most surprising things; I may almost say incredible things but I can't tell you about them now."

"Hugh! why not?" Her face was a study she looked so surprised. "Why can you not tell me what has happened?"

Her mother came in with a remark of her own.

"If you had the least idea, Hugh, how anxious Catherine and I have been you wouldn't try to put us off by saying you can't tell us what has happened. We're both of us burning to know."

"All the same, Mrs. Fraser, I can't tell you now, at least in detail. I haven't time. I'll just give you, Catherine, some idea of how the land lies, and later on I'll tell you the whole strange story. You'll be amazed." She looked as if she were amazed before I had told her a single thing. "To begin with, I've lost my situation."

They both exclaimed in chorus; exactly which of them said what I do not pretend to know.

"Lost your situation! How ever did you do that?

Has anything gone wrong with the firm? What shall you do?"

"The first thing I am going to do is to go to America."

"But what's the use of your going to America? How are you going to do it? Have you enough money to pay your fare, and how about having enough money when it comes to landing? I thought they wouldn't let you land in America unless you had a certain sum."

"My dear Catherine, you've got hold of the wrong end of the stick. I am going to America as a sort of agent for Mr. Stewart."

"Who is Mr. Stewart?"

"Really I can hardly tell you; I know little or nothing about him myself. I only know that he has offered, if I will take something for him to America and start to-night, to pay me five hundred pounds on my delivering it at an address which he is going to give me in New York."

The exclamation which came from Catherine! I do not remember to have heard her make a noise of that kind before.

"Five hundred pounds!" she positively shrieked. "Hugh, are you joking?"

"I do not know," I remarked, "why you should suppose I am joking. I cannot believe that I look as if I were joking, and I certainly do not feel it."

"But five hundred pounds!" Catherine was so agitated that she sounded as if she were hoarse. "Do you really mean that someone is going to give you five hundred pounds?"

"Of course I mean it! Am I in the habit of saying what I do not mean?"

"I don't understand. You must forgive me if I seem to be a little dull, but what you say is so unexpected, and so delightful. Fancy, Hugh, that's just the sum we've always fixed our hearts on. And you are so mysterious, and mother and I have been so upset. I've been up half the night--"

"And so have I." This was Mrs. Fraser. "I've hardly slept a wink for wondering if you had been run over by a motor omnibus and what hospital they had taken you to."

"So, dear heart," leaning close to me Catherine touched my cheek with her finger-tips and began to wheedle--she can wheedle if she likes--"if you were to give me some idea what this Mr. What's-his-name is going to give you five hundred pounds for, it would be--don't you think it would be rather nice of you? I do."

"Mr. Stewart offers to pay me five hundred pounds for conveying certain property of his from London to America."

Catherine knit her brows as if she were puzzled. As I looked at her the conviction was borne in on me, not for the first time, that she was distinctly pretty. I consider Catherine Fraser to be one of the best-looking girls I ever met.

"What can Mr. Stewart have to send to America for the carriage of which he is willing to pay five hundred pounds? That's what it comes to."

"I'm not sure that I'm at liberty to tell you."

"What's that?" The sudden change in her expression! "I thought it was agreed that we were to tell each other everything, that we were to have no secrets from each other. You're very mysterious! It's not like you the least little bit. Should I ask mother to leave the room?"

"I don't know why," struck in Mrs. Fraser, "you should be so anxious that I should leave the room. It seems to me as if Hugh were ashamed of what he's been asked to do."

"Is that it?" demanded Catherine. "Of course if Mr. Stewart has actually ordered you to say nothing then of course you must say nothing but has he?"

"I can't assert in so many words that he has." I looked at Mrs. Fraser; Catherine took the hint.

"I think, mother, that you had better go. I am sorry, but when a man and a girl are about to marry there must be things which they wish to talk about in private."

Mrs. Fraser looked black as she left the room, but Catherine opened the door and out she went. The moment she had gone Catherine turned on me.

"Now, Hugh, what is it? I know there's something, and you'd better tell me what."

"There's a great deal, but I can't tell you the whole story now. You shall hear all at the first opportunity I have. You know perfectly well that I have not the slightest wish to conceal anything from you, but this is a question of time. I expect Mr. Stewart here in an hour. I have agreed to be ready when he comes and to travel by the evening express from Euston, which will enable me to get on board the steamer to-night."

"I never heard such a thing in my life! You, who have never been farther from London than Margate, to talk about catching American steamers at Liverpool at half an hour's notice as if you'd been used to doing that sort of thing all your life. Now, Hugh, I don't wish to be disagreeable you know that; you also know what five hundred pounds would mean to me. But before you see your Mr. Stewart, or start for Euston, I should like to know something. I'm entitled to know something."

"I am perfectly well aware of that, my dear; I should like to tell you everything. I repeat, I wish to have no secrets from you."

"Never mind about telling me everything just now; tell me something. What is it you're going to take to America?"

"You'll smile when I tell you the whole thing sounds so ridiculous."

"Ridiculous? You can hardly be going to be paid all that money for taking something ridiculous to America. You only make me more curious by not speaking out. What is it? What are you going to take?"

"A case of pills."

"What! "It is no exaggeration to say that Catherine shrieked the word. "Don't be an idiot. You're mistaken if you think I'm in a mood to be played with."

"I told you you would smile. Nor am I in a mood for playing. I have it from Mr. Stewart's own lips that it is a case of pills which he wishes me to take to America."

"Hugh, if you're in earnest there's something mysterious about this."

"Of that I'm as conscious as you can possibly be."

"Why doesn't the man send his pills by post? Is it such an enormous case? Does it weigh tons?"

"No, it is quite a small case, capable of being carried in my waistcoat pocket. I do not know why he does not send it by post; I believe he has his own reasons."

"What kind of pills are they?"

"That is a subject on which he has volunteered no information, and, frankly, I'd rather not know."

She looked at me very intently, within her eyes a challenge.

"Hugh, I believe you do know."

"I do not know! I may have some sort of vague idea, which only amounts to a guess, but I'd rather keep it to myself if you don't mind."

"It seems as if it makes no difference if I do mind. Something has happened to you since you left this house yesterday morning which has made of you a different man."

"Perhaps you're not so very far wrong. The first chance I have I'll tell you all about it; now I must go and put a few things in a bag and get ready to start."

"You stick to your statement that you are to be paid all that money by a man you know nothing about for taking a case of pills mere pills; pills for human consumption from London to New York?"

"I did not say what kind of pills; I just said pills."

"Hugh, I suspect. You can't accuse me of being naturally suspicious, but there is something about this business of yours which I don't like."

"Candidly, there's something about it which I like as little as you do. Were the position an ordinary one I should refuse without hesitation; but it will take me perhaps less than a month to go to New York and back, and when I return to London I'm to have five hundred pounds. You know I've always told you that if I could only have the command of such a sum I would start in business for myself. I'm pretty well known in the dried fruit trade; I have what I may call a nucleus of a connection; I believe I could count on getting a certain amount of credit. I'm as sure as one could be of anything of the kind, that in a year I could get a good business together, and probably a comfortable home for you. We could be married, secure in the comfortable knowledge that I had ceased to be a clerk and that there was a decent prospect in front of us. Give me a chance and I'll make a rich woman of you, Catherine."

"I like to hear you talk like that, but I don't want to be a rich woman, Hugh; though I should like to feel that you were working for yourself as well as for me, and that someone else would not get all the fruits of your labours. I'd love you to have a business of your own and be your own master."

"Then let me take that case of pills to America and earn that five hundred pounds."

She shook her head and smiled I thought a little sadly.

"I should be very glad for you to earn that five hundred pounds; but for taking a case of pills to America it really is too ridiculous and, I might also say, too thin! No one pays such a sum for such a service! I wonder what kind of pills they are? After all, one can earn even such a sum as five hundred pounds too dearly." She paused to listen. "Whoever can that be at the front door?"

As I listened to the sound of the knocker I was conscious of the truth of what she said that one can earn even such a sum as five hundred pounds too dearly.

"Surely," she whispered, as if she were afraid of being overheard, "you have not been here an hour! That can't be Mr. Stewart."

It had been a feeble, hesitating sort of knock; not the boisterous rat-tat-tat which I felt might herald Mr. Stewart. I knew before Mrs. Fraser opened the door of my sitting-room that the visitor was not the man who had offered what to me was a fortune for going as he put it across the pond, NEW PAGE

CHAPTER X
THE OWNER OF THE COAT

At that period Mrs. Fraser had been my landlady for a good six years. She was the widow of a draper's traveller who had been in the employ of one house practically all his life, and who had met his death by falling off the top of a motor omnibus. Mrs. Fraser wanted five thousand pounds damages, but, acting on advice, to avoid litigation, accepted two thousand. It was unfortunately not so clear as it might have been that the fault was all on the side of the 'bus. I respect Mrs. Fraser; I may say I like her. I had considered the matter carefully and had formed the opinion that as a mother-in-law she might be a success.

At the same time I have never concealed from myself that she has her weaknesses. For instance, she has no nerves at all to speak of. If you drop, say, a pipe inadvertently from the mantelpiece she is apt to almost jump out of her shoes as if you had shot her. As soon as I saw her face in the doorway I knew the state she was in. Her cheeks were white, her eyes dilated, her lips twitching; she might just have had sentence of death pronounced on her, or she might just have learned that someone had broken her best china teapot either catastrophe might have made of her a gibbering wreck. She could hardly speak, just managing to mutter stammeringly, as if she were announcing something terrible:

"Hugh, there's someone to see you."

"Well, mother, who is it? Don't look as if the police had come to arrest him. Is it Mr. Stewart?"

Catherine, speaking lightly, had no notion how much within the range of possibility it was that the police had come to arrest me. Mrs. Fraser went on.

"I don't know who he is. I asked for his name but he wouldn't give it. He's a queer-looking man: I should say a foreigner. There was something about him which made me feel--"

What that something had made her feel she had no time to tell us. The hall door is only a few feet from my sitting-room; apparently the visitor had shown himself across the intervening space without waiting to be invited. Suddenly Mrs. Fraser looked over her shoulder, and whimpered with a sort of catching in her breath:

"Here he is."

She drew aside to make more room; whereupon there appeared in the doorway an individual whom she had not incorrectly described as a queer-looking man. Undoubtedly he was a foreigner; no Englishmen put themselves into such clothes or wear their hair so long. He was a small man short, meagre, thin; I doubt if he would have turned the scale at seven stone. His head, in proportion to his body, was so large as to be almost monstrous. He had a long, cadaverous face, with hollow cheeks and a big mouth. His thick lips did not seem as if they would quite meet; yellow teeth peeped out from between them. Enormous eyes, set far back, looked out from under a kind of penthouse shaded by eyebrows which overhung and were nearly as bushy as some men's moustaches. He had a broad, high forehead, which was crowned by an extraordinary growth of hair. I have never seen hair like it. It was not only that there was such a quantity, it was so coarse and greasy, and so untidy. He wore an old, queer-shaped top hat when he came into the room; when presently he took it off he seemed all hair. One wondered if he had ever used a brush or comb in his life, it was in such an amazing tangle. It hung down in a disorderly mass right over the collar of his coat, covering his ears.

Obviously Mrs. Fraser had been justified in her description. I know I stared at him in amazement, and so I believe did Catherine. He stood there, his old top hat in his right hand, and stared at me. Then he said, in good English, with just the trace of a foreign accent:

"Mr. Hugh Beckwith?" I admitted that I was. Then he looked at Catherine and Mrs. Fraser. "Can I speak to you alone?"

"What about? What is your name?"

"It does not matter what is my name. I wish to speak to you on a little private business if you will ask these ladies to be so kind as to leave us."

I was reluctant to do anything of the sort; I was not willing to allow him to speak to me, having an instinctive feeling that he had nothing to say which I wished to hear, and that he was the sort of person with whom it would be wiser for me to have nothing to do. While I was searching about for a form of speech in which to say so, Catherine took the words out of my mouth, and answered for herself.

"Come, mother, let us leave this gentleman and Hugh alone together. You will remember, Hugh, that you have an appointment with me in a few minutes; you must not allow this gentleman to keep you long."

As she followed her mother out of the room she favoured me with a glance whose significance I did not altogether understand. When the door was closed the visitor, his great head hanging a little forward, stood and looked at me as if he proposed to do nothing but stare. I was the first to speak curtly enough. Somehow he reminded me of a picture I had seen somewhere of an evil-faced Jew who dealt in second-hand clothing.

"Well, sir, what is it you wish to say to me?"

"You have something of mine."

He spoke in a thick, husky voice, as if there were something in his throat that impeded his utterance.

"I have something of yours? What do you mean? I have never seen you in my life before this moment."

"Yet you have something of mine."

"Pray what have I got which belongs to you?"

"You have a suit of my clothes."

"The Lord forbid!" The words were out of my lips before I had meant them to come; but the idea of wearing anything which had ever belonged to him was not a pleasant one.

"Mr. Beckwith, I come to you as a friend. I know that some badly-behaved people of whom I know very little have not treated you well: it is because of them that you have what I come for: it is a suit of clothes belonging to a drosky driver in St. Petersburg."

Then I began to understand. All sorts of imaginings came rushing into my head. Apart from his actual appearance no wonder I disliked the look of him. He was redolent of evil; he might have been Fagin the Jew.

"So you are one of that gang of scoundrels and you dare to come here."

"No, Mr. Beckwith, I am not a scoundrel I am not what you call one of that gang; on the contrary I am of the highest respectability, well and favourably known to ladies and gentlemen of wealth and of position, in all the countries of the world even to princes and to kings to sSy nothing of queens. Not for anything would I have you think that I am connected in any way with those creatures who conducted themselves so infamously to you. They have treated me as badly no, worse than they have treated you. That suit of clothes which I ask you to return was sent from Russia to me."

"Then you are Isaac Rothenstein?"

The change which took place in the man! I have never seen a person with St. Vitus's dance; I can only say that the muscles of his face began to twitch as if he were afflicted with some complaint of the kind. He turned right round, and I thought he was going to rush from the room. But since he made no movement towards the door, but simply remained with his back turned to me, I fancy that, conscious what a sight of horror his twitching muscles made of him, he was doing his best to get them under control before again confronting me. I know that when he turned once more his face was in repose, though there was a gleam in his eyes and a grin about his mouth which made me feel that it would need but little provocation to make him behave like a wild beast.

"Who did you say I am?"

"You heard me quite well. You say that those garments were addressed to you in which case you must be Isaac Rothenstein."

"How do you know?"

"Because they were enclosed in a wrapper which was addressed to Isaac Rothenstein."

"Did they break the wrapper, those those thieves?"

He asked the question with a sort of latent fury which was more impressive than any outburst of rage.

"The wrapper was, as you put it, broken already."

"Then how do you know it was addressed to me?"

"Because the name was on it Isaac Rothenstein, in big sprawling writing more than once. What I admire about you is your impudence you know what happened that you should dare to show yourself! Mr. Rothenstein, leave this room and this house! I'll have nothing to do with you!"

"Mr. Beckwith, be reasonable, I beg of you, my good friend."

"You call me your friend you!"

"I wish to treat you as a friend. My intentions towards you are of the very best. I am all eagerness to apologise for what those fellows did; although I had nothing to do with their bad conduct I am willing to compensate you to compensate you."

"How do you propose to do that?"

"It is only natural that you should feel angry, aggrieved, that you should wish, indeed, to be revenged. But, Mr. Beckwith, it is better to receive compensation for your injured feelings than to be revenged. Give me back my clothes and I will give you, as compensation, any reasonable small sum you care to mention. I will give you, say, five pounds."

"I doubt if your clothes, as you call them though you offer no proof that they do belong to you were worth five pounds."

"Oh, yes, indeed, they were my property, though, as you say, they were not worth five pounds nothing like it."

"I suppose there was nothing about them which was worth the money?"

"What do you mean by putting to me that question? What should there be about them which would be worth five pounds?"

"That you know better than I do."

"Mr. Beckwith, there was nothing about them which was worth anything at all. I give you my word there was nothing. It is only that they belonged to a dear friend, to a relative indeed. I will be frank with you, Mr. Beckwith. They belonged to a cousin "I wonder he did not say a brother! "to whom I was greatly attached. They were intended to be a memento of that attachment."

"A singular memento, Mr. Rothenstein."

"Yes, true. He was very poor that suit was all that he had."

"He must have been poor indeed!"

"It is not becoming to jeer at poverty, Mr. Beckwith."

"With that I agree; the sentiment does you credit. Unfortunately for the truth of your story, I am told that that suit of clothes was worn by the man who assassinated Stepan Korsunsky, the Prefect of Police worn by him at the moment when he committed the murder." The visitor's facial contortions began again. "You appear to suffer from some affliction of the muscles, Mr. Rothenstein."

He barked at me as a hyena might have done, showing his yellow fangs.

"Who told you that my name was Rothenstein? You think yourself too clever, Mr. Beckwith. Who told you your story told a lie--a lie! My cousin was a drosky driver who had no more to do with that affair than you had. He was poor, but he was an honest man. He never raised as much as a finger against authority; he was incapable of such conduct."

"The police seem to be of a different opinion."

"The police? What do you mean by the police?"

"When I handed over that drosky driver's uniform to the authorities at Scotland Yard they gave me the impression that it had been worn by the assassin, and on that account had been smuggled out of Russia."

My visitor's muscles began to twitch again; in fact, it seemed to me that he was in a sort of agony as if every muscle in his body twitched. Although his lips moved no words came from them. When he did speak it was in a hoarse whisper which made his voice sound as if he were speaking from a distance.

"You gave them to the police?" At first that was all he said. A sort of paroxysm seemed to tie his tongue. Then after a perceptible interval, with a convulsive effort he managed to add, "Do you do you mean that you gave my clothes--my clothes!--to the police--the pony-skin coat?"

"To whom else should I give them, Mr. Rothenstein? I had to report the outrage to which I was subjected in the proper quarter. Your cousin's 'memento' was, in its way, proof of the truth of what I said."

I feared that my visitor was about to have a fit; he seemed to be struggling with some internal convulsion, writhing and twisting as I had never seen anyone do before. Much though I objected to the fellow, I had to show some sort of human interest in his physical sufferings.

"You are ill," I told him. "Shall I call in my landlady? She has a friend who is an epileptic; she knows a good deal about the symptoms."

He clenched his fists: rage was added to his other troubles. If he could he would have hit me.

"I'm not ill," he gasped; "it is a little trouble to which I have always been subject. It is because you agitate me."

I watched him; it was not pleasant to observe how he seemed to be fighting for self-control.

"What," I asked, "have I done to agitate you, Mr. Rothenstein?"

"You tell me that my pony-skin coat is in the hands of your police, and you ask what you have done to agitate me? I would not have had it happen for a thousand pounds."

"You must have been much attached to your cousin if you value his mangy coat at such a sum as that. Half the hair had come away from the skin."

"What does it matter? Do you think it is the skin I care for? Oh, God of Abraham, what fools there are in the world! What stupidity! The fruits of a life of labour lost because of an English blockhead!"

"If your cousin's ancient garments are of such importance to you as that, possibly if you go to Scotland Yard they will be returned to you."

"I go to Scotland Yard! I go! What does he mean, this fellow? What does he speak? Does he wish me to put my head into the lion's jaws, that there should be an end of me?" Presumably he noticed that I was watching him intently, and on a sudden regretted the words which, in his heat, he had used. "I do not wish you to take me literally; of course--of the police I am not afraid--how should a respectable man be afraid of the police? But you must understand for yourself, that at my time of life I do not wish to be associated with people of the kind. All that I want is my coat, which has been sent to me from Russia." He paused, inclining his great head toward me, eyeing me from under his hairy brows as if he would read my thoughts. "You are sure that you have given it to the police at Scotland Yard--you are sure of that?"

"Mr. Rothenstein, I am a busy man; you have come here uninvited on what seems to me to be an impudent errand--"

"Why is it an impudent errand? How do you make that out?"

"You pretend to come after some some outlandish, wretched, rotten, ragged, filthy garments, which were forced upon me by your friends--"

"They are not my friends! Do I not tell you they are not my friends?"

"--in exchange for some quite decent clothes of my own. I say that is an impudent thing to do."

"I want my coat--my pony-skin coat!"

"Then go and get it. If you do not like to go to Scotland Yard go where you please. It is not in this house. I would not give such a disgusting relic houseroom. That will do, Mr. Rothenstein, I have heard enough; I am interested neither in you nor your cousin's memento. Take yourself off! I don't wan't to be discourteous, but you make me."

"Give me back my pony-skin coat!"

"How can I give you what I haven't got?"

"Did you did you find anything in it?"

"How do you mean did I find anything in it?"

"In the pockets or or anywhere?"

The anxiety which was behind this question in its way was tragic.

"Certainly there was nothing in the pockets. I had my hands in them half through the night, so I ought to know. What was there to find? There seems to have been something mysterious about that coat: I must give a hint to the police to examine it minutely."

"No! no! no!" He almost danced in his excitement. "You will do nothing of the kind! You will tell them nothing not a word! not a syllable!"

"Very well, as you please. I was only thinking that if there is something hidden in that old coat, as you appear to suppose, a little investigation will enable the police to find out."

"I do not wish the police to concern themselves in the matter. I beg you, Mr. Beckwith, if you are a gentleman, as I see you are--"

I cut him short having had more than enough of the man.

"That will do, Mr. Rothenstein; you have said all that before, or something like it. Allow me to open the door."

He placed himself in front of it so that I could not reach the handle.

"Before you do that allow me to say to you one word--one only."

"Very well--one only. It ought not to take you long to do that."

"No, it will not take me long, but I advise you to pay particular attention. When I see a man I understand him better than you suppose it is my business to understand. I do not pretend to understand you--what is in your mind and your heart, and so on--but I have a feeling that about my pony-skin coat you know more than you would have me think. That coat represents more to me than I can put into words--that I say frankly. I will soon discover if it is in the hands of the police at Scotland Yard. If it is not I shall understand you better. Look out for yourself! I will not lose sight of you either by day or night until that coat has been returned to me just as it was. Once more I ask you: is it in this house?"

"It is not. If it were not for my engagements I would take you all over it so that you might see for yourself that that is true."

"Very well, I accept your word; I daresay that is true. Is it at Scotland Yard?"

"Go there and inquire for yourself; no doubt they will inform you."

"In a few hours I will know. If it is not there mind, I do not say it is not, but I have my ideas then look out for yourself! I will discover where it is. I have ways of doing that of which you do not dream. As sure as you are alive, if you are deceiving me, telling me what is false, trying to rob me of what is mine you will be sorry. As sure as I am standing here and you are standing there grinning at me, Mr. Beckwith--there is something on your face which I do not like!--you will be sorry." NEW PAGE

CHAPTER XI
CATHERINE'S IDEA

I saw him out of the front door; he paused a second to take one more glance at me. Catherine came into my room before he had reached the pavement. Closing the door, she stood with her back against it.

"What," she asked, "is the meaning of this?" Before I could reply she went on. "Before you say a word I ought to tell you that I have been listening outside the door. Perhaps some people wouldn't think it a nice thing to do, and it isn't. But you're going to be my husband and I'm going to be your wife; you know perfectly well there's nothing in this world I would not do to help you. I didn't like the look of that old man, I didn't like the look on your face when you heard that there was someone to see you. I knew he had not come as a friend, and as up to yesterday morning you had not an enemy you're not the sort who makes enemies I felt that there was something going on that I ought to know, and I meant to know it. So I listened, and I heard every word that was said; perhaps you didn't know how loud you were talking. Hugh, what was all that about the pony-skin coat?"

I balanced myself first on my heels and then on my toes, and back again, as it were to give me time to pull myself together, her onslaught was so sudden; but Catherine mistook my intention.

"It's no use your trying to find a way to evade giving me a plain answer to a plain question." That was what I could not but feel to be the unjustified way in which she addressed me.

"You put that old man off with shuffling answers--I never thought you had it in you--but you're not going to put me. Once more, what is it about that pony-skin coat?"

"It's a long story, Catherine."

"Well, let's have it."

"I've been outrageously used in a house near Newington Butts--"

"Outrageously used? Who outrageously used you? How came you to be in such a house?"

"I can't go into details now. I'll just give you enough of the story in outline to enable you to see that nothing is farther from my wish than to keep anything from you; only please don't ask questions; they only cause interruptions, and interruptions mean delay. In this house, which I entered very much against my will, they robbed me of my clothes--perhaps you have noticed that this suit is not mine."

"Do you take me to be stone blind? I noticed it the very moment you came in."

"As I say, they robbed me of my clothes--every stitch!–and they put on me instead a dirty, filthy drosky driver's uniform."

"Whatever's that?"

"A drosky driver is a sort of Russian cabman; it appears that he wears a sort of uniform, as is the case with most of the drivers of our taxi-cabs--and in a disgusting state this one was."

"If they put you into that where did you get that suit from?"

"If you'll have patience I'll tell you. Then they locked me in a cellar, where, hungry, thirsty, and in darkness I spent the night, without even so much as a stool to sit on."

"Of all the extraordinary things!"

"In the morning that is to say two or three hours ago I got out."

"If you got out then why couldn't you do it before?"

"The people in the house were criminals hiding from the law. It seems that the police got on to their track, forced their way into the house, looked all over it, and then came to the cellars. They opened the cellar door; I didn't know that they were the police I thought they were those ruffians come back to do me further injury. I dashed out, rushed at them, knocked one them over, jumped through a window, and dropped to the ground. Being in the drosky driver's uniform, they took me for one of the men they were after. They fired at me--"

"Hugh! did they really fire at you?"

"They actually fired, in cold blood, but fortunately they missed. I found my way into a street beyond and jumped into a motor car."

"Whose motor car was it?"

"Would you mind having a little patience, Catherine? There was a motor car; I stumbled into it. I may mention that a lady helped me to get into it."

"A lady! What kind of lady?"

"Catherine! I was too done to notice anything, even where the car was taking me. It stopped before a house I went into it."

"You went into a house! Whose house was it?"

"I can't tell you whose house it was, but it was occupied by a person whose name I learnt was Stewart Paul R. Stewart."

"Did the lady go in with you?"

She did."

"Was she Mrs. Stewart?"

"That I can't say. Mr. Stewart addressed her as Darya."

"Darya what a name! Was she English?"

"I imagine she was Russian."

"Was she young?"

"She was not old perhaps under thirty."

"I don't call thirty old do you? Shall you think I'm old when I'm thirty? I'm not far off it now. Was she pretty?"

"She was not unattractive. She was beautifully dressed."

"Really, Hugh, you do appear to be having some adventures. W T hat happened to you in that house?"

"Aren't I trying to tell you? I do wish, Catherine, you'd let me get on. They gave me some breakfast--"

"You, a perfect stranger why?"

"For one reason, I take it, because they saw I was perfectly starving. And I fancy Mr. Stewart was in some way connected with the people in that horrible house."

"You mean those criminals who were hiding from justice? Perhaps he was a criminal himself. I felt that there was something wrong with the man. Go on."

"What's the use of your stamping your foot, and wanting me to go on when you won't let me? When I was locked up in the cellar I had on the drosky driver's coat. It was made out of a shabby old pony skin. I had nothing to do, so I put my hands in the pockets. In the right-hand pocket I felt there was something in the lining. I could not make the thing out, but when I had finished breakfast at Mr. Stewart's it came out all at once, and I held it up in my fingers to see what it was,"

"What was it? Anything particular? You seem to have been dealing in nothing else but mysteries 1"

"Mr. Stewart stooped down to look at it, and directly he saw it he snatched it out of my fingers, and made no end of a fuss."

"What did it look like can't you tell me?"

"It was a dark brown colour it looked like a pill; it was about the size of a pill and was round like a pill. Mr. Stewart said it was a pill. But it was certainly no ordinary kind of pill, or Mr. Stewart would not have made the fuss he did. He took me to his bedroom; I slipped out of the pony-skin coat and into a suit of his clothes instead this is the suit. When I got back to the room in which I had had breakfast, he presently came in and made me the offer I told you of he promised to give me five hundred pounds if I took those pills to America."

"Pills were there more than one?"

"I believe that while I was changing into his clothes he cut the pony-skin coat open and found, concealed in the lining somewhere else, other pills twenty-two of them altogether. It is those he wants me to take to America."

"But Hugh, what can they be? Of course they're not pills."

"The presumption is that they're not the kind supplied by a chemist."

51

"Then what are they? This old man who has just been here the thought of having lost them seemed to be very nearly driving him mad. So far as I could make out that coat is his property."

"That's no affair of mine. Those scoundrels robbed me of my own clothes and gave me that pony skin coat in exchange."

"Then, in that case, it's yours and the pills?"

"Catherine, you take my advice that's a point in which you won't inquire too closely. All I know is, that I've been offered five hundred pounds to take them to America; and, situated as we are as I am it would be absurd of me to lose a chance which may never occur again."

"Do you think you'll ever get to America with those twenty-two pills?"

"It won't be for the want of trying if I don't: don't try to put me off, my mind is made up. I'm quite aware that I'm not going to earn five hundred pounds for nothing at all; no doubt I shall have to run a certain risk; it is only reasonable to expect it."

"You won't earn the five hundred pounds never!"

"What induces you to say such a thing as that? I tell you I will."

"I tell you, you won't. You're a marked man, Hugh. You told that old man, Rothenstein, that you'd taken the coat to Scotland Yard; he'll find out that you haven't you remember he warned you that he'd find out where you did take it. Of course, it's what your friend Stewart calls the twenty-two pills that he's after whatever they may be. If he suspects that they're in your possession or in your charge whichever way you like to put it I've an uncomfortable conviction that he'll get them from you, if he has to take your life to do it. Anyhow, you'll never get them to America."

"We shall see. You seem to take it for granted I'm a perfect fool."

"I take nothing for granted. But don't you see for yourself that you must be a marked man? I don't use exaggerated language, but it's pretty those so-called pills represent a great deal to old Rothenstein, to say nothing of Mr. Stewart. The way in which they were brought to England shows that. You say yourself that those friends of Rothenstein's looked like scoundrels; do you think they'd stick at a trifle in dealing with you?"

"I admit that I don't. But what do you suggest I should do? Do you want me to lose the chance of earning the money which would make all the difference in the world to us? I should never forgive myself if I did. It may be weeks, even months, before I get another berth; and if I do as Mr. Stewart proposes, in a month I may be the owner of five hundred pounds. I ask you again, what do you suggest should be done?"

"I'll tell you what I suggest. As I stood outside the door listening to that old man shrieking at you, threatening you with all sorts of unpleasantness if he found out that you had told him a lie and you have the idea came into my head at once."

"What idea? Catherine, do speak plainly."

"It's good for you to talk about speaking plainly, considering I can't get anything from you that's in the least degree plain about what has been happening to you since yesterday morning."

"I've done my best to be plain, Catherine; I swear to you I've done my best. Will you tell me, if I refuse Mr. Stewart's offer, what idea you've got into your head?"

"I'll tell you, Hugh; don't get excited. My, idea is, that I should go to America instead."

She took my breath away. For a moment what she said seemed almost impudent. She, a girl, who knew less of the world than I did, having practically never been out of London in her life, to talk about going to America on such an errand! But the more I looked at her the clearer it began to dawn on me that perhaps, after all, her words were not so wild as they sounded. I have sometimes told her that she ought to have been a man. Unlike her mother, she does not know what it is to be nervous, to lose her presence of mind, her self-possession. She loves what she calls adventure. When she is in one of what I call her moods she has more than once lamented that there is so little of real adventure in the world to-day. I have the greatest faith in Catherine's resourcefulness; I have had experience of it. When I find myself in a position that is new to me I am a little slow and dull, not quick in adapting myself to new conditions.

Not so Catherine. Her wits move more rapidly than mine; she will always be at her ease. In no emergency would she be likely to be found napping.

"If it were not for your sex," I told her, "I should feel that there was a good deal in that idea of yours."

"What's the matter with my sex? Can't a woman do what a man can a woman of to-day? Don't talk nonsense, Hugh, or think it. You know better than that. As you say, we want that five hundred pounds, and we're going to have it. I'm not marked; Rothenstein would not know me if he saw me again."

"I'm not so sure of that; nothing escapes his eyes. I saw him look at you."

"Pooh! look! He looked at me for perhaps two seconds, not long enough for him to really see. They'll be on your track directly you leave this house till they've got from you what they want, while nobody will think of paying any attention to me. What's that?"

That was a knock at the door. We both of us paused to listen. Her voice dropped.

"Do you think that's Mr. Stewart? If it is I'm going to stop and talk to him, and you back me up. There's mother opening the door; there he is. Now, be a sensible darling, and follow my lead."

Mrs. Fraser opened the door to admit someone, but it was not Mr. Stewart; it was the girl he had called Darya. She looked at me and then at Catherine. Catherine also looked at me; I acted on the hint she gave me.

"I do not know your name," I said to the newcomer, "but this is Miss Fraser, the lady to whom I am engaged to be married."

"My name is Galstin--not a common name in England; but then I am not English. I am very glad to make your acquaintance, Miss Fraser."

"I have been telling Miss Fraser," I went on, "that Mr. Stewart wants me to start for America to-night. He is coming?"

"Mr. Stewart will be here directly. We did not think that we had better come together."

She looked at Catherine, who looked at her; I fancy that each woman was trying to take the other's measure. Something in Miss Galstin's manner suggested that she at least was not dissatisfied. She asked Catherine a question. I wondered if Catherine found her personality as attractive as I did. It was a pleasure to hear her speak.

"What do you think of Mr. Stewart's idea, Miss Fraser?"

"As matters stand, I think nothing of it at all."

Miss Galstin seemed to be surprised by Catherine's outspokenness.

"But why? Do you not wish Mr. Beckwith to go to America? Has he told you what he is to receive for a mere jaunt to Sandy Hook?"

"No sum of money can make it worth a man's while to lose his life."

"But why should Mr. Beckwith lose his life in a six or seven days' run on board a crowded steamer?"

"When Mr. Stewart comes, Miss Galstin, I will tell him why."

"Mr. Stewart is here tell him now."

And there was Mr. Stewart, standing in the doorway all smiles.

"I did not hear you knock at the door," I exclaimed. "I was looking out of the window, but I did not see you come in at the gate."

"I did not knock at the door, nor did I come in at the gate; I sometimes find it better to enter a house by a way of my own. I took the liberty to enter this house, Mr. Beckwith, by the back door, which I reached by the simple process of climbing over the wall which divides your garden from the one behind." NEW PAGE

CHAPTER XII
TWENTY-TWO

It did not seem to occur to Mr. Stewart that by entering the house in the way he said he had he might have been trespassing. I knew nothing of the people in the house behind: they were complete strangers. He certainly had no right to pass through their garden and climb over their wall into my premises. As I was about to point something of this sort out to him he showed that he had heard Catherine's last words by remarking:

"What have you to tell me, young lady?" He looked at her with what appeared to be that perpetual smile of his; then he turned to me. "This, I apprehend, Mr. Beckwith, is the young lady of whom you told me Miss Fraser. Very pleased to meet you, Miss Fraser. What is it you wished to tell me when I came? I heard you allude to something you wished to say."

Catherine has very frank, shrewd eyes of her own, and a trick of fixing them on the face of any person to whom she may be speaking. She gave Mr. Stewart glance for glance. I think her manner amused him.

"It is no use Mr. Beckwith going to America on the errand on which you wish to send him."

"That's all you wish to say to me? It seems to be a pretty good deal, Miss Fraser. Pray, why is it no use? Do you not wish him to go is that it?"

"It is not. I should like him to go. He will not get what you propose to entrust him with safely to America that's all."

"That again is a pretty good deal. Why won't he? Have you no faith in the man you propose to marry."

"Of course I have, or do you think I would marry him? I'd trust him with millions."

"Has he told you what I propose to trust in his charge?"

"He said something which I didn't understand."

"Did he say anything about a case of pills?"

"He did."

"Even granting that they're not quite of the usual kind, they're not worth millions. If you would trust him with millions, why shouldn't I trust him with pills?"

"The man to whom those pills belong has been to this house. If you had come a few minutes earlier you would have seen him leave it."

Mr. Stewart eyed her as if he were puzzled. He asked me:

"Mr. Beckwith, what does Miss Fraser mean?"

"Catherine is a little quick at jumping at conclusions, Mr. Stewart; a person whom I believe to be Mr. Isaac Rothenstein--"

"Rothenstein? been to this house? Are you sure?"

"He is a little man with a huge head, and a great mass of tangled hair if that describes Mr. Isaac Rothenstein he has been here."

"That sounds like Rothenstein." It was Miss Galstin. She and Mr. Stewart had been up to their former trick of exchanging glances, as if they wished to telegraph to each other an unspoken message. "How can he have found you out?"

"You know they robbed me of my clothes; in a jacket pocket there were some letters addressed to me. I take it that Mr. Rothenstein has had access to those letters and found my name and address on the envelopes."

"What did he say he wanted?"

"He said he wanted his pony-skin coat."

"How did he make out that it was his?"

"He said it was sent to him by his cousin in St. Petersburg."

"His cousin!" Miss Galstin smiled and Mr. Stewart laughed. "Did you tell him what you had done with it?"

"I told him that I had handed it over to the authorities at Scotland Yard."

Catherine interposed.

54

"And he did not believe it. He said to Hugh that he would find out if his story was true, and he threatened him with what he would do if he found that the story was false. He does not want the pony-skin coat; he knows what was in the lining he asked Hugh if he had found anything there. He wants what you found there you and Hugh together those pills, as you call them."

In his turn Mr. Stewart interposed.

"What do you imagine they are? You say 'as I call them.' What have you been telling this young lady, Mr. Beckwith?"

Catherine would not let me answer, she spoke for me without being asked. She seemed to dominate the situation I had never seen her in such a mood before; she seemed to be so full of vitality.

"Mr. Beckwith has told me nothing he knows nothing. You do not suppose that one need be told anything to take it for granted that no one is going to pay five hundred pounds for taking a case of pills to New York. Don't you see, Mr. Stewart, that Hugh's a marked man?" She moved to the window. "There, do you see that man at the corner he has his eye upon this house. When Mr. Rothenstein finds that that pony-skin coat is not at Scotland Yard, and never has been, he'll not let Hugh out of his sight until he knows where it is. If he starts with your 'pills' for America he'll have them taken from him long before he gets to New York. Can't you see that for yourself?"

"You seem to be a live young woman, if you'll allow me to say so, Miss Fraser. There's something behind your words. I'm wondering what it is. It's a matter of some importance to me that these trifles should get to New York by a certain day. It struck me that our friend Beckwith was the man to get them there. If you don't think so, who is?"

"Is a man necessarily wanted?"

"He's better than a monkey."

"But not so good as a woman."

"No? That's your considered opinion. This is the day when a woman fills the bill, but where am I to find the woman who would take this job on?"

"Here! I will! I'll take those 'pills' of yours to America."

"You're a sound woman, Miss Fraser, that's for sure."

"And I'll deliver them at the place in New York which you appoint, and undertake that nothing shall happen to a single one of them on the way?"

"You will that? Maybe you don't know it's a fair-to-middling tough contract you're taking on."

"I do; I know that if Hugh has charge of them, if he wants to keep his life he'll lose them quick. They'll have them from him dead or alive. They won't have them from me; I'll deliver them in New York."

"And pray why won't they have them from you? What more can you do than Mr. Beckwith, if they talk to you as you seem to think they'll talk to him? Your sex won't help you; they don't hold chivalry worth a cent."

"Never mind that's my secret, and with your permission I'll keep it. I'll just tell you that if you trust me I'll be on the spot with the goods up to time."

"Same terms?"

"On the same terms. You to pay all expenses and give me five hundred pounds in cash when I've carried out my share of the bargain."

Mr. Stewart turned towards me and laughed it seemed to be a habit with him. "It occurs to me, Mr. Beckwith, that when you do get married you'll get a wife." I guessed what he meant though.his language was ambiguous. "Our friend hasn't done much moving," he was standing in front of the window and nodded his head towards the man who was leaning against a lamp-post at the corner of the road. "Ever seen him before? Was he among that lot?"

I took his reference to be to the scoundrels who had so maltreated me.

"He is not one of those six ruffians, if that's what you mean. As far as my recollection carries me I've never seen him before."

"He's not English; yet I don't know he might be Scotch. Anyhow he looks as if he had time to burn. Do you think they'll find out that that ponyskin coat isn't at Scotland Yard?" There was a twinkle in his eye as he looked at me. "If they do, I shouldn't wonder, Beckwith, if there's trouble. When Isaac Rothenstein gets set on a thing it isn't easy to beat him off. I have heard stories about him which would surprise you law-abiding Englishmen. He's a law unto himself, is Rothenstein. What do you think of Miss Fraser's proposition?"

I had an idea that he had been leading up to that question from the first, and replied with perfect candour.

"I have," I told him, "great faith in Catherine's resourcefulness."

"But if she goes to New York and gets the dollars, what about you? I've a sort of feeling that it's to you I owe those pills, and if she cuts you out of your job where do you come in?"

Again Catherine did not wait for me to answer.

"Hugh knows perfectly well that I shall hand every farthing of the money you give me over to him. He wants the money for a certain purpose, and I only suggest that I should go instead of him because I believe that I shall be more likely to earn it. That is owing to no fault of his." She seemed to be in haste to add that. Between you he has had bad luck, to say the least of it, and I don't want him to have any more."

"I don't know what you mean, Miss Fraser, by saying that between us he's had bad luck."

"I mean, Mr. Stewart, what I say, and if he's not careful he'll have more. I'm not sure that he wouldn't have been wiser in the first place to do as he said he had done take that coat to Scotland Yard."

"The Lord and all the States in the Union forbid I Miss Fraser, you don't know what you're saying or you wouldn't say it."

"And I don't want to know, in the sense you mean. Anyhow he didn't take it, so it's no use talking. Are you going to accept my offer, Mr. Stewart?"

"I am, right now, with a difference. You shall both go, and you shall each get five hundred pounds."

"Do you mean that Hugh and I are going to travel together? What will be the use of that? It will only double the risk."

"That's not quite what I do mean. I shouldn't wonder, after what you've told me, if it's the intention of certain parties to follow Mr. Beckwith round the world if they think he's the guardian of those pills. Well, he won't be. They'll be in your charge."

"Then why should he go?"

"To divert attention from you that's one reason. There's a state cabin waiting for him on the boat which sails to-night."

"Is it engaged in his own name?"

"It is reserved for a passenger named George Peters. I have reasons for believing see how frank I am! that certain persons have already an eye upon that cabin; it's odd how well posted some people are in every little thing I do. If that cabin is not occupied they'll wonder why. They may look about the ship to learn if there's anyone else on board who is perhaps taking the place of Mr. Peters. I don't want them to light on you. It's not likely, it's a hundred to one chance, but I prefer that the odds against it should be a thousand to one."

"Am I to travel by the same ship?"

"You are as a second-class passenger."

"Do you mean to say that you had engaged a cabin for me before you knew I was going?"

"It's not a cabin, it's a berth. It was engaged for another lady who it was thought was going."

"I am that lady, Miss Fraser." This was Miss Galstin. "Until this moment I did not know that I was not. Mr. Stewart changes his plans and those of others very rapidly."

"My dear Darya, don't you worry. No one knows better than you that I am the sport of circumstances. Anyhow, Miss Fraser, you will occupy the berth which was taken for Miss Galstin. If the cabin reserved for Mr. Peters is also occupied he will be the object of attention; no one will give a moment's thought to anyone else. So you see that is one reason why Mr. Beck with should travel as well as you. You'll be strangers to each other; the first-class passenger will know nothing about the girl in the second. Then, also, I have a sort of feeling that it will do Mr. Beckwith no harm to get a trip across the water, and another five hundred pounds won't hurt either of you. Have you any objection, Miss Fraser, to my making the prize five thousand dollars?"

"That's equivalent to a thousand pounds. I've not the slightest objection to your doing that. At the same time one cannot help wondering how much those 'pills' of yours I understand that there are twenty-two--"

"You understand correctly; that's the number."

"are worth, and what the service you require really means, when without a moment's hesitation you pass from five hundred pounds to a thousand, as if the difference between the two amounts didn't matter in the least."

Mr. Stewart waited some seconds before he answered; he seemed to be summing Catherine up. The whimsical smile which was on his face as he observed her seemed to be a cover to a great note of interrogation. One felt that he was asking himself questions to which he was seeking to find answers as he looked at her.

"Miss Fraser," he said at last, "there's one thing I'm not paying you for curiosity. I'm not so simple as to suppose I can prevent your being curious, but please be as little as you can at my expense. I am just asking you to be a messenger, that's all. When a messenger in a department store is asked to take a parcel to a customer, he's not expected to carry his curiosity as to what that parcel contains to too great limits. You understand? Although you say nothing I can see you do; a young lady of your keen intelligence would. Here are the twenty-two pills I'm committing to your charge." He took a small wash-leather bag from his waistcoat pocket. "They are to be delivered to Ezra C. Bennington, 32 Paper Buildings, John Street, New York, if possible within ten days from this, and anyhow inside a fortnight. Here is the name and address, Miss Fraser; you had better keep it."

He handed her a scrap of paper; she looked at it carefully and then folded it up. He watched her keenly I thought anxiously.

"You won't lose that address, Miss Fraser; it's a little important."

"I will lose nothing." She looked at me. "Hugh, you shall have a copy of this."

"I don't think," commented Mr. Stewart, "that that's absolutely necessary. Mr. Bennington doesn't want more visitors than need be. If Mr. Beckwith goes to Raymond's Hotel on Sixth Avenue he'll find a room waiting for George Peters; when you're quit of your charge, Miss Fraser, you might join him. You'll find me. Raymond's Hotel is not grand, but it's clean and well managed; there we shall be comfortable together. Here's your charge, Miss Fraser. Would you like to look at it? You can."

He handed her the wash-leather bag. She crushed it up in her fingers as if it and its contents were things of no account.

"Thank you; I won't lose it now."

"There's one thing; you might at least make sure that it does contain twenty-two pills. It's the number I want you to verify to avoid misunderstandings later."

She looked at him as it struck me oddly; then she took off the mantelpiece a small round china ornament which I used as an ash-tray, untied the piece of pink tape which secured the neck of the wash-leather bag, and emptied its contents into the ash-tray which she had placed upon the table. After what Mr. Stewart had just now said I did not want to show any undue curiosity, but from where I stood I used my eyes to the best possible advantage. On the tray there was a small heap of what certainly did resemble pills. They were of a deep chocolate brown, all of the same size, precisely like each other. Catherine took them up one by one, returned them to the wash-leather bag, counting each out loud as she did so. As Mr. Stewart had said, there were twenty-two. Catherine announced the fact.

"The number is correct; you need fear no misunderstanding. They will be delivered to Mr. Bennington at the address you have given me."

"You perceive that they are pills?"

"I perceive nothing." She raised her eyes and looked him very straight in the face. "I prefer to perceive nothing. I agree with you this is a matter in which it will be better, on all accounts, to show no curiosity. When do you wish me to start?"

Mr. Stewart referred to his watch.

"The train leaves Euston in a little less than fifty minutes. I should like you to travel by it, Mr. Beckwith. Can you manage to do it?"

"I can. It won't take me long to put a few things in a bag; a taxi-cab will take me to Euston in twenty minutes. But you, of course, understand, Mr. Stewart, that I have no money and no ticket."

"Here is money ten five-pound notes. Here's your steamer ticket. You'll take a first-class ticket from Euston, and pay for it. You will also have to pay for any drinks you may have on board and the extras of any sort; you will also have to tip the steward and that sort of thing. I don't know if you're a good sailor; if not you'd better hire a deck chair you'll be able to get that on board. Even if you are generous you ought to land at New York with money in your pocket. I shouldn't advise you to play nice little games with pleasant, sociable gentlemen in the smoking-room, or anywhere. The steamer ticket is out and home. Whatever happens it will bring you back to your native land, where, as you know, you'll find five hundred pounds waiting for you at the City of London Bank. But nothing will happen. You'll get news from me at Raymond's Hotel, ten days from this, and also of Miss Fraser. You will be able to join forces and come back home together with a bagful of money. Now, Mr. Beckwith, is everything clearly understood?"

"Clearly, so far as I'm concerned. Catherine, where's my brown leather bag?"

"It's in the box-room; I'll give you a hand with it."

"As for you, Miss Fraser," continued Mr. Stewart, "I have quite a nice motor car. I propose to run you down in it, with Miss Galstin to chaperon us, a little way out of London to a station where you'll be able to catch a train which will land you at Liverpool in good time to get on board before the steamer starts. As I pointed out to you, you and Mr. Peters are strangers, and it's just as well that you shouldn't start by leaving London by the train by which he is going to travel. Mr. Beckwith, is that contemplative gentleman still leaning up against the lamp-post?"

I looked out of the window, and there he was. So far as I could judge he had not moved since I had seen him first.

BOOK II

CATHERINE'S STORY

CHAPTER XIII
THE FIRST STAGE OF THE JOURNEY

My name is Catherine Fraser. I am twenty-five years of age. And when I say that I have never been farther from London than Hampton Court Palace on one side and Southend on the other, and that all my life I have longed with a longing which cannot be put into words to see the world, all its great cities and queer places, and to start off on all sorts of splendid adventures, and to do things which no one has ever done before, you will understand what it meant to me to have a chance coming to me so suddenly that it might have dropped from the skies to go off to America all by myself on the most mysterious errand I had ever heard of. Not only was I to travel free, all my expenses of every kind were to be paid if they had not been paid I should never have been able to go but also I was actually paid for going, a sum of money of which I had never dreamed that I should become possessed. Five hundred pounds! Think of it! for doing one of the things in the world which I most wanted to do. The start was splendid. I did not catch the train in London, but at Bedford, and Mr. Stewart drove me down to Bedford in his motor. Lots of people would think nothing of that. They drive in motor cars every day all day long if they like. But I had never been in a motor car before not even in a taxicab. You cannot call a motor 'bus a motor car.

And to make it more splendid we drove at night Mr. Stewart, Miss Galstin, and I. It was an extraordinary sensation. I don't know which way we went, but in less than no time we seemed to have left the lights of London behind, and were out in the country real country! in the darkness. How we did rush along! I did not choose to let Mr. Stewart guess it, or Miss Galstin, but I was excited. When we got to Bedford, which is quite a town, I knew that I was then entering that land of romance which I had often feared I should never see.

I was left to find my own way to the train. There were reasons why Mr. Stewart and Miss Galstin did not wish to be seen in my society. It was quite a big station, and there were lots of people. When my train came in it was an enormous train, I could not see the end of it I got into a third-class carriage. As I opened the door I noticed a girl with very fair hair, dressed in a long travelling coat, move to where I was and stand and stare as if she had a mind to speak to me. If she had she changed it, and walked on. She got into a first-class compartment farther down the train. I wondered why she had stared at me. When Mr. Stewart had put me down just outside the station, as I was walking away from him she was on the pavement. Then she had looked at me as if she were disposed to speak.

The girl's peculiar manner rather worried me. It was silly, but I hoped she had not seen me speak to Mr. Stewart there were particular reasons why I did not want anyone to do that. Perhaps it was because of the little fluster I was in that I did not observe that there was anyone else in the compartment I had chosen.

The fact is that there was no one exactly in it, but just as the train was starting I perceived that there were some things on the opposite seat which obviously belonged to someone else. My inclination was to jump out and find an empty compartment. But there was not time; I should only have stopped behind if I had tried. The train was off. We had gone some little distance when the other passenger came through the door at the other end. It was a corridor train. I had not seen one before, but of course I had heard of them, and I wished there had not been such things. The man it was a man had evidently walked from goodness knew where, just as if the train had been standing still, and was returning to his seat.

Directly he appeared I caught up the book which I had brought with me and began to read; but I believe he noticed that I had not started reading till he did appear, and I daresay he formed his own conclusions. He placed himself in the corner opposite me. I did not look at him, but I knew that he was a big, weedy man, with dark hair and a long, hatchet-like face. If I dared not look at him, he did at me; it was not pleasant. Then in about ten minutes he spoke to me quite civilly, in a voice which somehow reminded me of Mr. Stewart.

"If you would like to see a picture paper I have some."

That is what he said. He did have some, I should say about a dozen. But although I like picture papers I was not going to take one from a stranger. I was as civil to him as he was to me.

"Thank you," I said. "I have a book."

"Is it a live book?" he asked. "Some books are awful dry reading."

He had no right to speak to me after I had given him to understand that I would rather he did not. Besides, how could I tell if it was a "live" book when I had not finished the first page? I told him so.

"When I have read more I may be able to give you the information you require; at present I have read none of it."

I was barely civil to him, but he did not seem to mind in the least. He immediately told me a story.

"When I was travelling from Naples to Rome the other day I hadn't so much to read as a patent medicine throwaway. So I went to the stall and I explained how it was. I said to the woman who was looking after it there's more employment for women in Europe than in the country I come from; I saw a woman harnessed with a cow to a plough not so very long ago that I wanted some kind of a book that I'd have to read till sleep took me. She couldn't speak any civilised language, and I am no Dago, but she gave me a book. I didn't look at it, because by the time I'd paid for it my train was slipping out of the station; as there's only about one every other week I couldn't stop to chatter. When I had planked myself down I looked to see what book she had given me. It was one of those interesting works in which they tell you how to swear at your hotel bill in twelve languages. Now that was a live book, because that's a handy thing to know. I have seen hotel bills which I should have liked to swear at in forty languages. Still that was not the kind of work I wanted, and I was alone with that book for the better part of that live-long day. I gave it to the conductor of that train the first chance I had. I believe he gave himself a crick in the jaw trying to ask me what I meant. I should have liked to look into that book to see if it told me how to explain, but it was no longer mine, and I didn't want to ask a favour of a man I didn't know."

That was the story he told me. It reads pretty flat when you have got it down, but I thought it rather funny perhaps it was the way he told it. But I did not dare to smile for fear he should tell me another, and I did not want to have a perfect stranger telling me stories all the way to Liverpool. I told him quite plainly that I would rather not talk, and he pointed out to me what a nuisance the stranger you meet in the train is who likes the sound of his own voice and thinks you must too. It seemed to me that that remark told rather against himself, but somehow I did not feel as if I could say so.

I did get to Liverpool, and I got on board the steamer, and when they showed me to my cabin I could just have hugged myself. There was an air of adventure about everyone and everything which made me want to dance the hornpipe. But I did not. I merely told myself that this really was a much better world than I had ever supposed it to be. I have not a word to say against the Fulham Palace Road, but at that moment I had a kind of notion that there were better places even than that, especially when you have lived in Grove Gardens for eight years without ever going ten miles away from home. Then I knew that I was going to get some practical idea of low big the world really is. NEW PAGE

CHAPTER XIV
ABEDNEGO P. THOMPSON

My cabin had two berths. I had the upper one. The lower berth had been engaged for a Miss Sadie Lawrence, so the woman told me who showed me to my quarters; she informed me, without my asking, that she was my stewardess and that her name was Mrs. Harrison.

When she had gone I examined my cabin. It did not take me long to discover one thing there was not a place in which to lock up anything; nothing in the shape of a lock and key, nowhere in which to keep anything private. It was awkward; I had not known what to expect, but I was not prepared for this. Not a nook or cranny in which one might keep anything one had which was of value. There were cracks in the woodwork in which tiny trifles could be crammed; under the mattress in my berth a scrap of boarding came away, that might be used as a hiding place at a pinch, though it was not a kind that appealed to me. Whoever made the bed might come upon that piece of loose wood just as I had done, and anybody of an inquiring turn of mind would soon discover what was supposed to be concealed behind it.

"If I had my way," I told myself, "and I were to build a cabin on a ship like this, I would have it properly fitted with strong cupboards lined with steel and secured by good locks, in which one might keep one's money and rely upon its being safe."

However, when I began to think matters over I saw that a cupboard on those lines would not quite do for me. If anyone knew that I had in my possession something worth having, and really wanted it, of course the first place in which they would look for it would be that strong cupboard. If the person was a desperate character, with his head screwed on, and had any tools worth talking about, he would force that cupboard open in a very short time, and where would its valuable contents be?

No, it was possibly just as well that one should be made responsible for the safety of one's own possessions. How one was going to safeguard them was not easy to say. So far as I could perceive the best way if they were not too large was to keep them about one's person. But then if one did that one had always to remember that a true desperado, bent on attaining his own wicked ends, would not stop short of personal violence; see what had happened to Hugh. Where should I be if they treated me as those conscienceless men had treated him? I am a pretty good fighter, for a woman, against fair odds; but suppose they took my clothes as they had taken his, what protection should I have against robbery then?

Obviously it was not altogether an easy problem. While I was thinking things over Miss Sadie Lawrence came in.

"I am Sadie Lawrence," she remarked before she had put her nose through the doorway, so of course that was how I knew who she was. "You're Miss Forester."

Mr. Stewart had booked the berth for Miss Forester, which was rather lucky, because of course the initial suited mine. Every single article of underwear I have is marked C. F.

"Often crossed before?" inquired Miss Lawrence, so soon as, so to speak, we had exchanged the time of day. When I told her it was my first time she gave a sort of shriek. "What! your maiden trip! I wish it was mine. I have crossed to the land of the stars and bars and the negro minstrels without burnt cork more times than I care to think. I am Sadie Lawrence, that's who I am."

She produced from a handbag a printed poster which she held up for me to look at.

"That's me," she said. She pointed to what was on it, reading aloud, as if I could not read it for myself. "'Sadie Lawrence. The World-famous Song and Dance Artist. Champion Clog Dancer, Sand Dance Queen.' If there's any lady artist now living who thinks herself a sand dancer I'm willing to match myself against her for any sum from five dollars to five thousand. I'm the winner of fourteen silver medals, that's what I am."

I had never seen a real artiste before, not, that is, in private life, and I cannot say that I was struck by the look of her now that I did. Not that there was anything against her, but there was not well, there was not so much style about her as I had expected to find. She was about

61

my height, but she was plumper and not anything like so healthy looking. She might think herself well dressed I found out before very long that she did but her ideas were not mine. She had the tightest frock on I ever had seen, which, considering her figure, was a mistake. It was too short both ends; cut low in the neck, which was red underneath the powder, and too high above the ground. She had on lemon-coloured shoes, and stockings which were meant to match, but the colour had run in the wash and they were just the wrong shade. She wore a long, grey fur which was not so new as it had been, and a violet velvet toque which was nothing like large enough for a woman with her sized head and face.

"Got much luggage?" she asked, as a man came in with a battered old leather trunk, which seemed to me to be falling to pieces.

"Not me; I've only got a handbag."

She looked at me sharply.

"How long are you going to stop on the other side?"

"Oh, no time; maybe a week."

"You must have money to burn. Isn't there anywhere nearer home where you can go for the weekend cheaper? What are you going for?"

"To see a friend who wants me to join her in the millinery."

I had quite expected that people would ask me what I was going for, and as an air of mystery was the one thing I wanted to avoid I had made up my mind what tale I would tell. But somehow, when I talked to Sadie Lawrence about the millinery it didn't seem to sound right. She looked me up and down, in particular she looked at my hat.

"Millinery!" she remarked. "Are you going to make the hats? Who made yours?"

As it happened I had made mine myself, and I was not ashamed of it either; but somehow there was something about the way in which she asked the question which seemed to make it difficult to answer.

"I'm not going to do the making," I said. "I'm going to look after the business side."

"Perhaps that's just as well," she replied, "though they do say that milliners never do put a decent hat on their own heads. I suppose you have got some money with you?"

I was surprised. I think I showed it.

"Why do you say that?"

"Well, if you're going to buy a millinery business--"

"I didn't say I was going to buy it."

"Well, take a share in it it comes to the same thing."

"Nor did I say I was going to take a share in it; I am only going to look." Since the only way to stop her asking questions seemed to be to ask them myself I put one to her. "Going to America to fulfil an engagement?"

"An engagement? Gee whiz! I'm going to work the McCulloch circuit four months on the road. Talk about one night stands! people don't know what that sort of thing means till they try America. You do two shows a night, and maybe a matinee; then you do the same thing at some place four hundred miles away to-morrow, with no connection to speak of, so that the Lord only knows how you get there. It's a dog's life, my dear, you get that tired and I have done my stunts when I've been three parts asleep. And talk about food! you can't get any, and what you do get you can't eat. And you don't see a bed for days together. But the money's good. Vaudeville does draw them in some of those back blocks which are going to be some place some day but just at present aren't on the map."

She had taken her toque off and was doing something to her hair with a sort of nail-brush, on to which she had poured some stuff out of a bottle.

"Don't you ever," she remarked as she eyed herself in the small looking-glass which was to do for both of us, "go in for vaudeville. God help you if you ever let yourself get older than twenty-five; the trouble with me is that I've been twenty-two so long that I shall have to make it twenty-three before I'm very much older. You stick to hats."

She could talk. She fixed up her things in what was going to be our cabin. She asked when I was going to turn in. When I told her about ten or half-past, she wanted to know if I would mind her making it two or three hours later. As a compensation I might get up first she never turned out till noon. She confided to me that she hoped to make a little money on the way over by giving what she called "impromptu sing-songs," to which everyone was welcome, but a "silver collection" was more welcome still.

"I've just about blown it all in," she said. "Someone will have to pay for my drinks on board, and if I don't get some hard cash somehow before I put my small threes on dry land, it will be padding the hoof for me and lacing myself up tighter."

I did not see how she could do that, as it seemed to me that she must have been poured into her corsets, so that I wondered how she managed to breathe but I had a sort of idea that I knew what she meant.

Sadie Lawrence was not the only conversationalist on board. I never met a friendlier and more sociable lot of people than there were in our part of the ship; everyone spoke to everyone, and it seemed to be the one idea of most of the people who spoke to me to tell everything about themselves and find out everything about me. I liked the first part of the idea better than the second. All the while I had a sort of uneasy feeling that people or at any rate some of them were more interested in me than I was ever likely to be in them and that for good reasons. There were no end of foreigners on board, but there was not one I did not look at out of the corners of my eyes, wondering if whoever it was was looking at me.

One of the first persons I noticed was the man of the train. He was not only quick to notice me; he greeted me as if we were old friends. I am bound to say that I could not help rather liking him; he was such a friendly kind of creature and so transparently sincere. That he seemed to me a little wrong in the upper story made no difference at all. He seemed to have been everywhere and done everything. There was not a thing he had not been. He declared to me that he had followed every trade and profession there is; and, as if that proved it, he produced a list of all the things he had been, with the dates when he had been them. His chief avocation, he declared, had been that of drummer, which it seemed was what we call a commercial traveller. There was nothing bought or sold which he had not represented on the road according to him. Sometimes several of them at once.

"One time," he asserted, "I travelled in Bibles, in shot-guns, rye whisky, and a patent preparation warranted to cure anyone of the drink habit though between ourselves that whisky was more likely to do that than anything I've ever met. I did hear of a man who, having bought a dozen bottles of my rye, passed away inside a week. So after that I added coffins to my other lines. They paid as well, if not better, than any of the others. I carried baby linen and wedding rings, and a little series of popular handbooks on popular subjects, like How to get Rid of your Wife, and How to Divorce your Husband, and that sort of thing. I may say, without fear of contradiction, that that trip I stood for ai varied a lot of goods as any drummer on that road."

His name, so he said, was Abednego P. Thompson, and whether he was telling the truth, I never even tried to guess. I do not believe that he recognised that there really is an essential difference between truth and falsehood. He embroidered truth till you couldn't tell it from lies, and his falsehoods were so well done that they sounded as if they might have been true.

On the second morning after we had left England I had a shock. I was talking to Mr. Thompson, or rather he was holding forth to me, when who should I see on the other side of the deck but the girl who had stared at me on the platform at Bedford station. I don't know how to describe it, but I had had a feeling that she would be on the boat. Mr. Thompson was there, and probably others in that train were catching the boat so why not she? The discovery that she was there did not therefore take me by surprise. All the same the sight of her gave me a little shivery-shakery sensation which I would not own to on any account.

She had on the long travelling-coat which she had been wearing on the Bedford platform and the most becoming little fur cap; as she leaned back against the railing I thought how nice she looked which does not mean that anything about her appealed to me, because it did not.

Mr. Thompson, followed the direction of my eyes, and made a sort of whistling sound through his breath.

"What's the matter?" I asked.

It was a second or two before he answered; then he turned right round, so that his back was towards the girl and his face to the sea. He spoke more softly than he had been doing. As a rule he spoke in one of the most penetrating voices I had ever heard. It was a surprise to find that he could modulate it so well.

"I've seen that young woman before. I've a good memory for faces, I wonder if she has?"

"Perhaps you saw her on the train which brought you to Liverpool?"

"Was she on it? I didn't know. Where I saw her was I wonder if she'd remember where it was if I asked her?"

I recognised that it was no affair of mine; still, curiosity pushed me.

"Where was it?" I asked.

There was a look in his eyes which rather startled me. I wished I had not asked the question.

"You're a friend of mine," he began, which annoyed me.

"How can I be a friend of yours when I don't even know you?"

"You wait and let me say my piece. I say you're a friend of mine."

"And I say I'm not."

"Well, if you'd rather have it that way you're not; only I kind of feel drawn to you, as the writers of the stories say, so I'll tell you something which I wouldn't tell anyone else."

I resented his tone and hinted as much.

"Thank you, I would rather you didn't tell me any secrets in confidence. Secrets are things I don't care for."

"Then you are the first girl I ever met who doesn't. There are girls who like secrets other people's secrets better than candies. You can feed them with such stuff from the rising up of the sun to the going down thereof."

"You couldn't me make no mistake. I'm not interested in your lady friend; I'm sorry I mentioned her."

My intention was to snub him, but it was not easy to do, when he said something as if casually which made me prick up my ears.

"I wonder if she's mixed up in the Korsunsky scandal?"

"What do you mean?"

"Not much. It's this way. It's put about that that Russian Prefect of Police, Korsunsky, was killed for political reasons by what the newspapers call Nihilists; but I have heard it whispered that it was nothing of the sort. Korsunsky was very fond of the ladies."

"How do you know?"

"I have been to Russia more than once, and more than twice. When I was last in Moscow there were all sorts of tales going round about Stepan Korsunsky and his women."

"Had he anything to do with the girl over there?"

"You had better let me tell you my story and then hold your tongue, in case of trouble."

As he had made me curious, I let him not that I intended to believe a word he said. He was looking at the sea again, and spoke as if he were thinking out loud.

"It all comes back as plain as if it had happened yesterday instead of more than four years ago."

"What! more than four years ago! However old is she?"

"As young as she looks. I never knew a woman who was older. In Moscow it was. There was some sort of religious procession going through the streets; they are whales on that sort of thing out there. The police were holding the people off the road. All at once something happened. The police and the soldiers stood up. The procession was stopped, and moved to one side. A carriage came along, driven at a smart pace. The proceedings were interrupted till it had passed. The police and soldiers saluted. The carriage was open, a man and woman were on the back-seat. The man, I heard afterwards, was a near relation to the Czar: the woman that's the woman over there."

Without moving his body he pointed with his thumb behind him.

"As the vehicle came abreast of me one of the horses shied; the driver lost control; people lost their heads; the whole caboodle would have been into the crowd if I hadn't caught hold of the reins it wasn't hard to do; another two or three feet, and the horses would have been trampling on yours truly. I can hold a horse. Horses like me. The woman stood up, glanced over the coachman's seat, and looked at me. I took stock of her. I guess we saw each other pretty well for just long enough to remember what we looked like. I've a good memory for faces; I wonder whether she has the same?"

"Have you ever seen her since?"

"Yes, twice; that's it why, I wonder if she remembers?"

Something in his tone made me glance at him.

"Where was it your second meeting?"

"In gaol. I can't give you the name of the place, but it is a big prison just outside Moscow. I had got a permit to look over it it's one of the usual travellers' sights. In the women's quarter was our friend over there. She had a cell all to herself. They unlocked the door to let me see her she was their sensational exhibit."

What he said was unexpected; it startled me.

"Are you sure? People ought to be very careful how they say that sort of thing, unless they're absolutely certain."

"I am. I remembered her, and she remembered me. I felt awkward, but she didn't seem to mind a little bit. She just smiled. They told me she was awaiting her trial on a charge of being mixed up with a gang of crooks who had been flying at some very high game. What became of her I never heard. You don't hear much about what happened in a case of that kind when you're outside Russia. But I wondered, and for a row of beans I'd ask her."

"You'll do nothing of the kind what a monstrous notion! Even if you're right, and it is the same girl, don't you dare to breathe a word of what you've said to me to any other soul upon this ship."

Again several seconds passed before he answered.

"Your sentiment is pretty, Miss Forester, and does you credit. No man wants to be down on a woman, but I have heard that there is some very valuable property being carried on board this ship. There are jewels in the first class worth more than a dime; their owners wouldn't trade them for a dollar; maybe more. One of the greatest troubles the nice kind gentlemen who run these ships have got to fight is the passenger who hopes to pick up a little bit of someone else's on the way over. Gangs of international crooks look upon an Atlantic liner as their happy hunting-ground. Now suppose, Miss Forester I put it to you I just say suppose that the lady over the way has friends on board, and there happened to be on this boat something very specially worth having. A little fact like that isn't announced in the daily papers; it's perhaps only known to one or two, but that gang may have got hold of it. Wonderful noses people of that sort have!"

Mr. Thompson removed his glance from the water, turned round, stood up and put his hands in his overcoat pockets. It seemed to me that he was taller than I thought he was.

"Once there was a man who had something which he rather valued which he didn't want to let anyone know that he had got, and did want to get info God's country without anyone knowing what he was after. There was a leakage somewhere. One person knew, and that was the one who before all others he would rather didn't. That one got together a little gang and the little bit of property was missing when the ship sighted the Statue of Liberty and it's been missing ever since. That sort of thing takes place every time a boat crosses. Don't you think that I'd better drop a word in the proper quarter that there may be sneak thieves on board, and that a special eye had better be kept upon a certain lady? Suppose now, Miss Forester, you had something you rather valued, don't you think you'd like to be warned in time in a case like that?"

I did not answer. I fenced, and I changed the conversation. I was in rather a funny state of mind when I left Mr. Thompson. My opinion of him was inclined to change. Perhaps after all he was not so simple as I supposed. There had been something about him the whole time he had been talking which made me wonder if he knew a little more than he cared to let me think. There is this about me, I do know what I don't know; I was quite aware that my experience of the world and its ways and its people was just nothing. Mr. Thompson might be aware of this even more clearly than I was. He might even have arrived at the conclusion that my ignorance, great as it was, was not so great as my stupidity. If he had, then I rather fancied he was wrong.

That day I kept seeing a good deal of the girl from a distance. One can't help seeing a good deal of the people who are on the same ship that carries you, especially if they have your own fondness for haunting the deck. Several persons spoke to her, men and women. Probably some of them were entire strangers who, in introducing themselves, seemed to be following the custom of the country. Men in particular seemed to find something attractive even about me. I should say that the male creature who wasn't attracted by her appearance was an unusual specimen. All the same, although probably the majority of those to whom she talked were strangers, there was one whom I felt sure she had met before. He was slight and thin, with very dark hair, and an enormous moustache, and would have been quite handsome if it had not been for a disagreeable expression which gave one the idea that he did not know what it meant to be in a decent temper. I felt convinced that he and I would quarrel inside ten minutes, because the one thing I cannot bear is a bad-tempered man. That they were old acquaintances I felt convinced, although, so far as I knew, they did not exchange more than half a dozen sentences.

I had rather an odd experience that night. I was lying asleep in my berth, when all of a sudden, although I was asleep, I became conscious that something was happening. I suppose everyone knows how, sometimes, one realises that a dream is a dream realises it in the middle of one's sleep. All of a sudden there came to me the idea that I must be dreaming a dream which was just beginning. I had an eerie notion that something was touching me so softly, imperceptibly, that I could not even feel the touch, as sometimes is the case in dreams. And yet I was unhappy. An intangible something seemed to be passing right over my body not in the least degree painfully; yet I was afraid. I hoped, still sleeping one does do that sometimes that I was not going to have a nightmare. The touch kept on; the oddest thing was that I could not make out which part of me was being touched. I lay perfectly still, wanting to move, yet incapable of motion. It was horrid.

Then something occurred which broke the sort of spell against which I was struggling. The touch became very tangible indeed, reached my throat, pinched the skin. In an instant I woke up.

The cabin was in darkness. I heard and could feel what I had learnt was the movement of the propellers it always seemed to me to be just beneath our cabin; the throb of the engines; the faint swish of rushing water and the snoring of Sadie Lawrence in the berth below. There was not another sound. I stretched out my arm to feel if there was anyone standing near my berth. Apparently there was not; my fingers passed through vacant air. I sat up and listened more intently. Then my ear did seem to catch something. I had a sort of notion that the cabin door was being softly closed. I felt certain that I heard the click of the latch ever so faintly, but beyond a doubt. I sat up straighter.

"Who's there?" I cried. "What do you mean by coming into our cabin?"

It did not occur to me that if whoever had been in had gone out it was unreasonable to expect an answer. I kept quite still, wondering what I ought to do. The switch of the electric light was by the door. I had to climb down from my berth to get at it. It was a nuisance, yet, since the visitor might have left a trace of his presence, it might be as well to discover what could be seen.

I got down on the floor, having to rest my foot on the edge of Sadie Lawrence's berth to do it. Then I reflected that the sound which I had heard might not have been the visitor leaving. For all I could tell he might be still in the cabin. If I moved, he might attack me.

I had to chance that. I did move, quickly, to where I supposed the switch was. The darkness confused me; I could not find it. I seemed to have come into contact with every single thing before I got it.

When I did reach that switch in about one-tenth of a second the cabin was flooded with light, and there was not a thing to be seen nor anything to show that there ever had been anything to see. Sadie Lawrence's clothes were lying just where it seemed she was in the habit of throwing them before she got between the sheets she had no notion of neatness and she herself was lying in her berth with her back towards me snoring like a grampus. I did not know when she had turned in, and it was perhaps not surprising that I had not disturbed her since she had certainly not disturbed me. I must have been pretty sound asleep about as sound asleep as she was. In spite of all the clatter I had made she snored placidly on.

I had asked her to bolt and lock the door when she came to bed, not fancying leaving it for anyone to come in who chose. A momentary glance showed that she had done nothing of the kind; anyone outside had only to turn the handle to walk straight in. I turned the key and shot the bolt, so that, should the visitor be minded to pay us another call, he might not find entry so easy the second time as the first.

I should have been driven to the conclusion that my imagination had played me a trick, though I do believe that I am the least imaginative person that ever was, and that no one and nothing had touched me except in dreams, had it not been that as I eyed my bedclothes in search of I knew not what, I saw something lying on the tumbled quilt. I gave a snatch at it. When I had it in my fingers I couldn't make out what it was.

Then it dawned on me that it was a tiny pair of tweezers attached to a silken thread. NEW PAGE

CHAPTER XV
HUGH'S NOTE

The next morning there was weather. When I woke up again I could not make out what had happened to my berth; one moment I seemed to be trying to stand on my feet and the next on my head. It was most surprising. Then there were various noises to which I was not accustomed, among them some singular sounds from below. It was several seconds before I understood that they were coming from Sadie Lawrence. She was making the most doleful din. I inquired over the edge of my berth if she was in pain.

"What's the matter with you?" I asked.

"Ring for the stewardess and tell her to bring some brandy."

She spoke in a voice which I scarcely recognised as hers, with a sort of involuntary pause between each word.

"What do you want brandy for at this time of the morning? Are you ill? Do you want the doctor?"

"Stewardess brandy," was all she seemed able to gasp. Then with a kind of rush, "I'm as sick as a cat."

Then I understood. Outside there was weather, and my fellow-passenger had an attack of the seasickness of which I had read so much. That surprised me. She was an old traveller. According to her own statement she must have passed a large part of her life in making voyages, and here she was groaning for brandy, while I, who had never been to sea before in my life, was not conscious of the least discomfort.

I was still more surprised when I found what the state of things on board seemed to be. So far as I could make out I had the bathrooms nearly to myself, and the breakfast-table, instead of being uncomfortably crowded, was practically empty.

"What has become of the others?" I asked the steward when I saw that at my table, which was meant for twenty, there were three of us.

"Sleeping a little longer than usual, miss," he said, and grinned. "There's a bit of a swell outside, perhaps you haven't noticed it. Some ladies and gentlemen don't like it when the boat starts dancing."

It was all so funny. There were things on the table to keep the plates and cups in their places fiddles the steward told me they were called, though I don't know why; in spite of them the coffee would keep splashing over, so that it was not easy to drink. When I had finished breakfast and I ate quite a good one the weather or something seemed to have made me hungry the steward tried to prevent my going on deck.

"It's blowing a gale," he told me. "You won't be able to keep your feet, and you won't find another lady up there."

"You'll find me," I informed him. "I haven't come to sea to be kept downstairs." I could not get out of the habit of calling "below" "downstairs."

"I have never seen a gale in my life, so if there is one blowing I'm going to see what it looks like."

And I did. It was not so bad as that steward had made out. The deck-chairs had vanished that was the worst of it but if you kept tight hold of something and did not try to move there was not much risk of your going overboard. And there was a wind ! When it came right at me, as it sometimes did, it seemed to blow the breath out of my body, especially if it caught me with my mouth open.

But it really was a sight worth seeing. What amazed me was that I was the only person there to see it. What was making other people feel so queer, I could not make out. If it had not been so hard to move about, there wouldn't have been a thing to find fault with. All the same, I did manage to get about to some extent. Then I became aware that, after all, I was not the only person on deck. It seemed that I had been on the wrong side, on that on which the wind was. Quite a number of persons were on the other side, under shelter. And then something which I had not at all expected happened.

The first-class passengers seemed fond of what I was told was called a hurricane deck. It was higher than ours, and I thought when I looked up at it how much I should like to go up there: one would be to some extent above the waves, and you would get a better view of the way in which the tumbling waters seemed to be doing their best to boil. But no second-class passenger dare place so much as a foot on the first-class deck, so I had to be content to look up and want.

As I looked there came to the side of the deck nearest to me Hugh Beckwith my Hugh. I had taken it for granted that he was on board because it had been arranged that he should be, but I had not been able to find out that he positively was, and, indeed, I had not even ventured to ask. The last thing I wished people on board that ship to suspect was that he had any connection with me.

So the sight of him on that hurricane deck was the first intimation I had that we really were fellow passengers to New York. The joke was that though I saw him he did not see me; I was looking in his direction, but he was not looking in mine. I was rather glad, because, although of course I should have loved to catch his eyes, Hugh is emotional it's not the slightest use denying it; if he did see me, the surprise and pleasure might be so great that in his excitement he might lose his head and do something which would show that we had met before.

So I was rather glad that I had not been recognised, and sneaked under the sort of roof which sheltered the approach to the stairs which led down to the cabins, resolved to leave the deck until the risk of being seen by him was gone. But it chanced that luck was against me.

I was just on the point of going down the staircase when, of all things in the world, he called out to me. How he made his voice carry was a mystery; he must have just hit a lull in the wind and shouted in a peculiar tone.

"Catherine! Hullo-o-o!"

That's what I heard coming at me. I was so startled that I nearly tumbled down the staircase. Luckily I did not quite or he would have shouted again. I did not want the whole Atlantic Ocean to learn that he was on sufficiently intimate terms with me to call my Christian name at the top of his voice. I had had no notion he had such powerful lungs.

Rushing on to the open deck again as fast as I could, lest, under the impression that I had not heard him yell, he should do it again, I stared up to where he was leaning over the rail. I was in a furious rage. That he should behave with such insanity was madness. I was aware that Hugh Beckwith was not one of the wisest of men, which was one reason why I had volunteered to take his place as Mr. Stewart's messenger we did want that five hundred pounds; but that he could have done anything so abjectly stupid as to stand up there against the sky-line calling at me, I should not have credited.

I made signs to him to try to behave with some sort of common sense, and I will do him the justice to say that when he saw my gesticulations it did begin to dawn on him what an idiot he was. When I turned my back upon him and walked so far as one could walk in the other direction, I rather imagine that I drove my meaning home. I walked right up to the end of the deck, holding on to whatever I could, and staggering anyhow; then paused, as if I were admiring the prospect instead of grinding my teeth with rage, turned, walked back, just giving one glance as I moved up at the first-class deck.

Hugh was still there, all alone. I was surprised at that; because, when I learnt how many people were upset by the weather, I said to myself, that if he were on board he was probably among those who, as the steward had put it, were sleeping a little longer. Somehow I had had a sort of feeling that he was just the kind of person who at the first chance he had would be sea-sick.

Instead of which, there he was standing as straight as anyone could, clinging with both hands to the railing, and looking down at me.

He had on his mackintosh, buttoned close up to his neck, and a cloth cap crammed down over his eyes, which cap must have been new because I had never seen it before.

I was in mortal terror lest he should speak to me when I got near enough my idea was that if he did not, but allowed me to come and go unnoticed, folks might be induced to think that that first wild yell had not been meant for me. So, after that momentary upward glance, I kept my eyes carefully averted, ignoring him utterly. I thought I had succeeded; that the impression might get abroad that, after all, we were entire strangers, because even when I got directly underneath him he did not breathe a syllable, so far as I could hear, though I admit that the wind was making such a noise that he might have bellowed and yet remained inaudible. However, I do not think that he did attempt to address me; he did much worse; he dropped me a note. I saw something fluttering in the air, glanced up to see what it was, perceived it was a scrap of paper. I did not for a moment realise what it meant; then caught his waving hand, and my blood turned cold.

The scrap of paper was for me from him. The wind was whirling it off the ship and out to sea; then it suddenly changed its mind, brought it back right into my face. It struck me with such force, in fact, that it positively stung. I made a grab, crushed it in my hand, gave one vicious upward glance, retraced my footsteps, staggered under cover. Under no circumstances would I give that absurd man an opportunity of adding to his blunders.

When I was under cover, I dived for my handkerchief and wiped my face; my wet cheeks smarted with the salty spray. As I dried them, who should come up but that girl I had seen at Bedford station. Where she had sprung from I could not guess. She had not been visible hitherto. Yet that she had been somewhere close at hand was sure, because the moment I caught her eyes I knew that she had not only heard Hugh shout, but also seen him drop that scrap of paper. She spoke in a voice which was not only pleasant, but in anyone else I should have called it musical. Nothing about her ever could be musical to me: instinct told me that. She might be a foreigner, but her English was perfect, her accent most refined. Whatever her moral character might be, the instant I heard her speak I had no doubt whatever that she had been born and bred a lady.

"You are a good sailor? You like wind, and the rough sea?"

That was the remark she made, when all the while I felt that she had her eyes upon that scrap of paper which I still held crumpled in my hand.

"I'm sure I don't know," I told her, "if I am a good sailor or not, since, as you are probably aware, this is the first time I have been to sea, and it is yet too early for me to judge."

That was my reply to her; that it was not very civil or tactful I know as well as anyone can tell me. There was I will call it an atmosphere about that girl which not only filled me with a feeling of dislike, but also with what was almost terror. I once saw a butcher kill a pig, and cut it up, and do all sorts of horrid things. The sight was horror to me, but I was a small child, and could not drag myself away. The worst part was that I knew the butcher liked what he was doing; that one of his ideas of pleasure would be killing pigs and other creatures the whole day long. I could see his cheerful grin and hear his merry whistle, which betokened his enjoyment of the job.

That girl recalled the butcher; I could see her using me as the butcher had done that pig. I had not the faintest notion what might be the cause of any spite she had against me; perhaps she had none, but would enjoy stringing me up by the feet and cutting my throat, and that sort of thing, just for fun. I knew that the consciousness of her presence upon that boat would spoil the pleasure of the trip for me, whatever happened. I suppose that that was why my answer to her was so rude and tactless.

I went down to the cabin where people were supposed to write letters and read, and be quiet. There were some people in it, but not many, and some of those who were there seemed to me as though they would have been much better somewhere else. They seemed to be both ill and unhappy. I found a chair in a corner, away from anyone else, looking round to see that I was not being watched by anyone in particular. Then I read that scrap of paper which had come fluttering down from the hurricane deck. Hugh had scribbled on it in pencil:

"Glad to see you are not ill. I am not actually ill, but am feeling beastly. Don't like the sea. Comfortable cabin, but am spied upon by someone. I don't know who. Yesterday afternoon someone went through all my things, looking, I take it, for you know what. Don't suppose they were satisfied with the result. If that sort of thing is going on till we reach New York, and I believe it is, I'm in for a time. Hope I shall get to America alive. Glad you are in charge instead of me. I do not like to think of the risk you are running. Feel most dispirited; hate the ship; wish I had never seen Mr. S. Want to kiss you bad. You don't know what it feels like to see your own girl, and not be able to kiss her. Send me some sort of a message please. Fancy I'm kissing you. HUGH."

That was what that ridiculous person had scribbled upon that scrap of paper. If, as instinct told me was the case, that girl was on board for a particular purpose, fancy what might have happened if that note had been blown to her instead of to me. In what he said about my being in charge, Hugh gave the whole thing away. It was all very well for him to talk about not liking to think of the risk I ran; but if that scrawl had got into other hands, that risk would have become certainty. That the persons who were shadowing him would not hesitate to cut my throat if they even suspected that I had what they wanted, I was most unpleasantly convinced. It was very nice of Hugh to say that he would like to kiss me; I was quite with him there. All the same, when, looking up, I saw that girl standing in the doorway, glancing at me, a shiver went down my spine. NEW PAGE

CHAPTER XVI
A MEMORY OF MOSCOW

Two days passed, and nothing happened. The weather went as suddenly as it had come; indeed, that same evening the wind had practically gone. Nearly everybody appeared at dinner, there were no "fiddles" on the table; and when I went to bed the sea was nearly calm, and there seemed to be little or no danger of my having to sleep in turns on my head and feet.

Sadie Lawrence, who had spent the day in her berth, was just getting up when I turned in. She was a disturbing person to have as a fellow passenger. Her habits were her own; she told me herself that she liked to turn night into day which is not my idea of decent living.

"Do you know," she told me, putting the finishing touches to what she flattered herself was her smart hat while I slipped out of my skirt, "something rummy seems to have happened in this cabin last night. I wonder if I was sprung when I turned in."

"How am I to know," I told her, "since I was fast asleep when you came to bed? I don't know if it was the sea air or what, but last night I seemed to sleep unusually well. What do you mean by you think something happened in this cabin?"

"I remember hanging my hat on a peg when I came in, but this morning there it was upon the floor against the door, looking as though someone had used it as a carpet. Didn't you notice it when you went out?"

"I noticed that all your things were on the floor, but I took it that that was how you liked them to be."

"The stewardess picked up my hat when she came in, and she said, 'Someone's been trampling on this pretty hat of yours, Miss Lawrence. They've broken the feather. I suppose it wasn't broken when you took it off!' One can't be dead sure after one has had three or four very last drinks, but I'm betting twopence that that feather was all right when I came in here, and I swear I hung the hat upon the peg. It's my belief that someone asked himself in when we were both asleep, and did a step-dance on all my clothes. I shouldn't wonder, my dear, if it was someone after your coin; no one could be such a ninny as to think that I've got anything worth taking. Everyone says that you've got bags of gold."

"Who's everyone?" I was startled.

"Some gentlemen friends with whom I was having a chat last night chaffed me about sleeping in the Safe Deposit Company. When I asked what they meant, they said you had got things hidden away in this cabin which are worth more money than anything in the Bank of England. Of course I knew they were only rotting, but if you do happen to have anything worth sneaking, money or money's worth, I should take it to the purser. He'd give you a receipt, and it would be safe with him till you set foot on shore. You may take it from me that they're not all saints and angels who travel on an Atlantic liner."

It was close on ten o'clock when she went out of the cabin; where she was going to, or what she was going to do at that time of night, I couldn't think.

Ten o'clock is my bedtime, or it is no fault of mine, and if I were to start my day when sensible people are going to sleep, there would soon be an end of me. Sleep from ten to six is what suits me.

That time I did not go to bed as soon as she had left me. I had been struck by what she had said. Somehow, although I had only been on the ship as it were five minutes, an idea seemed to have got about that I was a more interesting person than I wished to be Who was it that had told Sadie Lawrence that I had got something worth having? I had expected, when I made that arrangement with Mr. Stewart, that I might have a little trouble between Liverpool and New York; but it was beginning earlier than I had counted on.

I locked the door, and I bolted it, and I wished I could keep it fastened, and not have to leave it open to admit of Miss Sadie Lawrence's coming in which might not be, so far as I could make out, till it was nearly time for me to get up. I had read, of course, of cabins with several berths, and had wondered how one managed if one's cabin mate had tastes and habits which were quite different to one's own. It seemed as if I should have that point settled before I reached New York.

When the door was fastened, I went very carefully over practically every inch of that cabin. If anyone had caught me, they might have been excused if they arrived at conclusions which were not complimentary to me. I even took a small screw-driver out of my bag, and with it drew the screws out of a small batten which was just above my berth, and from behind the batten I was just going to take something when I had the start of my life. Someone knocked at the door, and turned the handle. Most fortunately it was locked, or there might have been trouble. Passengers are not supposed to remove battens from the walls of their cabins.

"Who's there?" I inquired I dare say a little shakily.

"Me, miss, Mrs. Harrison. Could I speak to you for one moment?"

Mrs. Harrison was our stewardess. I got down from my berth, leaving the screws on the quilt, and opened the door as quickly as I could.

"Miss Lawrence sends her compliments to you, Miss Forester, but she has forgotten her purse. She can't think where she left it. Will you oblige her with the loan of half a sovereign?"

Mrs. Harrison's face was quite grave, and there was not a twinkle in her eyes, yet I felt that she appreciated the impudence of the request as much as I did. Left her purse behind, and didn't know where? That was pretty thin. To send the stewardess to borrow from me, a complete stranger, half a sovereign that wanted some beating! I do not lend money; in fact, until then nobody had ever asked me to. My impulse was to send Mrs. Harrison empty away. Then I compromised. I sent Miss Lawrence five shillings, which I hoped that I should get back in the morning.

When Mrs. Harrison had gone, I just peeped behind that batten, returning the screws to their places, undressed, and turned in too conscious of the escape I had had to resume my investigations any further. As a rule I sleep lightly; mother will tell you that the slightest sound wakes me up. It must have been the effect of the sea air, because again I slept right through Sadie Lawrence's coming to bed. That the process had not been a noiseless one, the state the cabin was in when I did wake up distinctly suggested. That time she had not only left the door unfastened, she had left it open. Any passer-by, he or she, could have peeped in and seen me in bed. Perhaps Miss Lawrence did not mind making herself a public spectacle; I did.

The way she snored! How I could have slept through the noise she made was a marvel. When I turned out for my bath, a woman came out of the next cabin, stopped me, and said: "Whoever is it making that dreadful noise?"

"Do you mean snoring? That's the lady that shares my cabin."

"Is she a friend of yours?"

"She is not; I never saw her till I came on board the ship."

"But what an affliction, having to sleep with a perfect stranger who makes a noise like that! But can you sleep?"

"That's the odd part of it it seems that I can. She does not come to bed till I am asleep, and then I am so fast asleep that I keep on."

"You are lucky. I should have thought that the noise she makes when she does come to bed would have disturbed anyone. It disturbed me. Surely she was not sober. Someone brought her to her cabin, and helped her to undress. I could hear the two voices talking."

That was a nice thing to be told that I had slept through a scene like that! What could have kept me from waking up? I made up my mind that I would ask to be given another cabin even if I had to pay something extra. But when I spoke to Mrs. Harrison, she told me that there was not another berth to be had; all the second-class cabins were full. When, after breakfast, I told this to Mr. Thompson I felt that I had to tell someone, and he seemed to be the most sympathetic person on board he said the ship was so full because we were taking home a large party of excursionists, who had reserved practically the whole of the second-class accommodation. The information did not reconcile me to the prospect of sharing a cabin for the rest of the voyage with Miss Sadie Lawrence.

"What strikes as queer," observed Mr. Thompson, "is that you should have slept through the din she made. My cabin is right away from yours, but I heard her. And you say you are a light sleeper."

"I am, as a rule. I cannot imagine how it was that I wasn't disturbed."

"I suppose it's all right." As he said this he rubbed his chin, and kept his eyes studiously turned away from me.

"What do you mean you suppose it's all right?"

Well it's funny. Your lady friend--"

"She's not my friend how dare you?"

"Your cabin mate turned in last night as if she were a band of music; sure to goodness, the whole ship heard it playing; it seems queer you didn't and you a light sleeper."

"Mr. Thompson, you're driving at something what is it?"

"Miss Forester, you were so good as to inform me that I was no friend of yours, since you've got to know a man a hundred years before he's got any right to call himself your friend and I've only known you fifty. So I find myself in a delicate position."

"Don't be silly! if you can help it! Tell me straight out, what are you driving at?"

"It's like this, Miss Forester; I take an interest in you which you may not think is justified. I've kept you under observation and made inquiries, and put two and two together which is like my sauce! and the result is that I have arrived at certain conclusions which you will resent."

"How do you know until you tell me what they are?"

"You are alone upon this ship; I have met no woman who has seemed better able to take care of herself than you are. I have an idea that you've as many eyes in your head as most of us, and more than some. At the same time, I wonder if you see everything there is to be seen."

"You're very mysterious, and I hate mystery."

"Yes, maybe we'll take it as said."

"What are you driving at? Please speak plainly."

The man annoyed me so that I should have liked to stamp my foot.

"You are the centre of mysterious interest to others, Miss Forester, I can tell you that."

"Indeed? Pray on what grounds do you make that statement?"

"The lady's name is Cara Oudinoff at least that's how she's entered on the ship's books though I don't fancy that that was her name when I saw her first."

"Are you referring to the girl you were telling me of yesterday?"

"I am. Just look behind you at the present moment. Miss Forester, there's been a queer thing happened in Russia. I have some friends over there who are in the know; I had a letter from one of them before I came away. There's been a big robbery, not a word of which has reached the public here for reasons. It is whispered that one of the persons chiefly concerned in the theft was the Prefect of the Police, Stepan Korsunsky. There was a misunderstanding between him and his accomplices they did him in. Rather than let certain facts become known, the persons robbed have preferred to say nothing they're in a position to say nothing. Orders have been issued that no one is to say anything."

"Are you connected with the police, Mr. Thompson?"

"No, Miss Forester, I am not, but my informant is a person who knows he's in a position to know he told me in confidence what I am telling you. I'm not afraid of you talking."

"Why ever not? Why shouldn't I talk? I haven't asked for your confidence. I've told you before that I don't like secrets."

"That's as it may be; you ought to know considering that you've a pretty big one of your own."

The man made me uncomfortable when he talked like that; there seemed to be a hidden meaning in everything he said. I cannot bear to have to look under a person's words to find out what he means. I told him so.

"A secret is a relative thing, Miss Forester. Probably nothing that ever happens in this world is known to one person only for long. When we say that a thing like that Russian business is kept secret, we mean that everything possible is being done to keep the knowledge in a certain narrow circle, each member of which is interested in letting it go no further. I can't tell you how many people are in this secret, but I rather fancy that they've all reasons of their own for keeping their knowledge to themselves. You have."

"I! Mr. Thompson, what do you mean? What nonsense you are talking."

"You know something; you don't want to know more; you don't want anyone else to know what you do know; so, though you're a woman, you're pretty certain not to talk."

"You say that I know something about a robbery which has taken place in Russia. If you only realised what ridiculous stuff you are talking! What do you suppose I know? Is it any use my telling you that until you said so I had not the vaguest notion that a robbery had taken place in Russia and I have only your word for it now."

"Exactly I'm wondering what Miss Oudinoff and the rest of them think you know. Miss Forester, I'm not trying to thrust myself upon your confidence I'd rather be kept outside of it. But there happen to be certain people on board this ship who are making a dead set at you, for reasons which you probably understand better than I do. And I'm asking you to take care that no one doses you with any drug just before you go to bed for the purpose of keeping you ignorant of what happens to you in the night. Here's Miss Oudinoff coming to ask what you think about the weather. I don't want to talk to her you can." NEW PAGE

CHAPTER XVII
MR. TROUNCER'S STORY

On the morning of the fifth day out, Miss Sadie Lawrence was awake when I got up which was surprising. The first intimation I had of the fact was when I was doing my hair. We had a little bit of looking-glass stuck against the wall where no light could reach it, so that, no matter how easy-going you might be, you might count upon losing your temper every time you tried to find out what you looked like from the back.

"Swearing at the looking-glass?" was the first remark she made.

"I was doing nothing of the kind," I told her; "no one has ever heard me swear yet. I was only saying to myself that I wish they'd put this mirror where one could see something."

"They won't; they never do." Presently she added, "I'm fed up with your old ship! Next time I cross, it will be by aeroplane."

I did not know if she was in earnest or not, so I said nothing. After a while she made a remark which I did not understand.

"There's been a bit of a barney in the stalls."

"What might you mean?" I asked.

"They've done someone in in the first class a party of the name of Peters done him in in style."

At that I did prick up my ears. Peters George Peters was the name under which Hugh was travelling. Could her allusion be to him?

"If you could only talk so that an ignorant person like me could understand what you say, I'd be obliged. What do you mean by they've done someone in?"

"Pretty nearly killed him, that's what I mean. I thought everyone could speak the king's English."

"Pretty nearly killed who?"

"Oh, chuck it! You want too much explanation. I was only going to tell you a little talk I heard last night, but I don't want to keep on saying things over and over again." She sat up on her elbow, and glared at me as if I had been in fault. "I tell you that yesterday they nearly killed a party in the first class state cabin he has named Peters."

The only thing we had in that cabin to sit down upon was a small folding chair with a carpet seat, which Miss Lawrence had got from the stewardess; so I sat down on that, because I had to sit on something and Sadie Lawrence screamed: "Take care! you're sitting on my hat!"

I was not; I had presence of mind enough to be aware that the hat was there, so I caught it up as I sat, and held it on my knee. She was not satisfied with the plain proof that it was uninjured.

"Put that hat down! Hang it up on a peg! Don't you know that's the only hat I've got, and goodness only knows when I'll be able to stand myself another."

"How do you know what you told me?"

"How? Bless the girl, how should I know? You look as if you'd had something to do with it."

I was conscious that there was something perhaps a little unusual about my manner.

"I asked you how you knew."

"Can you keep a still tongue in your mouth?"

"I can." The question coming from her was the height of the ridiculous, considering that she was perpetually cackling about everyone and everything.

"Then I'll tell you especially as I want you to lend me another five shillings." That would be the sixth five shillings she had borrowed in four days Mr. Stewart's money, not mine. "I've got a friend in the first class he's a steward, though, mind you, he's quite a gentleman he's got a cousin who's a major in the Royal Artillery. He might have been a soldier himself, only he says there's more money in stewarding, and I shouldn't wonder if he was right. I dare bet that there's more to be got at his game than there is at mine. Look at me never a dollar in my pocket always on my uppers. Though, mind you, if I had a hundred dollars this moment, I should be stony in the morning. Money always does run through my fingers like water--"

"You were saying that you had a friend in the first-class saloon."

"Yes Tom Trouncer; there now, that slipped out; I never meant to tell you his name not that it's one he has any cause to be ashamed of. Don't you breathe a word you'll get him sacked if you do."

"What did Mr. Trouncer tell you?"

"Mister Trouncer! fancy calling old Tom Mister. But that's by the way. What did he tell me? Why, he told me everything, every blessed morsel. You seem uncommonly interested, Miss Forester."

"You think so? Well, you can tell the story to someone else when I'm gone." I got up, and returned to the mirror. I knew that making cut that I didn't care a bit was the best way to make her go on. "Hope you slept better last night." I gave a dab with the brush at my hair. "I dare say there isn't anything in your Mr. Trouncer's story, or it would have been all over the ship by now."

"Would it? That's all you know. There's only one or two who know, and they won't blab. The captain doesn't want it to get about for fear of frightening the passengers."

"It seems to me there's really nothing to get about."

"Oh, isn't there? You know a lot, don't you? There's a man been killed, that's all."

"Killed! Do you say he's been killed?"

"As good as. Most likely he'll be dead before tonight, if he isn't dead already."

The idea of Hugh dying, or anything like dying, all alone in that state cabin by himself, with me close at hand and not able to do a single thing to comfort him or even send so much as a message that did take it out of me. No wonder I wanted to sit down on that carpet chair again. But I wouldn't I kept standing up. I wanted her to go on.

"I don't understand your story in the least. What did you say was the name of the person to whom this has happened?"

"I told you his name was Peters so far as anyone knows. Tom says he's a card. He's got a fine state cabin which cost a hundred and twenty pounds, and he doesn't seem to have five bobs' worth of clothing."

"Whatever does your Mr. Trouncer mean?"

I knew of my own knowledge that the clothes Hugh Beckwith had were worth more than that.

"Just got one bag, one shabby old leather bag, which didn't cost more than a guinea when it was new, which was about the time of the ark. And all he has got, Tom says, is the suit of clothes he wears; his boots are the very commonest and cheapest; reach-me-downs, Tom says his suit is perhaps cost fifty shillings when it was bought."

I happened to know that the suit which Hugh was wearing cost fifty-five, so for once in his life Mr. Trouncer wasn't so far out.

"There's a mystery about the fellow, Tom says always has been since he came on board. Tom thought he might be someone who was doing a bolt from the police."

"What right had your Mr. Trouncer to say a thing like that?"

"I don't know that he did say it, he only thought though I don't know why you should snap at me even if he did. The other morning he told Tom a rare yarn; how someone had come into his cabin in the night, and run the rule all over it. But as Peters admitted that the door was locked when he got up though Tom says that locking your cabin door's a mug's game; where would you be if you wanted to get out in a hurry? anyhow Peters owned that the door was locked, so how anyone could have got in without unlocking it he couldn't explain. Tom looked upon the yarn as a try on."

"What did Mr. Trouncer mean by that?"

"Why, it's a common game on board ship. Somebody says they've been robbed, and lays a claim for damages when they never had anything in their life worth prigging they're just trying it on. That's what Tom meant by thinking it was a try on."

"Then how dare he think anything of the kind?"

"Upon my word! You do talk! To listen to you anyone would think that this Mr. Peters was a friend of yours. Does he happen to be?"

"I never knew a person named Peters in my life."

It was perfectly true, though, of course, I was keeping something back. I was not going to blurt out things to Sadie Lawrence.

"It's a queer start anyhow a chap like that in a state cabin which cost a hundred and twenty pounds. Everybody's noticed it it isn't natural; the steerage is more in his line." I did not like to hear these things said about Hugh, but I didn't know how I could stop it. I just kept on brushing my hair. "Tom is his steward, and nice and sore he was about it. He's always looked upon that cabin as worth a fiver to him, but he didn't expect to make a dollar out of Mr. Peters and now they've done him in."

I had to put down that brush, and hold on to the shelf which was in front of the mirror. It was all I could do to keep my voice steady.

"What do you mean by they've done him in? What have they done?"

"When Tom went in yesterday morning to say his bath was ready it's a regular suite, private bath and all there was Mr. Peters lying right across the bed, without a rag of clothing on him. He didn't wear pyjamas, but an old-fashioned night-shirt twill cotton it was made of." Considering that I had made it I knew all about Hugh's night-shirt. "The nightshirt had been torn right off him. The funny part about that night-shirt was that H. B. were the initials on it that does not look as if his name was Peters. When Tom saw them, he wondered if the fellow had murdered Mr. Peters and was taking his place; but according to Tom he didn't seem to have grit enough to murder anyone."

That was a nice sort of thing to say! As I listened I felt that I would give a trifle to have a word or two with Mr. Trouncer.

"I was not aware," I managed to get out, "that not being of a murderous turn of mind was against a man."

"Who said it was? How you do go on! When Tom saw him first, he thought that he was dead, he'd been handled something cruel: his head was twisted right round on his body, so that, as he lay on his stomach, his face was upwards. He was black and blue with bruises and every bone in his body seemed broken as if they'd dragged him round and round the cabin and banged and smashed him against everything they could, to say nothing of kicking him to a jelly."

That was nice sort of talk to have to listen to, without even daring so much as to wipe my eyes. I had to sit down again on the chair.

"Was he--" my voice would break "--was he dead?"

"What's the matter with you? If what I'm saying upsets you, I'd better not go on."

"I think I must be a little out of sorts this morning, that's what it is; and the idea that this should have happened so close to all of us, and no one gone to gone to the poor fellow's assistance is a little upsetting."

"Very nearly, but not quite. The doctor says the chief trouble is concussion of the brain. Whoever did it must have had a grudge against him; they seem to have done everything to him they could. Why he didn't cry out and call for help was because they'd twisted a cord or something round his throat so tight that if they hadn't taken it off just when they did, it would have been a case of strangulation there was a great weal round his neck where the cord had been. He couldn't have uttered a sound while it was on, do to him what they might, and the life was all out of him by the time they took it off."

I tried to speak when she paused, but for a moment it was beyond me; I had to put up my hands to hide what was on my face and in my eyes, and I shuddered. Never before had I felt as I did then.

"Good gracious, you must be a bundle of nerves to make such a fuss. I suppose by any chance it wasn't you who did him in. There's something funny about you somewhere. If you haven't got a guilty conscience, what have you got?"

"It's so so awful! to think of it happening so close to us."

"Oh, stuff! That's for a tale. If you go through life carrying on like that every time a chap's done in, you'll be a howling maniac before you've done."

I said nothing; I just put all the restraint on myself I could, and after a while I pulled myself together.

"I am foolish, I admit. It isn't like me to be upset like this about a trifle." A trifle! when drops of blood seemed to be draining from my heart. "What I don't understand is, if this took place yesterday, why has no one heard of it?"

"Don't I tell you? Tom's been told to hold his tongue, and the staff has been dropped a hint that if the story gets about there'll be trouble. It's quite easy to have a thing like that kept dark. Why, I was once on a steamer going to South Africa when a man was murdered in his berth, and not a passenger knew anything about it till we landed at Cape Town. Then it came out that not only had the man been murdered, but they'd got the chap who did it; they'd kept him locked up somewhere forward all the while."

"Have they any suspicions about who did this?"

"Can't say Tom thinks not. Every blessed thing in the cabin had been turned topsy-turvy; the furniture had been broken open, the woodwork stripped off the walls; someone had been looking for something for all they were worth. What it was they were looking for, and whether they found it, there was nothing to show. Tom thinks not and because they wanted the chap to say where it was, and he wouldn't, they did him in."

"But the whole thing must have taken some time; how was it that no one heard anything suspicious?"

"That's the wonder. The cabin is on the upper deck, right amidships. Tom says how anyone got in without being noticed is a puzzle; one reason why he didn't believe the chap's yarn about someone having run the rule over the place was because he didn't think it possible that anyone could have got in. The whole thing's a puzzle. Of course, as Tom says, there are any number of people on board who would be willing to cut anybody's throat for a couple of dollars, but there seems to be nothing whatever to point to the particular parties who did this."

"But surely, if the story was made public, they'd have a chance of finding out who were the guilty persons."

"Tom doesn't think so. There's an inquiry going on all the while don't you think there isn't; you're being watched, and I'm being watched, and we're all being watched on the quiet. So long as nothing is said, the parties who did it--"

"You think there were more than one?"

"Sure; no single person ever handled a chap the way he was. Get them to think that nothing's doing, and they may do something to give themselves away. We shan't know it if they do perhaps Tom mayn't; they've got their own way of doing things on a ship. They may have someone locked up somewhere at this very moment, we should never know it. A person's missed; you ask about him; they tell you he's ill, the doctor's looking after him. He can't see visitors. How are you going to prove that it's a lie you can't even begin. People die on board, and nobody knows, except the captain and his lot. Passengers don't like to hear about such things and they don't."

"Do you mean to say that this person may have died, and nobody know?"

"Rather; from what I can make out, the chances are that he is dead. Tom doesn't know anything for certain, but he understood that he was pretty bad last night; that may have been his last night on earth. What's the odds? When a chap's been handled as he was, it's sometimes just as well that he should die. I knew a party who had his head burst in; they kept him alive somehow; that's ten years ago, and all that time he's never moved or spoken, or known a single thing. He's lain like a log of wood. All he can do is swallow the food they put into him through a silver tube. What's the good of that sort of life? Would he be worse off if he was dead? It may be the same with that chap who calls himself Peters; whether he lives or dies, he'll never be much good in this world again. Here, you'd better skip. I'm going to get up. There isn't room in this dog-hole for two people to dress together."

I what she called "skipped." That is, I took myself outside the cabin; I found a quiet corner I knew my way about the ship by then and how I did cry! I had always told myself that I was not a crying sort; I knew better then. If I could only have got within reach of Hugh, it might have been something; but I knew that even if I asked them, they wouldn't let me. There was nothing for me to do but cry. NEW PAGE

CHAPTER XVIII
CATHERINE'S TROUBLE

The sense of utter helplessness was, I think, the worst part of it; the consciousness that I knew nothing definite. I placed not the slightest reliance on anything Sadie Lawrence had said. I had seen enough of her to be aware that probably she herself often did not know if she was speaking the truth. I should have liked to be able to get within reach of Mr. Trouncer; he might have been able to tell me a good deal that I should have liked to know; that I should have been happier for the knowledge was another question. Situated as I was, ignorance seemed worse than unhappiness. As I ate my heart out, I almost felt that bad news was better than none.

One person I did find to talk to, Mr. Abednego P. Thompson. I certainly did not seek a conversation with him even in the midst of my trouble. He dogged me. I was restless, could not keep still, seeking for that mental peace which I could not find. Wherever I went, Mr. Thompson seemed to have resolved that he would go, from end to end of the ship, from side to side, from cabin to cabin; wherever I went, there, sooner or later, he came.

At last I could stand it no longer. I had taken refuge under a lifeboat, where I did think I might avoid his persecution; then, all of a sudden, looking up he was there. It was too much!

"Mr. Thompson," I exploded, "may I ask why you are hunting me?"

If my manner was unusually warm, his was almost painfully cool.

"You are in trouble; you want a friend; you mayn't know it, but I do."

"You appear to know me better than I know myself."

"Sometimes that's dead easy, where a woman is concerned, since herself is often the last thing she does know. What has happened?"

"What is likely to have happened? You profess to know such a deal, don't you know that?"

"That's what I'm asking myself. Don't tell me if you'd rather not; just a chat may do you good. I've known a mountain of worry melt in a mist of words."

I was silent. I did not know what to say. I wanted to talk I owned it to myself. He was a sympathetic soul, but how was I to begin torn as I was in a dozen different ways? From one point of view, the one thing I ought not to do was talk; though my darling Hugh was lying dead, I ought to hold my tongue, I ought never for an instant to allow myself to forget that my one object on board that ship was to allow everyone to suppose that I was absolutely alone, and had no connection of any sort or kind with any other passenger, or with any member of the crew.

And yet I had to obtain information from Mr. Thompson on one point. I tried to get it with the most casual sort of air, as if I had no real interest in it either way.

"Do you know the names of any of the stewards in the first-class cabin?"

Mr. Thompson had a trick of fixing his glance on one object say, for example, the sea and then, without altering his position in the least, all at once turning his eyes towards you just for an instant, then back again; and one had a feeling that in that instant he had seen more than some people would in an hour. Before he answered my question, his eyes rested for a second on my face, and I had an uncomfortable feeling that in that second he had found a key which he had been seeking, and had learnt more than I intended.

"Any particular steward in your mind, Miss Forester? There are as many as several in the first-class quarters. I've travelled in the saloon myself, so I know. In fact, I don't mind telling you that I've a first-class ticket for this very trip."

"Then why are you travelling second?"

"I'm not the only one who's doing it. Here's a list of first-class passengers." He showed me a sheet of paper. "See here, 'Single berth cabin No. 20, Miss Cara Oudinoff.' Next to her is a single gentleman who has a fine state cabin all to himself, Mr. George Peters. Now I wonder why Miss Oudinoff prefers to travel second?"

"Do you say that Miss Oudinoff originally had a cabin next to Mr. Peters?"

"That appears to be so. She appears to have vacated it in favour of a Mr. Whitaker Smith. What inducement he offered her, there is nothing to show. I guess she didn't do it for nothing."

"Are you really a first-class passenger?"

"I am--here's my name." He pointed to where his name was printed on the paper. "I quit for the sake of a lady. I saw her for a short while one night on a train. I met a friend on the way from the train to the boat. I said to him 'What class are you going?' he replied, 'Second,' I inquired, 'Would you like to go first?' he observed, with a snigger he's a sniggering sort 'What do you think? Rather!' So we did a deal on the spot I passed on to the second. Would you like to know the lady's name?"

"I've not the slightest wish to do anything of the kind."

"Then I'll tell you."

"I say that I do not wish to know. I'm not in the least interested in your private affairs."

"You are the lady, Miss Forester. I have no wish to thrust myself into your private affairs, but I happen to know that you're a centre of attraction to some people whom I should like to sell at less than ten a penny, and I had a feeling that I might be able to look after you better in the second class than in the first."

"You may think yourself very chivalrous, Mr. Thompson; but how did you know I wanted looking after by you or by anybody else? I think you've behaved with great impertinence."

"Maybe. But that don't worry me worth a cent. We understand each other better than you care to allow. We'll say that I take an interest in Miss Oudinoff, and leave it there."

There was, as always seemed to be the case, something behind his words which affected me in a way I could not explain. In my then state of fluster, very little was needed to upset my nerves. It was actually only after swallowing what seemed to be a lump in my throat that I was able to speak.

"Mr. Thompson, do you know any steward named Trouncer?"

Again that sidelong glance towards me. "Why do you ask?"

"Why don't you answer? Do you or do you not know a steward named Trouncer? Can't you give a simple answer to a simple question?"

He was silent so long that I was on the point of asking what he meant by his rudeness. Then an answer came which was so unexpected that it seemed to knock the breath all out of me.

"Miss Lawrence has been talking to you."

I stared at him; for some moments it was all I could do.

"How do you know that?"

"Would you mind telling me, Miss Forester, what Miss Lawrence told you?" When I hesitated he was taking me completely by surprise! he added, "As you must be aware, I can get the information from Miss Lawrence if I can't get it from you. For two dollars, she will turn herself inside out." When I continued silent, he went on. "Not that it matters. Unintentionally, you have told me all that she told you. I wondered if she had been talking. Trouncer's a fool. If he must chatter, he might have chosen a sieve with smaller holes."

"Mr. Thompson," I gasped when I could speak, "what position are you supposed to occupy on this ship?"

"The same position as you do; I'm a passenger. It's very odd, Miss Forester, how one thing leads to another. I saw that Russian young lady on the platform at Bedford Station, and I saw you. I noticed what an interest she took in you. That was the beginning of something which is going to end I'm beginning to wonder where. Most great discoveries are stumbled on haphazard. Miss Forester, what is or perhaps I ought to say what was, since Miss Lawrence has been talking the real name of the individual who occupies the state cabin reserved for Mr. George Peters?"

The form in which he put his question was disconcerting.

"Why," I asked, "do you speak in the past tense? Is is the person to whom you refer dead?"

Another lump came into my throat as I added the last word. I think it is because he noticed it that Mr. Thompson replied so quickly.

"No, he's not dead; at least he was still alive half an hour ago."

"How do you know that? How do you know anything about him?"

Again there was an interval of silence; my heart, or something, was jumping about inside me in a way which was horrid. It would only have taken a very little to start me blubbering like a fool. Before I left Grove Gardens I should have declared that nothing could make me behave so stupidly. There was something about that man which had an uncanny effect on me, he was so altogether different from anything I had thought so big, so calm, so mysterious, so secretive, so strong. I had an uncomfortable feeling that, if he chose, I should be like putty in his hands. He evaded my question even when he did speak.

"When a man undertakes a task which spells adventure, how shall he know what will happen to him on the way? When you started out, only the other day, on the road which passes through the land of the unusual, did you guess it would mean to you what it has done?"

He paused. What he meant, I had no notion, except that I had a vague idea that he might be using words as a cloak for his thoughts. What his thoughts were about was beyond me altogether. Presently he asked a question which certainly, as far as it went, was clear enough.

"Miss Forester, would you like to reach America alive?"

"Mr. Thompson, I should as at present advised."

"Though Mr. Peters be dead?"

"What do you know about Mr. Peters? Tell me! Don't be cruel. What have they done to him, and who has done it? Is he very ill?"

"They will not impossibly do to you as they have done to him."

It was not because I was afraid that something seemed to have gone wrong inside, it was because there was such a creepy-crawly air of assurance about the man.

"What do you mean? Why should they do anything to me?"

"I imagine that whoever treated the occupant of Mr. Peters' cabin with such discourtesy was seeking something which they believed to be in his possession."

"How do you know that? How is it you know so many things? Well, whatever it was they were looking for, I'm told they turned the cabin upside down, besides nearly killing him so I suppose they found it."

"Was it there to find?"

On the surface it was a simple enough question to ask, but that was on the surface only. As matters stood, it presented possibilities to me which made my blood run cold. I longed to ask him all sorts of things on my own account whether he knew Mr. Stewart, and Isaac Rothenstein, and what happened in that house to Hugh; but somehow I dare ask nothing. Possibly this was to some extent because I realised that in asking things I might convey information which I was most anxious to withhold. As I hesitated some words of his made me wonder if, though he kept his eyes studiously turned from me, he was reading what was passing through my mind.

"Say nothing, Miss Forester, which might commit yourself. A woman often says so much more than she means. Have you ever played a game called 'Hidden Meanings'? We used to play it when I was a kid at home. Someone asked a question; you had to say all it might mean to you. I was quite smart at it. I got so that I could draw a vivid picture from the life out of nothing at all. Folks used to say I was a conjurer. Better not give me a chance to score off you."

For the first time he drew himself up and turned towards me.

"Maybe, Miss Forester, you and I are in the same line of business. I don't say we are and I don't say we aren't; I just put it to you as possible that if we were our interests might clash."

"You told me that you were a drummer, or whatever the thing is called I certainly am nothing of that kind."

"Sure? You travel with something, don't you, Miss Forester? A drummer is a fellow who travels with samples; don't you? Now, I might have got to know that you travel with samples of goods which I'm dead keen to keep off the market; what then? I might not be certain that you've got these goods about you, but be anxious to know. If anything you've said, quite innocently, were to tell me what I want to know I should be awkwardly placed. I like you, Miss Forester, I just like you. I'd hate to have to strangle you in the way of business."

"You do say the most extraordinary things. Strangle me! What have I ever done to you that under any possible circumstances you could wish to do anything so dreadful to me?"

"They strangled the party in Mr. Peters's cabin, not because he'd done anything to anyone, but apparently because certain persons suspected that he had in his possession certain samples of goods which, it might be, they had very special reasons of their own for wishing to keep off the market. Don't you see what follows?"

"No, Mr. Thompson, I don't, and I'd rather not see. I only know that I seem to have misunderstood your character entirely, and that you now appear to be a very dangerous man."

I turned to go. He placed his finger on my shoulder.

"A dangerous man, Miss Forester, may in a moment of danger prove an excellent friend."
NEW PAGE

CHAPTER XIX
CHANGED

I have had some shocks in my life; particularly I have had more than one during the brief period which has elapsed since I left Grove Gardens; but I do not believe that I ever did have such a shock in my life as when I returned to my cabin after the extremely unsatisfactory interview which I had had with Mr. Thompson. I wanted a proper wash, which it was not always easy to get in the ladies' lavatory, as the women were crowding in to get ready for lunch. I had been crying, and doing all sorts of silly things, and was aware that I might require more than a couple of seconds to make myself presentable. So far the cabin had been occupied by Sadie Lawrence until an unconscionable hour, she seeming to make it a practice to lie in bed all day, and stop up all night. But on that occasion she had got up as I was going out, so I took it for granted that as she could hardly take more than two or three hours over her toilette, and it was then more than four hours since I had seen her last, there was a possibility of my being able to use the cabin to get ready for lunch.

So I went down to the cabin, opened the door, and walked in, expecting to find it empty. What was therefore my surprise to find that it had an occupant of all persons the one I most desired to avoid, the girl I had seen at Bedford Station, who, according to Mr. Thompson, although she had booked as a first-class passenger, was travelling second under the name of Cara Oudinoff.

My first impression was that I must have mistaken the number and entered someone else's cabin by mistake. I stared, feeling a little bewildered, and was just about to stammer an apology when, speaking as if she were an old and dear acquaintance, she addressed me.

"Good morning, Miss Forester. The weather is very fine this morning." Then she smiled. "As it does not blow a great gale perhaps you do not think so."

What she meant by speaking to me like that, or what she was doing there at all, I could not understand. A cursory glance round made it clear that the mistake was not on my side.

"Haven't you made some error?" I asked. "Aren't you in the wrong cabin? This is not yours."

"No, it is not all mine; we share it together, you and I."

"We share it together! what on earth do you mean?"

"Did not Miss Lawrence tell you?"

"She told me nothing at least she told me nothing which could explain your presence here. I do not know if you are aware that the berth with which you are making free is hers."

The girl shook her head and laughed.

"Not at all. It is you who are mistaken. Miss Lawrence has been remiss if she has not told you of the arrangement we have made."

"Arrangement? What arrangement have you made? What are you doing in this cabin?"

"It is very simple. We have made an exchange, Miss Lawrence and I; I have given her the berth in which I have been sleeping, though it really is a better one than this, and she has given me hers instead."

Even then I did not grasp her meaning. It had not occurred to me as even possible that such a blow could fall upon me. I knew so little about a ship that I had supposed that arrangements made before she started had to remain unchanged until the voyage was done.

"This cabin is not only Miss Lawrence's, it is also mine; she has no right to let anyone enter it without first of all consulting me."

She looked at me as if I had said something funny.

"I do not follow you. Surely Miss Lawrence can change her quarters if she chooses without consulting anyone. I don't wish to suggest anything in the slightest degree rude, but I'm afraid I don't see what her movements have to do with you. I hope you do not object to my taking her place."

"But I do very decidedly."

I spoke right out, on the spur of the moment, I admit; I admit also that Sadie Lawrence was not the sort of person I would have chosen to share a cabin. Goodness knows she was not faultless, but compared to that smooth-faced young woman she was an angel on earth. Miss Oudinoff, holding what looked like a pair of silken pyjamas in her hand, which she had apparently been arranging on the coverlet of the lower berth, stood smiling at me as though I were something almost too funny for contemplation.

"Why do you object to me, Miss Forester?"

"On every possible ground."

"Really? Is your feeling so strong as that? Since, possibly, if all goes well, we are only forty-eight hours from New York, you won't have to put up with me long."

"Forty-eight hours are forty-eight hours too long. I don't mean to have you in this cabin at all if I can help it, and you'll find I can."

"Miss Forester!" She knitted her brows and eyed me with an air of polite amazement for which I could have hit her. I knew I was rude; I had doubts as to the wisdom of the course I was pursuing. But I could not help it. I felt that I would sooner be shut up with a cabinful of snakes than with that woman. I longed to tell her so. "May I ask you what I have done to fill you with such a singular dislike of me?"

"You know as well as I do I Do you imagine I'm such a simpleton that you can throw dust in my eyes? Instinct would warn me against you if nothing else did."

"Is that so? This is interesting. I do not remember to have seen you, or to have been conscious of your existence till I came on board this ship. Are you an occultist? Have the unseen forces advised you not to let your path cross mine? Is that the explanation of your extraordinary attitude?"

"I am not going to have you in this cabin if I can help it."

"You can't help it. You can leave it if you choose I shan't."

"Then I will leave it."

"Do. At least you might try. You will not find it easy. You must understand, Miss Forester, that I had to share a cabin with an unclean old woman who, I really believe, is a dangerous lunatic. I have not had one night's sleep since I came on board. As I cannot do without some sleep, I have been leaving no stone unturned to induce someone to change cabins. Miss Lawrence was the only person I found open to persuasion, and I made it worth her while."

"Then I'll make it worth her while to come back."

"Will you? I don't see how you'll be better off with a lunatic than with me. Still, try; you may find it amusing."

"It's all nonsense about your lunatic; I don't believe in her! You had a first-class cabin: why did you change it for a berth in a second? In order that you might have the pleasure of sleeping with a lunatic? I'm going straight to Miss Lawrence to offer her my berth in exchange for the one you have given her. I'll chance the lunatic."

"As you please; but, before you go, one word. Who told you I had a first-class cabin?"

"What business of yours is it who told me? I know. I know a great deal more about you than you perhaps think. You don't suppose I object to you for nothing. You call yourself Oudinoff. I don't know whether that is your name; it is not the one you were in prison under."

"In prison under I What do you mean?"

"I want to have no discussion, to have nothing to do with you or your affairs. Take yourself out of this cabin: don't attempt to force yourself upon me and I'll say nothing. But you may take it from me, I don't mean to have you in this cabin, even if to keep you out of it I have to tell the truth."

"This ship seems to be full of lunatics! You appear to be as mad as the woman I have already endured. However, I'm as little desirous as you are to have what you call a discussion. Pray do not let me detain you from doing anything you please."

She unfolded her pyjamas they were of light blue silk, gorgeously embroidered and laid them out over the coverlet as if they were part of a scheme of decoration. I had always flattered myself that it wanted a good deal to ruffle my calmness, but hers was beyond me altogether. It almost maddened me. I had an absolute conviction founded, I own, on very little that was tangible that this woman had something to do, that, indeed, she was the leading spirit, in what had happened to Hugh; I knew as certainly as if someone had told me from the skies that if she only had the shadow of a shade of a chance, she, and her friends oh, I knew that there were friends of hers on board! would do to me what they had done to Hugh that they would stick at nothing to get at the charge with which I had been entrusted. As I observed her smiling demeanour fooling with her silk pyjamas a feeling was growing up in my heart that, if I could not be rid of her, rather than become her helpless victim I would be the first to start. I was not so wholly defenceless as she perhaps supposed I would rather cut her throat than that she should cut mine.

I nursed a lingering hope that I might still be able to drive her from the field by informing her of certain facts with which I had become acquainted and adding to them little additions of my own. Looking back, through the haze of horror which followed, I can see that it would perhaps have been wiser to play her game of hypocrisy. I should probably have lost nothing by taking up her attitude of pretended friendship. I should scarcely have been worse off by allowing her to suppose that she deceived me; by, metaphorically, taking her to my bosom. I see that now. But I could not have done it then. Had I been prepared for the position perhaps I should have met it better but I was not.

Had Sadie Lawrence dropped the faintest hint of what she proposed to do, if by out-bidding that woman I could not have made it worth her while to stay where she was, I might at least have been ready for what was coming. It was to some extent the unexpectedness of the thing which caused me to lose my mental balance. So far as I was concerned pretence was out of the question; all I could do was to fight or try to. And I tried my very best. I struck at her with every weapon I could.

"I have already told you that I have not the slightest wish to place the authorities on board this ship in possession of information which you would probably rather have kept private."

"That's very good of you. I should not have thought you would have been so punctilious."

She had ceased to play with her pyjamas and was smoothing out the creases from one of those arrangements of lace, ribbon, and muslin which some women nowadays wear on their heads in bed.

"But understand me clearly I have no intention of sharing my cabin with a thief, even if I have to tell everyone on board that you are a thief."

She looked at me with the end of a piece of pink ribbon held between her finger and thumb, smiling all the while.

"Who told you I was a thief? You use some very blunt language. A person who associates herself with the conveyance of stolen property isn't there the taint of a thief about her?"

Her words stung and made me more resolved to fight her. But somehow words would not come to my tongue. There was a volume which I wanted to say; but for some cause at the moment the faculty of fluent speech was denied me. I do not know if the strain I had undergone was telling on me, but as I stood with my back against the door, confronting the laughter on her face and the scorn in her eyes, the consciousness was forced upon me unwilling though I was to admit it that at least on that occasion she was more than a match for me. In her cool, easy, refined tones she asked questions which I found it difficult to answer.

"Is it too much to inquire who has been telling you those dreadful things about me? You are one of those simple, slightly stupid English girls, with dull brains and with no knowledge of the world outside their own front doorstep; such libellous falsehoods can hardly be the creatures of your imagination. Someone has been telling you lies. Come, Miss Forester, tell me who it is. Who has been prejudicing your mind against one whose sole wish so far as she can be said to have a wish in the matter is to be your friend?"

"They are not lies. You know you are a thief, and that you have been in prison. Do you deny it?"

"It is as I suspected. I have watched you and your angular American friend; for some reason of his own he does not appear to like me. I don't know why, but he has evidently been poisoning your mind. For every poison there is an antidote I may possibly find one which may be effective against that instilled by Mr. Thompson. I allow no one to circulate lies about me with impunity."

"Are you going back to your own cabin, or am I to take measures to make you?"

"My dear Miss Forester, take what measures you like." She held up her concoction of silk and lace. "What do you think of my nightcap? Do you not call it a nightcap, you English? Is it not pretty? You will see how charming I look in it at night. Do you wear no nightcap, Miss Forester?"

I could not answer her or even attempt to find words to fling at her. I flung myself through the door and left her in possession of the cabin. NEW PAGE

CHAPTER XX
AN UNSOLICITED INTRODUCTION

I forgot all about lunch; even when people went streaming past me towards the dining saloon, some of them nodding as they asked if I was coming, I somehow did not grasp the fact that they were all of them moving towards the mid-day meal. I was not hungry, although I had had no breakfast. I was bewildered, confused, in what mother used to call a state of moither; conscious that I ought to do something, and that quickly but what it was I could not think. Chance put me in the way of doing one thing.

As I was moving aimlessly along, Mrs. Harrison, our stewardess, came towards me with a tray in her hand. The sight of her brought back some of my senses.

"Oh, Mrs. Harrison," I exclaimed, "I want to speak to you."

Apparently she did not want to speak to me she said as much.

"Sorry I can't stop now, miss. I'm taking Mrs. Isaacs her lunch, in No. 19, and from the way she goes on if I'm five minutes late you'd think I'd committed a crime. Why she can't get up and have her lunch in the saloon I can't think; she's as well as I am."

I took hold of her arm as she was trying to edge past me.

"Mrs. Harrison, I must speak to you, I must!"

I suppose she saw the state I was in and relented though not much.

"Well, miss, if you must you must. What is it?"

"That awful woman has forced herself into my cabin, and won't go."

Mrs. Harrison opened her eyes wider, as if doubting that she had heard aright.

"What awful woman? Mrs. Isaacs' lunch won't be improved by being kept waiting nor will her temper."

"I'm told that she calls herself Cara Oudinoff--"

Mrs. Harrison did not wait for me to continue, she concluded my sentence in a way of her own.

"Oh, yes, I know; she's changed berths with Miss Lawrence. You certainly won't lose by that. I don't want to say a word against any lady passenger, but Miss Lawrence!" She pursed up her lips and she stopped. "Is that all you've got to say, miss? I must get on."

"Mrs. Harrison, I can't occupy the same cabin as that woman it's impossible! I won't!"

"Sorry to hear that, miss. You'd better speak to Mr. Harding. He is the one who looks after the berths. Sorry I can't stop, miss."

"But, Mrs. Harrison, you must stop a moment please. You don't understand. Rather than occupy the same cabin with that woman I'd sooner sleep on deck."

"There's no reason why you shouldn't, miss or in one of the cabins, or somewhere; the only trouble is that you'd get woke up early. You must let me pass, miss you've no idea what Mrs. Isaacs is like when she's kept waiting."

I had to let her pass--she was clearly not to be detained by anything short of physical force. Nor did I see what there was to be gained by stopping her, if all she could do was to tell me to go to Mr. Harding. I don't know what those kind of people are called on board ship, but so far as I could understand, Mr. Harding was head steward of the second-class cabin. I dare say he was all right when you knew him, but his manner was grim. I did not feel the least drawn to interviewing him. I had spoken to him once about having the looking-glass put in a position in which one could see. He then told me that every lady who came on board wanted to have the ship rebuilt to suit herself. He had, he said, mentioned this on several occasions to the company who owned the boat, and they had, he regretted to state, come to the conclusion that it was not easy to do this every time the vessel went to sea. Of course this was rude, and I believe it was meant to be rude: I did not want to have the ship rebuilt, I merely wanted to have the position of the mirror slightly altered it was not the least necessary for him to be snappy. But since he was disagreeable about a thing like that I could quite fancy what he would be like if I asked him to see that that woman went back to her own cabin.

Rather than that I should subject myself to rudeness from him without getting any satisfactory result it would be better that I should sleep on deck or in a corner of one of the general cabins. Two considerations prevented me from doing that. In the first place I doubted if I should be any safer; in the second I did not want her to have the run of my cabin, or pull it to pieces in a sort of game of hide-and-seek.

It always seemed to me on board that ship that you never saw a steward without a tray in his hand; he was always carrying something either to eat or drink.

As I was pacing up and down the deck like a caged wild thing one of them came along with a tray in either hand one sometimes met them with two trays in either hand. The steward I met then was a freckled, ginger-haired man, who had been quite polite to me more than once most of the stewards were civil, not like Mr. Harding. At sight of me he stopped, not as Mrs. Harrison had done, because I took him by the arm, but of his own accord, and he said: li Aren't you going down to lunch, miss? You'd better: they're all at table. Nothing like a good lunch to keep you going till it's time for dinner. It's not good for you to be hungry on board ship."

He grinned, nodded, and passed on. I stopped tramping up and down, looked after him, and acted on his suggestion. I went down to lunch, realising that, as he said, it was not good to go hungry, and I had had nothing whatever to eat that day, but also that I might have a chance of arranging with Mr. Thompson to speak to him as soon as possible. He never missed a meal. His seat was at the next table to mine: I would sometimes look up and find him regarding me between his mouthfuls with an appearance of interest which I resented. As I entered the cabin I looked for him in his accustomed place. His chair was empty.

I cannot describe what an odd effect the discovery that his seat was vacant had on me. He was such a constant attendant at every meal, coming first and leaving last anyhow I always found him when I entered and left him when I went that it did seem queer that on the first occasion on which I really did want him he was absent. As I took my place the strangest and even unreasonable sense of loneliness came sweeping over me. It was with sensations, which I myself found a little startling, that I realised that I had come to look upon this man as something more than a mere acquaintance as the one friend I had upon the ship. As I tried to eat the food that an attentive steward placed before me, I knew that I had grown to regard him as a protector; one to whom, in a tight corner, I might turn with the certainty of receiving help. It was perhaps because I was at that moment in such a tight corner that I missed him in a fashion I had not dreamed would have been possible. It was dreadful to feel that there was not one creature in all the crowd who cared in the very least what happened to me, or who would regard it as anything but an agreeable topic of conversation if I was torn to pieces or my throat cut from ear to ear.

There was Hugh lying between life and death, maimed and torn did anyone care? The captain's main object seemed to be to keep the fact secret, lest, if it got abroad, it would put the other passengers off their food. A nice idea! I was a woman I thought I was strong, but I knew better now; I was a weak and unprotected woman. There were creatures on board that ship, I was perfectly certain, who, if I would not give them what they wanted, would tear me to pieces to get it.

Yet if I stood up and said so that hungry horde would regard me as a lunatic. The stewards and people of that sort would perhaps lock me up in some secret place, as Sadie Lawrence had said was often done. The one thing they would not do was to give me adequate protection. If I was killed, the captain and his officers would do their best not to have the passengers' appetites spoilt till they reached New York that was all they would do.

Who among the lot would care a pin's head what happened to me?

No, my only help was to come from Abednego P. Thompson. The more clearly I realised this the more I began to worry about his non-appearance. The sooner I appealed to him for advice and protection the better it would be. I might possibly know some sort of peace of mind again. I should probably go grey before I reached New York unless they killed me or merely, as in that story of Sadie Lawrence's, made of me a log of wood, capable of doing nothing but swallowing food pumped into me through a silver tube.

I could stand the strain no longer; I had to speak to the man who was waiting on me.

"Where is Mr. Thompson?" I inquired.

"That's the long gentleman with the thin face who sits at the next table?"

That steward was not very complimentary, but the description was fairly accurate. I told him so. The man leant closer towards me; he dropped his voice.

111 he is so I hear."

"What! "I twisted round in my chair so suddenly that I almost knocked my head against his.

"Took bad about an hour ago, uncommon bad; the doctor can't make out what's wrong. I tell you because he's a friend of yours I've seen you together. We're not supposed to tell everyone."

"But he was perfectly well an hour ago. I was talking to him."

"1 know you were; I saw you. The illness must have come on him directly you left him terrible bad he was. I'm told the doctor thought he was dying bad attack of heart disease or something like that. And now he doesn't know what it is so I hear. Yes, sir, coming."

Someone else had called that steward; he moved off to wait on him, leaving me in a cheerful state. Not much more than an hour ago I had been talking to Mr. Thompson, who was to all appearances a great strong man, as fit and well as ever he was in his life. Directly I had left him, according to the steward, he was taken by a mysterious illness and was on the point of death and apparently still was. What did it mean? I had gone from him to my cabin, to find that woman playing tricks with Sadie Lawrence's berth. She possibly had reason to suspect my connection with Mr. Thompson. Could she, or her friends, have had a hand in striking him down? How had they done it?

What did it matter how they had done it if they had? The bare possibility was a terrible one to contemplate. It suggested what was waiting for me. So resolved were they to have me wholly at their mercy that they had disposed of the only being who could have protected me against them. There should be no one willing and able to lift a finger on my behalf.

I got up from the table and went on deck tumbled on deck would be perhaps the better way of putting it, because my legs seemed to be tottering and my feet did as they liked. Directly I got into the open air a voice addressed me.

"Well, old dear, how goes it? Done yourself a treat? Got room for any more? Have a tiddly?"

It was Sadie Lawrence. She was seated at one of those expanding tables, with a tray on top, which the stewards were always willing to place on deck for people who for any reason preferred to have their food on deck. An undesirable-looking male person was her companion. There was an empty bottle at his feet and a partially full one on the tray. It was from this Miss Lawrence invited me to have a "tiddly."

I did not want her drink, but I had something to say to her, and I said it.

"Miss Lawrence, there's a woman in our cabin who says you've let her have your berth."

"Quite right, my dear; absolutely correct. In two days we shall be ashore. She came to me and she said, 'I'll give you a hundred dollars if you'll change berths with me--that's twenty pounds.' I didn't do any beating about the bush; I said, 'It's yours!' What she wanted with my berth I didn't know, but I knew I wanted that hundred dollars. Sure you won't have one?"

Again she referred to the bottle. I ignored her invitation.

"If you'd let me know what she was after, I'd have given you two hundred dollars to stay where you were."

She paused with the bottle on its way to her glass to express her surprise.

"No! would you really? Two hundred dollars? You must be made of money. What's the game?" She turned to her male companion. "Sounds as if she were a lady millionaire, doesn't it?"

"Perhaps the lady thinks your society is well worth paying for it's a question of taste."

As he said this the man smirked at her and winked at me; he was a dreadful creature. She did not see the wink.

"Go on!" she exclaimed. "Hadn't you better order another bottle? This one's nearly done. Sorry, Miss Forester, you didn't mention that two hundred dollars before. I wouldn't have deserted you if I'd known you wanted me so bad."

"Come back now. You can still have the money if you let me have the berth which you got from that woman."

"That woman? Listen to her! Isn't she nasty? The lady seems to be fonder of you than you are of her. I'm sorry to say it can't be done; I'd like to, but it's not on." She turned to the man. "Will you order another bottle? You know they'll take a week to bring it."

I am sorry to say that she had been drinking. Hitherto she had confined her performances in that direction to the night; now she was at it in the middle of the day, on deck, before all the people. It was no use trying to get her to talk sense. I offered her more than two hundred dollars to come back to her original quarters, or to take my berth. She only sniggered and the man jeered. Finally she lost her temper.

"Look here, you get out of this. Who are you offering your dirty money to? Think I'm a dealer in berths? I'm an artist, that's what I am. I've come to an arrangement with the lady to sleep in her berth, and I'm going to. The sooner you take yourself off the better. You're casting a damper on a convivial meeting, that's what you're doing. Spoilsport, I call you."

As she was descending to abuse obviously it was time that I did go. It was no use arguing with an intoxicated woman; there would only be a scene, and there would be nothing gained. People were watching and listening as it was; I did not want to be made a public spectacle. Miss Oudinoff spoke to me as I was moving away of all people.

"Miss Forester, allow me to introduce you to a friend of mine; he has something which he rather wishes to say to you. I '

The insolence of the creature! There was the little, dark-haired man with the huge moustache and bad-tempered expression to whom I had seen her speaking more than once. He dared to address me, raising his hat and speaking with a strong foreign accent.

"Pleased to meet you, Miss Forester. I believe you know Mr. Stewart."

"Who told you I did, and what does it matter to you who I know?"

I was not so civil as I might have been: though I was conscious that my bad manners placed me at a disadvantage, whenever I came near that woman I could not help but be rude. I am not one of those people who can feel one thing and pretend another; I will not say I never can, but I could not then. The man looked as if he could have stuck a knife into me; looking back, I admit that he was not without excuse I was exasperating. His courtesy was greater than mine on the surface.

"Why do you speak like that? I am not impolite to you. I have a proposal to make on which I should like to have your decision."

"You can have no proposal to make to which I wish to listen."

"That is absurd. You do not know what you are saying."

"I know perfectly well that I wish to have nothing to do with you. Let me pass."

"No, Miss Forester, I will not let you pass, unless you make a scene. Then I will follow you, and at the first opportunity I will speak to you again. I intend that you shall listen to what I have to say, so if you are wise you will listen now and get it done."

He stood in such a way that unless I made what he called a scene I could not avoid him. I looked at his face and did not like him; but though the woman at his side was beautifully dressed and positively pretty, somehow I liked her face still less. I did not want to have the man following me about the ship I believed him when he said he would so I decided to listen to him then.

"What is it you have to say? Be quick! I do not wish to be seen in your company."

"Mr. Stewart has chosen a singular messenger. However, that is his affair, not mine; he chooses his own tools. You are carrying for him certain articles to America which are not his property at all. They are stolen; that is the truth. If I choose to give information to the captain I can have you arrested and held a prisoner till the matter has been threshed out in an American court of justice. You will then find that there is justice in America, and that there the law deals severely with the trafficker in stolen goods. However, it so happens that I do not wish to have any trouble. I do not even wish to have you punished, because I believe that to a certain extent you are innocent, that you have been engaged in this business without knowing what it was you were doing. How much money is Mr. Stewart going to give you for acting as his messenger? If you will be frank and tell me, you shall have no cause to be sorry." NEW PAGE

CHAPTER XXI
TWENTY-FIVE THOUSAND DOLLARS

While he spoke we had been moving slowly from the people towards the back of the ship. It was perhaps just as well that he did not say such things within the hearing of everyone, yet I had an uncomfortable consciousness that in that society publicity was the safest thing for me.

"Of course," I told the man, "what you say is false. I am not conveying stolen goods for Mr. Stewart; you have not the slightest justification for making such a statement."

I have seldom seen anything more disagreeable than the way in which that man looked at me.

"You think I speak of what I do not know you accuse me of lying? I will tell you what I do know, then perhaps you will not be so foolish as to say such things."

"Yes," chimed in the woman, "tell her what you do know, and then perhaps she will begin to understand."

"You forget," the man went on, "or perhaps you are so ignorant as not to be aware, that on a ship nowadays there is such a thing as wireless telegraphy. It happens that I had my suspicions of you directly you came on board. I know Miss Forester, the lady for whom the berth you occupy was engaged. You are not she, and you are not the least like her. I wondered what you meant by pretending that you were. I have been in telegraphic communication with England since we started; I will tell you what are the facts I have learnt."

I confess that the idea that he had, as it were, been talking to England all that way off across the sea finding out things without my having the faintest notion that he or anyone else was doing anything of the kind, made me uneasy. One thing he said was true I was ignorant. Of course I had heard about wireless telegraphy, but I did not understand its working. If that was the sort of thing it did, let people find out things behind your back thousands of miles across the sea, then I had a perhaps absurd feeling that it was uncanny, almost supernatural, and ought not to be allowed. The man went talking on, every word he said increasing my uneasiness. What made the matter worse was that I knew that woman was enjoying my discomfiture. Between the pair of them I felt what he said I was no thanks to him! a simple fool.

"Your name is Catherine Fraser. You are the daughter of a woman who lets apartments in Grove Gardens, Fulham Palace Road, London. She has one lodger."

"You do know that much, do you?" I said it with a gasp the man was taking my breath away. He spoke with a quiet malignancy which was horrible.

"Know it? Of course I know it. What is there I do not know? This lodger is a man named Hugh Beckwith; he is on board this ship."

"Who told you that?"

"Spirits of the air!" He pointed upwards.

What he said was in a sense so true that it silenced me. People may laugh, but to me just then it was all black magic.

"As for Mr. Beckwith he does not matter, he does not count. It was thought that he did, but it has been proved that he does not. He interfered in what was no affair of his and he has got his deserts. It is you who count. Through Beckwith all the mischief came now it is you who are responsible. Make no mistake, we know! I will show you."

And he did show me. If he had found out all that through wireless telegraph then all I can say is that the wonders of science are a bit more than I care for.

"Hugh Beckwith, through a series of disastrous blunders, got hold of property of great interest and value which was certainly no concern of his. Without knowing what he was doing he is the kind of creature who seldom does know what he is doing he passed this on to Paul R. Stewart, who is a dangerous man and one of the biggest thieves living. This property, which had no more to do with him than with Beckwith, had to be delivered in America by a certain date. He thought that if he could get it there by that date he might derive considerable benefit. He knew that if the rightful owners became aware it would not be allowed to continue in his possession a single hour no, not for a minute!"

The ferocity with which the man said that! He made me jump.

"So he desired, before all things being a wholly unprincipled fellow to keep secret the fact that he had what did not belong to him. He knew that if he attempted to take it himself it would never get there. He had two berths engaged upon this ship. He knew that the rightful owners of the property would be crossing in her. He formed a scheme to rob them of it that is the sort of man he is!"

The speaker held up both hands as if there were no words strong enough to express what he felt.

"In the meantime there came along this fool Beckwith, who actually handed over to him the property which he had formed such a desperate plan to get by force. It seems that his first thought was that Beckwith the fool! might take it for him to America travelling in the cabin which he had reserved for himself. Then it seems that he felt that though a fool might be required Beckwith was altogether too big a one to be entrusted with the charge. Instead he chose you!"

He hurled the "you" at me as if it were a bomb which he hoped would kill me. He seemed to be nearly beside himself with passion.

"Yes, that is where you come in, where you begin to figure on the scene. I suppose there is something in you Beckwith has not got which makes you a better tool. Stewart is a good judge of men and women; no doubt he had what he judged to be sufficient reasons for choosing you instead."

There, at any rate, the speaker was wrong Mr. Stewart had not chosen me at all, I had volunteered but I was not going to tell him so. Besides he was so amazingly right in other directions that he positively frightened me.

"So it came about that you travelled as Miss Forester in the berth which was reserved for Miss Forester. He thought that your identity would not be suspected, perhaps because you are so stupid and so ignorant that it seemed incredible that he, a clever man, should entrust property of such value, under circumstances of such danger, to your keeping. So incredible, when I saw you, did it seem, even to me, that I had inquiries made by wireless to know if it was possible."

The man paused. He stood with his hands held palms upwards, looking at me as if he sought to read my heart. I hated to have to meet his gaze it just fascinated me. His voice dropped he had not been speaking loudly before, but then he began to speak so quietly that it was even worse than if he had whispered.

"It is not only possible, it is sure it is absolutely sure. You have in your possession property the value of which you do not dream I will say so much for you; in no sense do you know what you are doing; and Stewart is so mad as to think that you will be allowed to act as his accomplice in getting what he has stolen to America."

"I'm not an accomplice you shan't say I am!"

"No? What, then, are you? At the same time you'll permit me to observe that I never said you were an accomplice I only said that Stewart wanted you to act as an accomplice. But I realise that you are an honest woman, and that the nefarious nature of the business in which he has ensnared you has only to be made plain and you will be quick enough to wash your hands of all his rascally schemes. Miss Forester as it is by that name you are known on board this ship I will make it plain that what you hold is not the property of the man who employed you. I will prove it to your completest satisfaction. You will then give it up?"

The words were a question which I left unanswered. The man's manner was more ingratiating than I had expected, but I was not so simple as to commit myself to anything at all. His words might be specious, but I believed they were lies: that at any rate they were not the whole truth. So little of it indeed that the only part which really counted, he was very careful not to allow to appear.

"I say to you that if I make it plain that this property with which you are entrusted belongs to others and has been stolen from the rightful owners, then, may I take it, that you, as an honest woman, will hand it over to those owners of whom I am one and this lady another?"

I began to have an inkling of the point at which he was driving. With candour which, as I look back, may have been unwise I told him so.

"I see; or rather I commence to see." He snapped at me like a terrier. "What is it that you commence to see?"

"Where you are getting to what all this you have been saying leads."

II Speak plainly to what does it lead? I say that I will make it clear even to your intelligence that this lady and I are two of the persons from whom it has been stolen well, what then? If you are an honest woman, what more do you require to show what is the right thing for you to do?"

"I don't believe you, that's all. What's your name?"

"My name--what does it matter what is my name?"

"To me it seems that it matters a good deal. I like to know to whom I am talking--especially when it is on a delicate subject."

"My name is Galstin."

"That again I don't believe. I know now that her name is not Oudinoff, as she calls herself, and that you also are not the person you pretend to be. That is something. One begins to have some idea of the kind of persons with whom one has to deal."

He turned to the woman. "What does she mean?"

She spoke to him in some foreign language which I dare say was Russian. A brief and animated dialogue was carried on in the same tongue.

"I suppose you two are telling each other," I said, "things which you would rather I did not hear. Since you both of you speak English, I have no use for people who do not wish me to understand what they are saying."

She replied, "I was telling this gentleman that I believe you've had some conversation with a person who calls himself Thompson--"

"Calls himself Thompson? It seems to me that on this ship all the passengers call themselves by names which are someone else's. I will call this person Galstin if he likes, it will make no difference to me. I have no confidence in him anyhow."

"My name," he broke in, "is Yashvin. But, as you said, what difference does a name make?"

"That is not by any means what I said but no matter."

He began to gesticulate with violence. Evidently he was not a person whose temper was at all under control.

"If I prove to you that we are part owners of the property which you are conveying for Mr. Stewart, will you give us what is our own? That is if we give you the sum which Mr. Stewart has promised to pay. We do not wish you to lose in any way by being honest."

My reply was blunt enough.

"No, I won't!"

The woman spoke he was inclined to be hot enough but it seemed that she was always cool. And she smiled sweetly and falsely.

"Mr. Yashvin does not make himself so clear as perhaps he might. He ought to have said that not only will we give you what Mr. Stewart has promised to pay, we will make it twice as much so you will gain by your honesty. Once more honesty will be shown to be the better policy."

"That is your idea of honesty? It is not mine. To betray my trust for gain! No, thank you! Try someone else."

"You look at the matter in a wrong light, Miss Forester." This again was the woman. The man stood scowling by; one felt that he preferred other means of persuasion. "It appears from what we have learnt that your simplicity has been practised on, that you have been tricked into a false position. A person comes to you in the street and says, 'Take charge of this money for me.' You discover that it was not his money at all, but belongs to persons who are in need of it. If these persons say to you, 'Give us our money; you shall not suffer loss by being honest,' how can you be said to betray your trust to a thief, by giving to them the money which is already theirs?"

"Unluckily I don't believe this money we'll call it money is yours. And, mind you, you are taking something for granted I have not yet said that I have it."

"We know that you have it that is sure." This was the man.

"If all the things of which you are sure are as valueless as that, you know nothing. I think, if you don't mind, I will leave you. I wish to get news of the person who calls himself Thompson, whom I believe you have poisoned."

"Believe we have poisoned! What does she mean? What does she say?"

How that man did glare; he looked like murder. The woman did not attempt to answer him, she merely smiled and spoke to me.

"Then are we to understand, Miss Forester, that the path of honesty does not appeal to you?"

"Nothing about you does appeal to me. When I first saw you staring at me at Bedford Station I said to myself, 'That's a dangerous woman.' When you talk about paying, I will make you an offer. Miss Lawrence tells me that you gave her a hundred dollars to let you have a berth in my cabin. I will give you two hundred dollars to change back again."

"Is that your answer to my question?"

"Is that your answer to mine? What you have done can only point to one thing danger! for me. You wish to have me at your mercy you and your friends. You say that what you have been talking about is not Mr. Stewart's."

"How can it be his when you know how it came into his possession?"

This was the man; he shook his hand at me as if it were a clenched fist. There could be no doubt about his rage, yet I was more afraid of the woman's calmness. I laughed at him.

"At the beginning of this agreeable little conversation you talked of handing me over to the authorities of the ship and explaining to them what kind of character I was. Well, do it! Tell them the worst things about me you can. Tell them that I'm in possession of stolen property and having told them, prove it."

"What do you mean by that? It is easy."

"That seems to be a favourite question of yours. I am sure the meaning of what I said was clear enough even to your limited intelligence. Between ourselves I'm thinking of going to the captain on my own account and asking him to keep me under lock and key until we reach New York. I should feel myself a good deal safer as his prisoner than as her travelling companion."

"How much is Mr. Stewart going to pay you? Some paltry sum?"

"Maybe; perhaps he's going to pay me nothing at all he won't have to. If, as I think is quite possible, I land at New York with my throat cut there'll be no one to pay it to!"

"Miss Forester, one final appeal to you." This was the girl, plausible and soft. "We will not talk of any little sum, so anxious are we to avoid unpleasantness--"

"Oh, that's certain! It is shown by Mr. Peters's little misadventure. After that you talk about being anxious to avoid unpleasantness."

"We will deal with figures which count. I swear to you, Miss Forester, that what Mr. Yashvin says is true. What you have in your possession is our property; not wholly ours, but in part. And no part of it belongs to Mr. Stewart. Yet there are reasons why we should not do as you say, and carry the matter to the captain."

"I can believe it first time of asking."

"You can surely conceive that there may be perfectly sufficient and honest reasons why we should wish to avoid scandal. There are such reasons in this case. And so I make you this proposition. We will give you five-and-twenty thousand dollars, now, within ten minutes, if you will return to us what is our own."

Five-and-twenty thousand dollars? That was five thousand English pounds. Certainly, as she put it, we were talking of figures which counted. It was some seconds before I realised the magnitude of the sum then I felt a little dazed. Her eyes were on my face; though they smiled, I seemed to see something behind them which warned me.

"Come be reasonable we offer you a fortune take it. Never again will you have a chance of earning one so easily."

For a moment I may have seemed to hesitate; it is possible even that I did waver. I have been hard up all my life; over and over again mother has not known where to turn for her rates and taxes, to say nothing of her rent. I knew what poverty meant and I had a very fair notion of what could be done with such a sum as five thousand pounds. I remembered that once when Hugh and I were talking about ways and means, I had said that there was nothing which I would not do to get money. Never in my wildest flights had I dreamed of such a sum as the one she mentioned and there it was within my grasp.

That is what I might have thought for an instant. The second after I knew that it was nothing of the kind; that, so far from its being in my grasp, it was not even in sight. I had said there was nothing I would not do to get money; I then knew that I was wrong I could not do that.

While she looked at me, and the man looked too, I saw it all quite plainly that her offer was one which it was impossible for me even to consider.

I just said nothing, and I walked away. NEW PAGE

CHAPTER XXII
THE FIRST NIGHT

I made inquiries about Mr. Thompson with not very satisfactory results. It was so difficult to find someone from whom one could get information of any sort or kind. It took me I don't know how many questions, and two half-crowns, to find out the number of his cabin. It seemed that he had one all to himself lucky creature! at least he would have been lucky if he had not been frightfully ill. When I knocked at the door, it was opened suddenly and a head was put out.

"Now, who's that worrying?"

That was the remark which was addressed to me by a man with very red hair and a square-cut red beard. He seemed to be in a state of agitation. When he saw me, instead of apologising, he was, if anything, ruder than before.

"If you want to know how the man is I can't tell you he's ill; if you want to know what's the matter with him I don't know; and if you want him to get better you go!"

That was what that red-headed person said to me before I had a chance of saying a single word to him then he shut the door in my face, possibly under the mistaken notion that he had given me all the information which was required. I looked about me a bit hazily everything seemed amiss that day. But what I had done to cause me to receive such a reception was beyond me altogether. There was a steward just behind me, grinning. I felt inclined to ask him what he meant by his behaviour I had to scream or scratch someone but just as I was about to speak a few plain words, that steward volunteered what was perhaps intended to be an apology for the man who had put his scarlet countenance through the cabin-door.

"That's the doctor, that is, miss; he hasn't what you might call the best of tempers, and when a passenger's ill he likes to be left alone to treat him in his own way. You can always tell how a patient is getting on by his manner: if he's getting well, the doctor is all smiles; if he's not, the doctor gets so that it isn't hardly safe to look at him."

"Is Mr. Thompson very bad? I'm afraid he must be if what you say about the doctor's manner is true. He nearly snapped my nose off just because I knocked at the door. I never said a word."

"No, miss, I know you didn't. That's the doctor's way. As for how Mr. Thompson is, he's very queer indeed. What upsets the doctor is that he can't make out what's up with him. Nothing makes the doctor so mad as to know he's gravelled."

"But Mr. Thompson was perfectly well only a little while ago."

"Yes, miss, that's just it. They found the gentleman in the smoking-room in a sort of a fit quite unconscious he was. It took the doctor more than an hour to get him round again and now he isn't what you might call really sensible like. He keeps having convulsions, and between them he just lies and stares; he hasn't tried to say a word. Each convulsion he has seems worse than the last, and I did hear the doctor say that if he can't do something to stop them he'll be snuffed clean out."

That was cheerful hearing. I could not tell the steward that, if I didn't know what was the matter with Mr. Thompson I could inform him what or rather who had been the cause of his illness. I should have done no good if the man had listened and believed me but I felt pretty sure he would do neither. What was wanted was practical information which would assist the doctor and result in Mr. Thompson's prompt recovery and that I could not give.

Oh, that was a cheerful day! There was a dreadful scene with Sadie Lawrence. I do not know how many bottles she and her gentleman friend had between them, but they reached a point at which the steward would serve no more. When still another bottle was ordered and refused the gentleman was willing to take no for an answer, but the lady was not. She made such a hullabaloo that the services of two or three stewards were required to assist her to her cabin. On the whole, as I heard the noise she made and the language she used as they helped her along, I was forced to the conviction that there was something to be said for having her in someone else's cabin instead of mine.

I went to bed early. There were certain things I wished to do while I had the cabin to myself, but I had not a chance to do one of them. I was just getting out the screwdriver when Miss Oudinoff put her head in. She professed to be surprised to see me.

"You are turning in already that's good. I go early to bed myself. Since there is not room for two to undress at once, I will return presently, before you are asleep, that you may not be disturbed."

She retired before I answered. No one could be smoother tongued than she was. It was in part her smoothness which made me feel that she was not to be trusted. I had a feeling that she had watched me go into the cabin, that she had listened outside, and had tried to take me by surprise by looking in to see what I was doing.

Her unexpected appearance so unhinged me that I did not venture to proceed with getting out that screwdriver. I even had to sit on the edge of her berth, not only to think things out, but also to get rid of the fluttering which had suddenly overtaken me. My mother had always been subject to "fluttering," but until I went on board that ship I did not know what it meant. Now I had it, I should think, quite a dozen times a day. I never dreamt that one's nervous system could be so easily upset.

I could not properly collect my thoughts as I sat on the edge of that berth. There were things which I ought to do, and quickly, if they were to be done at all. But the effort it required to do them was more than I could manage to say nothing of the presence of mind. To be caught in the act of doing them would be fatal. I did not want that woman to even guess what I would be at; and, clever though she thought she was, I was quite certain that, unless I did something to give myself away, she would not guess. The result of my endeavour to keep my head was that I decided that, rather than run any risk with that woman probably listening outside and catching a cold in the eye by trying to look through a crack, it would be better to do nothing at all. And I did it. I left the screwdriver alone; I undressed myself pretty leisurely; I climbed into my berth. Five minutes after I had settled myself between the sheets she came in, as usual all smiles and sweetness.

"You haven't been long getting ready for bed. I don't know if you sleep quickly. I do. Generally I am asleep almost as soon as my head touches the pillow. But I sleep lightly, the least thing wakes me, and I hate being disturbed. I'll promise not to disturb you if you won't wake me."

I said nothing. I was not going to be drawn into a conversation with one towards whom I felt as I did towards her. She took the hint and kept still. I do not know what she did I was not looking but I never knew anyone who was ready for bed quicker than she was. Whether she really undressed I could not say; she must have slipped out of her clothes by magic if she did.

"Good night," she suddenly exclaimed; "sleep well."

She laughed softly, as if in the enjoyment of some joke of her own. I heard her get into the berth below, and that was all. I never had a more restful night in my life. None of the things I had feared came about. The next thing I heard was Mrs. Harrison's voice.

"Tea, miss; it's half-past eight."

She was speaking to me. She had a tray in her hand. NEW PAGE

CHAPTER XXIII
"DEVIL OF A WOMAN!"

It was with the most prodigious sense of relief that I opened my eyes, woke up, and realised that nothing had happened. It seemed incredible! I had not even dreamed certainly my throat had not been cut. A voice ascended from the berth below:

"Are you going to have some tea? Mrs. Harrison, will you please bring me some? I'd love a cup of tea."

"I'm afraid I shall have to keep you waiting a few moments, miss. Miss Lawrence wasn't fond of tea. You ought to have ordered yours last night. There are five other ladies who did, and they'll have to have theirs first."

"Good morning, Miss Forester! Did you have a pleasant sleep?"

The woman spoke to me directly the stewardess had gone. It seemed to be so silly to persist in saying nothing, so I returned her good morning. As I sipped the tea I wondered if I had misjudged her. Clearly, as I have already said, my throat was not yet cut, and on the morrow we should reach New York. I got up first she seemed to be willing to give way to me in everything. At the breakfast-table I found that everyone was talking about how soon we were to land. Apparently everyone was in the highest spirits, inclined to congratulate each other on the excellent crossing they had had. The pervading air of cheerfulness was a little jarred when my friendly steward leaned over to inform me that Mr. Thompson, so far from being better, was, if anything, worse.

"I do hear," he said, "that Dr. Binstead expected him to die in the night. They won't let him land if he's still alive, the doctor doesn't think. Those health people won't let anybody land who's the least bit sick; they let them die on board, but not on shore."

That piece of information rather took my appetite away. At the same time I recognised the possibility of my having done that woman and her friends an injustice. It was conceivable that she was not responsible for Mr. Thompson's condition at least that was how I felt until something happened in the course of the morning.

Something else tried my nerves not only the difficulty, but the absolute impossibility of finding out anything about my Hugh. If what that steward had said was correct, then those health people would not let him land. That would upset my calculations altogether. What would be done with him if they did not let him go on shore? But the notion that they would not let an inoffensive stranger land because he had been nearly murdered on the way across seemed so monstrous that I did my best to refuse to entertain it. If I could only have learnt that he was still alive it would have been something, but I did not know how to begin to find out anything about him at all. I thought of going to Miss Sadie Lawrence and asking her for a consideration to give me some sort of introduction to her friend Mr. Trouncer. But it seemed, so the stewardess said, that she was not in a condition to receive visitors. I could believe it easily. Still what was I to do? I wanted to know something.

I was hardly in a condition to share the high spirits of the other passengers. It was something to find myself still alive, but after all there were other things besides mere life and presently I was worrying as hard as ever. I wanted to get into my cabin and be left alone in it for sufficient reasons. I hung about till I felt certain that the coast was clear. Then I started to see for myself.

On the way I was stopped by the man who had said that his name was Galstin and then that it was Yashvin. Although he took off his hat and bowed, his scowl was much more pronounced than his bow.

"One more chance I offer you, Miss Forester. Have you considered the question of that five-and-twenty thousand dollars?"

"I don't wish to speak to you," was all I answered but he did not seem to like it.

"Nor do I wish to speak to you--you may be very sure of that you common English female pig!" I never heard anyone so rude, and his manner was even ruder than his words. He lacked the polish of his female associate. "All I want is what belongs to me, and I am going to have it before you reach America. Tell me where it is; you will have your five-and-twenty thousand dollars, and you may positively count on never being spoken to by me again. Such a thing as you!"

The man presented a repulsive spectacle of what it is to have an evil temper. I felt how sorry I should be for any girl who had to marry him what an awful time the poor thing would have.

"Let me pass," was what I said. My brevity only made him worse.

"You utter fool!" was the courteous language he addressed to me. "Before I let you pass it will not be my fault if you don't understand clearly what the position is. The property which the thief Stewart gave you the charge of is not in your cabin." With that he waved his finger at me as if it were a lethal weapon I may be ignorant, but I know that lethal means deadly. "If it is, then you have hidden it with great skill. We have taken everything in your cabin to pieces--nowhere is it to be found. It is not to be found because it is not there."

"When did you do this?" I asked.

"Last night when you were asleep."

I stared. His frankness was surprising. If last night he had, as he put it, taken everything in the cabin to pieces, then I must have been asleep indeed.

"I don't believe you did anything of the kind. I sleep so lightly that I am woke by the slightest sound. Last night I was disturbed by nothing."

"Think so if you please. We took your berth to pieces; we searched the bedding, your bag, your clothes everything! It was not there. Yet I know you have it. Stewart was not so simple as he seemed; when he chose you to be his messenger, he knew what he was doing. Did I not know you had what I am seeking I should have said it cannot be but I do know! It is as certain as that there is a sky above us. If you will not tell me for twenty-five thousand dollars where you have hidden what belongs to me, then you shall tell me for nothing. That I promise you. If you suffer a little inconvenience, the fault will be yours and no one else's it will be on your own head. Now, once more, will you tell me for the five-and-twenty thousand dollars?"

"According to your own confession you appear to be a pleasant sort of person. The idea of making free with a lady's private belongings while she is asleep! I never heard of such a thing in my life."

"Answer my question--is it to be for the five-and-twenty thousand dollars?" He actually laid his hand upon my arm and pinched me.

"Allow me to inform you on one point! You may be a bully and a murderer, but I'm as strong as you, and if you dare to touch me with your grimy fingers I'll prove it."

I proved it to some extent then and there. I shook him off, and I caught his wrist between my fingers, and I gave his arm such a twist that he not only winced he squealed.

"Devil of a woman!" he cried.

"Don't use such language to me," I warned him. "I've been told I'm as strong as a horse, and if you're not careful I'll try on you how strong I am. To begin with I'll twist your arm out of its socket; to go on with, if you don't let me pass, I'll make you. Out of my way!"

With both hands I took him by the throat, and I spun him round, with the result that, taken by surprise, in his attempt to keep his balance he tumbled on to the floor.

"You may thank your lucky stars," I informed him, "that you're getting off so lightly. There are some things I'll stand from no man. By the time you've picked yourself up and got on to your feet again, you will perhaps have found out what some of them are."

He was picking himself up as I went striding off. As I glanced back over my shoulder he was feeling himself as if he were anxious to find out if anything was broken. NEW PAGE

CHAPTER XXIV
ALMOST WITHIN SIGHT OF LAND

I forget how many miles we were from New York when I turned into my berth that night. We had got into misty weather, which prevented the ship moving at full speed, but I understood that if the fog would only lift we might expect to land on the morrow. I was full of the strangest mixture of feelings. My voyage the great voyage of which I had dreamed but had not supposed would ever be possible to me was nearly over. It had lasted so short a time; it seemed only the other day that I had started with Mr. Stewart in his motor car from Grove Gardens. Of course, I had known that on a quick steamer one travelled from England to America in just over a week, but one has to learn from experience what, circumstanced as I was, a week means. In one way it had been the shortest week I had ever known; yet I realised that, in a very wide sense, it had meant for me the passing from one world to another I should never again be the Catherine Fraser whose horizon had been bounded for so many years by the Fulham Palace Road. From the moment in which I had first heard of Hugh's strange adventures in that mysterious house to that hour in which I was looking forward, with feelings of trepidation, to landing in what I had been informed was the greatest country on God's earth, I had been moving through a series of sensations which were so strange and so various, so unlike anything I had ever known before, that I could scarcely credit that they were real.

So far as I could ascertain the entry into America was to be a trying ordeal in itself. On the morrow I might expect all sorts of things to happen. The ship was to be boarded by officials who would take all the passengers into custody that, they said, was what it came to.

The most searching questions would be asked on the most delicate subjects, and they would have to be answered. If I made even the slightest error in one of my answers, goodness only knew what would happen to me. That was what I could not learn exactly what would happen to me. It was very important to know how inaccurate I might be.

"Above all things," a woman had told me only that very afternoon, "don't play any tricks on the custom-house. If you've got anything dutiable, declare it. They'll be down on you if they find you out in trying to do them out of a dime. Unless you're absolutely certain that you can do them and you never are don't tell them a lie."

The advice might not suggest a high moral standard, but I did not care to tell her so. I had been feeling lonely, worried in a way I never thought I should have been; it was good of her to talk to me at all. She was an agent for a Paris milliner. Some of the stories she told me of her own experience with the custom-house authorities were a little startling. I had no means of telling how true they were, but they made me wonder.

One thing she said did stick in my mind.

"If you do get anything through the customs you can never count on its being safe. I knew someone who got through with never mind how much, but a good lot of Brussels lace. She was met by a friend. As they were going to Brooklyn in a cab, the friend asked her what she had done about the lace. She said she had got it through. They got home. About two hours afterwards, as she was getting the last of the lace out of its hiding-place it had been pretty securely hidden three custom-house officers walked in two men and a woman. They had been talking louder in that cab than they thought, and the cabman had listened the wretch! He had driven straight back and told the custom-house people what he had heard, and they arranged a little surprise. They caught both women in the act, and they hauled them both up and wasn't there some duty to be paid! If you've anything on which you ought to pay, declare it and pay; you'll find it cheaper in the end."

It was all very well for her to talk like that, but my position was peculiar. I did not even know if I had anything on which I ought to pay; I could not pay if I had. That was a difficulty which, in my ignorance, had not occurred to me. Suppose it turned out that I was taking something into the country on which I ought to pay duty, and I said I was not, and they found out that I was whatever would happen to me? Suppose, to go further, the duty which I ought to pay was a lot it quite easily might be; from the hints dropped by Mr. Yashvin and his lady friend it might be a terrific sum; and through making a false declaration I had to pay it several times over. They might send me to prison. I should hardly dare to appeal to Mr. Stewart. He would pull a long face if he were dragged into the trouble, because, from his point of view, I had made a mess of things. If he had to hand over a bagful of money, he might consider his bargain with me off, and after all my high hopes I should have gone through all that worry and trouble for nothing.

If my ad venture were to result like that, I should never hold up my head again. Once having reached America it had seemed to me that all my troubles would have ended; now I feared that they would be just beginning.

I had this fresh worry on my mind, added to all the others which were there already, when on what I hoped was the eve of my introduction to a land compared to which my own country was as a drop in the ocean, I went into my cabin to retire for the night. It was not yet ten o'clock. A lot of the passengers were what they called "celebrating," though quite what they were celebrating I did not understand, but it seemed to involve a good deal of drinking and plenty of noise. The sounds of revelry came to me as I closed the cabin door. There was music in the saloon, where some sort of concert was taking place; somewhere people were dancing; laughing and singing seemed to be general.

Ordinarily I should have joined the revellers. I am as fond of a bit of fun as anyone. To my own surprise I was in no mood for it then. All I wanted was to make certain arrangements of my own, sleep the night out, and await the coming day. I should know no peace till I had handed over my trust to Ezra George Bennington, of 32 Paper Buildings, John Street, New York.

The cabin was empty, which I regarded as lucky. I did all I had wanted to do, undressed and got into my berth before anyone appeared. Just as I was dropping off to sleep I was conscious that Miss Oudinoff had come into the cabin. I realised how noiseless she was, opening the door without a sound, and standing just inside it as if fearful of disturbing me.

It seemed to me that she stood there quite a considerable time. My back was towards her, so I could not see what she was doing, but I had an odd feeling that she was listening for something, or someone.

Then she crossed towards me. I heard nothing, but I knew she had moved. She came into slight contact with the side of my berth she was leaning over the bed-clothes trying to make out if I was asleep.

"Miss Forester," she whispered, very softly. I said nothing. She addressed me again, a little louder. I continued to hold my peace.

There was a pause. Although I kept my eyes closed, so that even if I had been facing her I could have seen nothing, I knew that she was still leaning over the berth trying to make out if I really was asleep. Then, all at once, apparently for no reason, I was conscious of a curious feeling a feeling of dread. That woman at my side meant mischief the conviction was borne in on me with a force which there was no resisting. I was clear-headed enough. I did not wish to be caught like a rat in a trap what was I to do? How protect myself from the imminent danger? It was no use to be caught lying down. I suddenly sat up, turned and faced her.

As I did so the door opened, as noiselessly as before the man Yashvin entered.

"What do you want?" I began. I was going to ask, "What do you want in here?" but before I had gone further than the first four words, she reached out and caught me in some odd way by the windpipe so that I could not breathe.

"Be still," she said. I knew there was something shining in her other hand some sharp-pointed thing with which she pricked me. "Where are those pearls?" I heard the word "pearls" in a sort of haze; something had happened when she pricked me which made everything seem hazy. "I'll give you five-and-twenty thousand dollars if you'll tell us. If you don't, and we can't find them, we'll cut you open to find out if you've swallowed them there's a fog, and you won't be missed. Quick tell me, where are those pearls?"

I just managed to say something.

"How can I speak when you're throttling me?"

She removed her hand from my windpipe. Something very odd had happened; I could hardly speak even then. I knew that Yashvin was standing close to the berth; I had lost the power to order him to stand away. I heard his voice cruel, menacing, dangerous.

"Now, Miss Forester, you have no time to lose twenty-five thousand dollars or the sea which is it to be? Will you tell us where they are?"

"No," I stammered I could just stammer I won't!"

"She's had her last chance," I heard him say. "No more fooling! Give it her."

The woman stretched out the hand in which was that shining thing and pricked me again.

BOOK III

THE GREAT TEMPTATION

CHAPTER XXV
THE PATIENT

"Will somebody kindly explain where I am?"

The girl in the bed sat up. She leaned on her hands, looking about her with the air of one who wondered. The three other persons in the room gave jumps their movements really amounted to jumps and they looked round. The nurse one was a nurse in one of those becoming costumes which nurses sometimes do wear exclaimed:

"She's conscious!"

With her were two men, one of whom was Mr. Paul R. Stewart. He was a tall, broad, muscular individual, perhaps somewhere in the early forties, not ill-favoured, with a square-jawed face which somehow suggested that as a rule he knew what he wanted and did his best to get it. He remarked:

"Holy smoke! Land at last!"

What he meant was not plain. The other man was a doctor Dr. Hardicanute Rasselton. He was a person who might have been thinner with advantage, but looked as if he were contented to be stout, if only because his physical condition enabled him to wear an air of radiant satisfaction, which could not fail to impress the most woebegone patient with the conviction that things were not so bad as they might be. He settled his spectacles on his nose, looked at Mr. Stewart as if he wondered at his displaying so much emotion, and crossed towards the bed, observing, in what one has seen described as a "fruity" voice:

"Well! How are we now? Very much better."

The girl on the bed seemed surprised to see him, which she probably was. The nurse was at her side, trying to induce her to return to a recumbent position.

"Now, my dear, lie down be good. You'll tire yourself if you're not careful. You're so much better that it would be a pity to lose ground again now wouldn't it?"

The remark seemed banal, but those of nurses sometimes are. The patient who returns to consciousness for the first time after the lapse of a fortnight is seldom in search of the original or even the startling. Mr. Stewart came in with something which certainly was not commonplace.

"The sound of your voice beats any band I ever heard. It begins to look as if we were through the Straits of Najero."

Since what he meant was possibly not clear to himself, it was not strange that the girl on the bed looked puzzled.

"Haven't I seen you somewhere before?" she asked. "Leave me alone." This was to the nurse who was persevering in her efforts to induce her to lie down. Then she added: "Why doesn't someone tell me where I am?"

The doctor said: "You're among friends, my dear. And how are we feeling like the flowers which bloom in the spring?"

The girl paid no attention to this preposterous inquiry. She commented on the first part of his remark.

"I didn't know I'd got any friends."

She was a nice-looking girl not lovely, but pleasant faced, with pretty brown hair, clear, steady, sensible eyes, wide apart, curved lips, and a good chin a young woman whose appearance inspired confidence, suggesting that her head was screwed on properly at birth. The nurse seemed to think that her statement came of painful reflection.

107

"My dear, you mustn't say that; the world is full of your friends."

Is it? I don't know." The girl looked at that nurse with a simple directness which the woman possibly found a trifle disconcerting. "Why doesn't someone tell me where I am?"

"That's dead easy," exclaimed Mr. Stewart. "You're at Raymond's Hotel, Sixth Avenue, New York City, and if you want more comfortable quarters I don't know where you'll find them."

"What," the girl persisted, "am I doing here?"

The doctor, possibly feeling that he was being ousted from the position which a medical man feels he ought to occupy in a sick-room, took it upon himself to answer.

"You've not been very well, my dear; you must not overdo it. Come, lie down."

The nurse and the doctor between them got her on to her back again. The nurse drew the bed-clothes up to her chin. She lay, wide-eyed, pale-cheeked, but good to look at, gazing up at them. She said, speaking as a child who asks for information:

"Then have I got to America?"

"You have, my dear, you have. You've been in America just over a fortnight." This was the doctor. He added, "Now, Stewart, I'm afraid that I shall have to ask you to go. This young lady must not be allowed to excite herself."

That was a subject on which the young lady herself had a word to say. She looked at Mr. Stewart.

"You are Mr. Stewart. Of course, I remember. Don't go, please, until you've told me what I want to know."

She closed her eyes, and somehow when they were shut she looked singularly pale. The trio exchanged glances. Mr. Stewart asked a question with his eyes; the doctor shook his head; the nurse passed her hand lightly over the girl's brow, then she telegraphed something to the doctor.

"I think," he said, "if I were you I should try to get a little sleep and ask your question afterwards."

He looked at Mr. Stewart and jerked his thumb towards the door. The girl, opening her eyes, caught the gentleman as, in obedience to the hint, he was starting to move.

"You're not to go until you've told me what I want."

The girl shut her eyes again as if she were tired. Mr. Stewart telegraphed another question to the doctor, who returned an affirmative nod. He whispered in one of those noiseless whispers at which a doctor ought to be an expert.

"You'd better stay; she'll worry if you don't. Tell her what she wants, but nothing unpleasant."

The whisper might have been noiseless, but the girl heard. She unclosed her eyes and looked at the pair as if she had detected them in something improper.

"What are you two talking about?" The men said nothing; they might have been guilty. Once more the eyes were closed; with them shut the girl asked a question. "Where is Hugh?" When a reply did not immediately come, her eyes re-opened; she gazed at Mr. Stewart. "What has become of Hugh? Tell me."

The words were a command. She kept her glance on Mr. Stewart as if to drive it home. The gentleman fenced.

"Hugh? Do you mean Mr. Beckwith?"

"You know that I mean Mr. Beckwith." It was an accusation. "Where is Hugh?" she asked again. Mr. Stewart seemed to find it difficult to answer; he glanced at the doctor as if for inspiration. "Tell me!" she exclaimed.

"You know where Mr. Beckwith is, Stewart. Why don't you tell this young lady what she wants to know?"

As if taking advantage of the fact that the girl's eyes were not on him, the doctor winked at Mr. Stewart, who did not seem to find it easy to act on the suggestion which it conveyed.

"Mr. Beckwith? Oh, yes; of course, of course. He's all right."

"Where is he?" asked the girl.

"Where is he? Just so; where is he? He's down town."

"In this town?"

"Certainly he's in this town in New York right here. In what other town should he be?"

"You're quite sure he's in this town?"

"Absolutely dead sure. What does the girl mean? He was in this town when I saw him last, which was only this morning."

"Is he well?"

Mr. Stewart seemed unhappy. He glanced at the doctor as if for assistance which was cheerfully given.

"The truth is, my dear, that Mr. Beckwith has not been well; like you, he's been a patient of mine. Now, you really must compose yourself and try to get a little sleep. You're getting on so nicely that it would be a pity to get a set-back after all the trouble we've had with you."

"Will you tell me about Hugh, please?"

"There is very little to tell. Mr. Beckwith appears to have had an accident on board the steamer as you had."

"Did I have an accident?"

"Well, so far as I'm concerned, I'm scarcely in a position to say. I have been given to understand that you were found in your berth, on the morning of the day before the steamer reached New York, in a state of collapse from which it has taken you more than a fortnight to recover. I don't know if you are aware that Mr. Beckwith was on board the steamer which carried you."

"Oh, yes, I knew."

"You did know, did you?" This was Mr. Stewart, who spoke hurriedly. He addressed the doctor. "Unless you have a very serious objection, Mr. Rasselton, I should like to say a few words to this young lady in private. I think a little talk with me would do her more good than harm, and, anyhow, I'll set her mind at rest on certain points which otherwise may worry her. If you and nurse will both take yourselves away."

Dr. Rasselton glanced at the nurse.

"Our friend is peremptory; he wants to turn us both out. If he promises to say nothing upsetting I think he might have his own way. Would you very much mind, young lady, being left alone with Mr. Stewart, or would you rather I turned him out? I can do it."

"Let him stop. You go."

The words were plain enough. The doctor smiled.

"That doesn't sound very complimentary, but we understand. Come, nurse, let's leave them alone." He turned to Stewart. "I hold you responsible for the patient's condition. You'll only be allowed a couple of minutes with her anyhow, and don't you say anything to agitate or worry her. Remember she's not a great strong creature like you."

As soon as the nurse and the doctor were out of the room, Mr. Stewart drew a chair to the side of the bed and placed himself on it. Being seated, he drew a long breath which was very like a sigh it might have been a sigh of relief and he said:

"At last I have a chance of speaking to you. The strain of waiting has been almost too much for me. I wouldn't go through it again not for a peck of rubies."

The girl between the sheets was silent; then she merely said, as if she were turning a problem over in her mind.

"What about me? Don't I count?"

There were traces of heat in the man's voice as he answered:

"Of course you count--if you only knew for how much. I was beginning to fear that I should have your blood upon my hands. I believe I should have cut my throat if I had."

"Did they cut mine?" The question and the simplicity with which it was asked seemed to startle him.

"They? Who? Tell me just what happened. I am absolutely in the dark about everything, and a bully cloud of dust has been raised in consequence. This will be the last experiment on those lines I'll ever try if I live to be as old as Methuselah. During the last month I believe I've aged a century." NEW PAGE

CHAPTER XXVI
TWO FRIENDS

The noise of distant traffic was the only sound which broke the stillness. Apparently the bedroom was at the back of the house; it could scarcely have looked out upon a busy street. The girl's eyelids had fallen again. Mr. Stewart, leaning forward, was keenly noting the expression on her face.

"Aren't you feeling well enough to talk? You'd better not try if you aren't. At any rate tell me one thing if there is any humanity left in you. I mayn't look it, but I'm feeling as bad as you do maybe worse. Where are the pearls?" He waited for her to answer. Nothing came from her. She might almost have been inanimate. "Did you hear what I said? For God's sake tell me if you did. Where are the pearls?"

That time she did speak, but not in reply to his question.

"Is Hugh alive?"

"Don't let that worry you he's as much alive as you are. I don't know what did happen; it seems impossible to get the truth from anyone. I believe those steam-boat people are in a conspiracy to hold their tongues. And though I admit that, with the enterprising press over here, in some respects it's just as well, I don't want them to conceal the essential facts from me. Don't you see how you're keeping me hanging on a hook? Please tell me where are the pearls the twenty-two?"

She replied to his question with another.

"When can I see Hugh?"

"How in thunder should I know; you'd better ask the physician. I take it just as soon as you're fit. That's the sort of question he keeps asking when can he see you? He asks it about a dozen times a day."

"Does he? Dear Hugh! I wonder if he'll ever know."

Her tender tone was in marked contrast to his impatience.

"I'm wondering if I shall ever know. Be merciful don't play me like a fish on a line. Tell me where are the pearls?"

Her reply was, "Where are Cara Oudinoff and Mr. Yashvin?"

"Who in the name of blazes are they? People you met on board?"

"They said that what you entrusted to me belonged to them."

"Did they? Potiphar's wife! Can they have been that bright couple masquerading under another name?"

"I was masquerading under another name you arranged that."

"Don't I know it? I'm beginning to suspect that you're not so ill as old Rasselton thinks, and you've taken him in as well as me. Before you say another thing will you just answer my question." The stillness continued so long unbroken that he repeated his question. "Did you hear what I said? I know you heard, but will you answer where are those pearls?"

There was another lengthy interval, then all she said was:

"I think I've talked enough."

Nothing he could do induced her to speak another word. He hardly dared to lose his temper to any perceptible extent, with physician and nurse probably keeping watch and ward in an adjoining room, but he went some distance. He repeated his inquiry in varying forms perhaps twenty times; he even abused her under his breath; he told her frankly that he would have liked to treat her to a shaking. No result ensued of any sort or kind. The girl lay perfectly still, with her eyes fast closed, to all intents and purposes as deaf as a post. No weapon within his reach would move her. When at last he flounced from his chair, having exhausted all his patience, and finding himself incapable of sitting any longer, he hurled what he meant to be a parting shot.

"I believe you're up to some low-down game or other. I ought to have known better than to trust a job of this sort to a woman."

As he was moving towards the door she did turn her head, opened her eyes, looked at him, and gently said, "Give my love to Hugh."

He spun round like a teetotum, glared, then strode back to the bed. By the time he reached it her eyes were closed again and her face turned upwards. In spite of his ill temper he could not but admit that she was good to look at. He admitted as much.

"Your Hugh's a lucky beast; you're worth ten of him."

When he once more gained the door, a meek voice came to him:

"I'm nothing of the kind. Hugh's worth ten of me."

Encouraged, possibly by the evident fact that she had regained her power of speech, he paused to make a last appeal, speaking below his breath, yet with an eagerness which there was no mistaking.

"Will you tell me where those pearls are?"

Not a sound from the bed. The girl had apparently relapsed into sleep; the gentleman, after a momentary hesitation, dragged the door open and strode from the room a little more noisily than he need have done.

He marched straight from the sick-room to a parlour which was on the floor below. It was a private parlour which, for the time being, was reserved for him. On the way through the anteroom, in which was the nurse only, the doctor apparently having taken his departure, he made one remark:

"I've lessened her worries, but she hasn't mine."

When he entered that private sitting-room he banged the door, and exclaimed in a tone of voice which was not subdued,

"Confound all women! Why were they ever allowed to plague the world?"

A voice, which evidently came from someone to whom English was not his native tongue, but the anxiety in whose tone was obvious, remarked

"Never mind about the women! Where are those pearls?"

"Boil you, Rothenstein, for an idiot!"

"What fresh lie is that? You are all lies! Are you now going to pretend that she is not conscious? I know better! I met Dr. Rasselton; he said to me, 'She is all right enough. She seems to have come back into full possession of her senses. Mr. Stewart is having a talk with her. She seems to have something which she wishes to tell him, so I have left them alone together.' Those are the words which Dr. Rasselton used to me. In the face of them are you going to pretend that she is not yet conscious? Do not play the fool with me any longer where are those pearls?"

"Rothenstein, your career up to the present has been a striking illustration of what a mess an idiot can make of his affairs if he tries. If you suppose that merely because a woman is conscious you can get her to tell you what you want to know you display your ignorance. If you can help it don't be an ass!"

"Do you dare to say she will not tell you where those pearls are?"

"I do. You can go and tackle her if you like. You know the number of her room."

"I will; I go to find out from her what a liar you are."

"Go; the trip may do you good, especially if it is as fruitful of result as mine was. Who is Cara Oudinoff, and who is Yashvin? Acquaintances of yours?"

"What do you mean? I know no one of that name."

"Rothenstein, it is my turn to call you a liar. I hate to do it, but you are. You certainly know the lady and gentleman who travelled under those names on board the Columbia."

The little old man, in a queer-shaped top-hat, and a long frock-coat reaching almost to his ankles, opened the door as if to depart on the journey to which the other had challenged him. As he stood with the handle in his fingers something in Mr. Stewart's tone seemed to attract his attention. He shut the door; combed with his fingers the amazing beard which covered the whole of his chest; then moved slowly back towards the centre of the room. He was so small and so oddly formed that he seemed to be all frock-coat, beard, hair, and top-hat. His eyes, which were deeply sunken, looked out from under a penthouse of coarse hair; yellow fangs gleamed through the shock of hair below; he had a sideways, crablike motion as he moved; his hands did not look as if they had made the acquaintance of soap or water for years; altogether he did not present a pleasant appearance. He went close up to Mr. Stewart, who towered high above him, and he said, as if conveying a confidential announcement:

"They made dam fools of themselves, those two."

"Oh, they did, did they? How did they do it?"

"It is because of them she is as she is."

"I imagined it was the handiwork of some of your friends; travelling under aliases, I presume. Do I know them? Is Cara Oudinoff that charming and adventurous lady, Princess Kitty Vronsky, and the gentleman that decidedly dangerous friend of yours you have such friends, Rothenstein I Mr. Konstantin Ivanovitch?"

"That is so." The old man, raising his claw-like hands, shook them in the air. "It has been blunder upon blunder. I do not say that it was all your fault, but you have been chiefly to blame because of your love of getting the better of your friends."

"I suppose you are never moved by desires of that kind? That was why you wanted to keep me out of the deal and have it all to yourself."

"They were to have brought the pearls to New York."

"And they didn't."

"How could they when you had stolen them? Thief that you are!"

"Thank you; I can stand a good deal of you, Rothenstein, you are always so nice. Well, what did they do?"

"I sent them a telegram that you had stolen them, but that they were to cross all the same because you had given them to a fool named Beckwith to take to New York."

"I begin to understand; that is why Mr. Beckwith had a little misadventure."

"He had not got them. They supposed he was cleverer than they thought, so they nearly killed him, trying to make him tell them where they were. When they had nearly killed him they searched everywhere. Not only did they tear his cabin to pieces, they broke the furniture. The pearls were not there. They sent me a wireless message. By that time I had found out things for myself. I told them that at the last moment you had changed your plans, that you had given them to a girl named Catherine Fraser, who was on board the ship as Miss Forester; that the pearls were certainly in her possession; and that they were to get them from her."

"So they got them. The position becomes transparent. You're a nice bag of tricks!"

Mr. Stewart, leaning against the radiator, his hands in his jacket pockets, beamed down at Mr. Rothenstein as if he thought him a humorist of the first water. The little man, instead of appreciating the compliment, began to dance in such a fury of rage that his utterance was impeded. He screamed in a voice which sounded as if it had cracked:

"They did not get them they did not! That is where they blundered. Did she not have them? Did you not give them to her?"

"You were quite right, I did give them to her; they were in her possession when she was on board that ship."

"Then where has she hidden them where? They did everything to her they could, they left her for dead, but they could not get her to speak, they could not find them."

"I thought that girl had pluck. I am told that in the morning they found her in her berth, lying as if dead, the cabin torn to pieces, and the young woman who had been her cabin mate, missing. I take it that that was the Princess Kitty." Rothenstein gave an affirmative nod. "The dear soul! That young woman has had an adventurous career she should end well. And pray how did she and her associate get away from the ship? They were not on board. Did they throw themselves over?"

"That was part of the plan. It was arranged that they were to take the pearls from her that night. It was pretty certain whereabout the steamer would be her course is always the same; unless they had a wireless message to the contrary a tug would come out to meet them. They were to give a signal when they had done their business; the tug was to come close to the steamer; they were to be provided with lifebuoys of a peculiar kind; they were to lower themselves overboard; the tug would pick them up and land them at a point which was not New York with the pearls on them."

"That sounds a risky business. It was easy for the tug not to pick them up, and they say that on that night there was a mist."

"That did not matter. The tug knew that they were there; those buoys would keep them afloat for hours till the morning, when it was light enough for them to be seen."

"You are an ingenious person, Rothenstein. The idea of their landing at a point which, as you put it, was not New York was that I should be kept in ignorance of what had become of the pearls and you might diddle me after all. Is that so?"

"Diddle? Do you say that! Did you not diddle us? You traitor to your friends!"

"So it's an elaborate comedy you've been playing. You've been worrying me to learn from the girl what has become of the pearls, and all the while you have them. You'll have to account to me."

Mr. Rothenstein resumed his jigging up and down overtaken by another paroxysm of rage.

"I have not got them! I have not got them! We none of us have got them! It is you who have got them--you--you!"

"Are you in earnest? Do you seriously wish me to believe that those two choice spirits left that ship without the spoils for which they had done so much in their possession?"

"I swear they had not got them. Should I have come to you if they had?"

"You believe them when they say they haven't?"

"It is not belief I believe in nothing and no one! it is knowledge. I know that they have not got them. If you have not then the girl has you must get the secret of their hiding-place from her if you have not got it already."

"Don't be an ass if you can help it. Rothenstein, this is a case in which we've got to trust each other because there's no way out of it. Suppose they're still on board the Columbia and she has hidden them in one of those infernal holes and corners which would only occur to a woman."

"Has she said they are?"

"She says nothing. When I asked where they were she was smitten with deafness shut her eyes and went to sleep."

"She will have to tell, that is all."

"That, presumably, is what your friends said, but they don't seem to have made a great success of it when they tried to make her tell. Then there's the question of time. The lady's birthday is in seventeen days. Our client has made it a condition that everything shall be ready two days in advance. Although from one point of view even a dangerous lunatic, he's one of the most level-headed men in this great country. He's not buying a pig in a poke, and he no doubt has his own reasons for wishing to have everything ready in advance. Anyhow it's got to be it's in the contract. If they are still on that ship we shan't be able to get hold of them in anything like fifteen days. And what are we going to do with the Romanoff pearls if Van Groot won't have them; if they're not up to time he won't. Heaven only knows what we've done to get them, and I verily believe he's the only man in this world who'll pay for them enough to make it worth our while. You must remember that this is a question of half a million dollars, Rothenstein."

"Do I not know it! My God, do I not know it!" Instead of his beard, the little man was thrusting his fingers through his tangled mass of hair, which hung over his shoulders looking as if it had never known a comb. "If I do not get my share of the money I shall be ruined."

"We shall none of us be better off."

"The money must be divided into five shares; you have forfeited your share--"

"Don't talk like that or there'll be trouble."

"And Darya, she has forfeited hers--"

"You had better tell her so. The safest thing you can do is to play fair. If you'd begun that way there wouldn't have been this trouble?"

"What is the use of talking like that when we have not got the pearls? If we had them, and all expenses were paid, there would not be so much left out of my twenty thousand pounds to represent an adequate profit for the risk I run; but if I were to get nothing I am ruined a broken man. And all that has been done for less than nothing!"

"Rothenstein, we shall have to get those pearls quickly."

The little man seemed to read something significant in the other's words. He stared at him from under his overhanging brows.

"You'll not be able to pass off imitations on to Mr. Van Groot."

"I'm not such a fool as to try. Mr. Van Groot knows as much about the Romanoff pearls as you do and Bennington knows more. First of all we've got to find out from that young woman where they are, and then we've got to get them well on time if we have to use an aeroplane. My own opinion is that Catherine Fraser is as straight as a die and that anyhow she wouldn't try to play it off on me, unless your friends have put her back up in which case there's some excuse for her."

At that moment the door opened and a young woman came into the room, who was tall, slender, graceful, excellently dressed, and bore herself with an air as if she knew that she was someone. She looked at Rothenstein, and then she said:

"So you are here." Then to Stewart, "Any news of the pearls?" She added as if it were a postscript, "I've been to see Hugh Beckwith; I believe he's dying." NEW PAGE

CHAPTER XXVII
CALLERS

The girl sat up in bed; Miss Galstin sat on a chair at her side; Mr. Stewart, who seemed restless, was fidgeting about the room. Conversation hung fire, especially at first. Neither of the visitors seemed to know exactly what to say; or, knowing, how to say it. They received no assistance from the invalid, who, with her hands clasped outside the coverlet, looked steadily in front of her. After an interval of silence, which continued so long that it became uncomfortably marked, Miss Galstin made an effort to say something. Not the latest costume from Paris, nor the consciousness, which she must have had, that she looked charming, lent her an appearance of ease. She looked at Mr. Stewart as if she thought that he ought to speak first, and then at the girl in the bed; but as neither of them uttered a syllable the conclusion seemed forced upon her that she must. And she did. She had one of the greatest gifts a woman can have, a clear, soft, rounded, musical voice; the mere sound of it was good, and she said, as if she were breathing a sympathy which came from the bottom of her heart:

"I was so sorry to hear of your illness."

"I haven't been ill. I've been nearly murdered. That's all."

Miss Galstin seemed to find the instant response a trifle startling. She looked at the speaker as if she wondered what she meant. The girl made no attempt to look at her. She kept her glance fixed steadily in front. Miss Galstin turned towards Mr. Stewart, as if for assistance, but received none. At that moment, with his back towards her, he had stationed himself in front of the window and seemed to be enjoying the view; which was odd, as there was nothing to be seen.

"Anyhow, evidently you are very much better. Indeed, I think you are looking blooming."

This was a gallant effort on Miss Galstin's part, while avoiding delicate topics, to carry the conversation a step farther.

"Indeed? Am I? How does anyone look blooming?"

Anything less encouraging than the girl's manner would be hard to imagine. With a courage which did her credit Miss Galstin said something which was rather neat.

"If I had a mirror handy I should show you yourself in it; you would then understand how one can look blooming."

The remark scarcely received the reception it merited. There was silence. Then the girl shot at her one sidelong glance.

"Do you take me for a fool?" she asked.

In her softest, sweetest, most appealing tone Miss Galstin inquired:

"Miss Fraser, why do you speak to me like that?"

The proffered olive branch was rejected; the response was as uncompromising as it could have been.

"Don't you really mean, why do I speak to you at all? I don't know why you are here. I did not ask you to come. You're forcing yourself into my bedroom in sheer impertinence. It's adding insult to injury. It's through you I've been nearly murdered, and then all you do is to pretend that you know nothing about it and to simper that you are sorry to hear of my illness. Stuff and nonsense! that's what I say."

Perhaps the fact that the girl looked so bonny as she uttered her belligerent words had something to do with Miss Galstin's being taken so wholly aback. She appealed to the gentleman,

"Mr. Stewart, what am I to say to her?"

The gentleman, who had possibly had enough of staring at nothing at all, twirling rapidly round, exclaimed:

"Ask her where those pearls are."

Catherine did not wait for the question to be repeated by the lady. She addressed the gentleman.

"Oh, that's it, is it? I thought it was something of the kind. I felt sure that neither of you would have come merely to pretend that you sympathised with me. Your conduct throughout has shown that you didn't care one pin's point whether I was alive or dead."

"You'll do me the justice to remember, Miss Fraser, that I did not suggest that you should come to New York. You were an eager volunteer. I did not hide from you that the journey involved considerable risk. You treated my warning lightly, hinting that the idea of risk rather attracted you than otherwise. That being so, I don't understand your present attitude. What cause of complaint have you against me, or against Miss Galstin?"

"I wish to have nothing to say to you of any sort or kind thank you very much."

The gentleman, quitting his position in front of the window, came striding towards the bed.

"That's all very well, but I have something to say to you we both of us have. I entrusted a certain charge to your keeping. You promised in the clearest possible language that you would take care of that charge and deliver it at a certain address by a certain day. As it has not been delivered, what has become of it, Miss Fraser?"

"What did the charge consist of?"

"You know perfectly well."

"I don't; that's untrue to your knowledge. I knew nothing."

The visitors seemed a little at a loss; they exchanged glances, asking each other questions with their eyes. Then the lady observed:

"I thought it was understood that the charge entrusted to Miss Fraser consisted of pills--twenty-two, to be exact."

"Tell me what kind of pills they were and I'll have others like them made up at the nearest chemist's shop. A prescription I suppose you have--one can always be made up at any chemist's anywhere."

The girl could scarcely have been surprised that the reply did not satisfy her visitors.

"Don't play it too much on us, Miss Fraser. Do you mean to say you didn't look at those pills?"

"I did not."

"Sure? Not once on the road over?"

"Not once." There was a finality in the way she said it.

"Then you must be a remarkable example of your sex! I was to pay you a large sum to carry the mysterious something six thousand miles across the sea, and do you mean to tell me that curiosity never urged you to find out what the something might be?"

"I preferred not to know. I did find out something on the way over, and that knowledge I would rather have avoided."

"What did you find out?"

"I was told that you were a thief; that what you had entrusted to me was stolen property. I was accused of being your accomplice and a receiver of stolen goods. I did not like it."

Mr. Stewart seemed to be a little nonplussed by the lady's candour.

"Who told you that?"

"A man who called himself Yashvin and a woman who called herself Oudinoff. They both claimed to know you."

"Did they, the darlings! Did they claim the 'stolen property' as theirs?"

"They said that they were part owners that you had swindled them out of it."

"Did they tell you what it was?"

"They did supposing that I knew already; which I didn't. They said it was pearls."

"Now we're coming to the point. Did they say anything about the history of those pearls?"

"They didn't. They only kept on saying that you were a thief."

"That's false--they're liars."

"I was quite sure of that anyhow. I was conscious that I'd got among a gang of liars."

"Now come, Miss Fraser, don't you carry your innocence too far. When first I saw you in your house off the Fulham Palace Road, I only had to look at you for five seconds to know that you were shrewd."

"Don't you try to butter me up. You'll waste your time."

"I'm not going to try to butter you up. I only want you to be as frank with me as I am going to be with you. Didn't you know perfectly well when I offered you that commission that there was something funny about the whole thing?"

"I admit that I did. I felt that you were one of those plausible men with whom no honest person ought to have anything to do."

"That's not fair, it really isn't. You're not behaving with the fairness I have a right to expect from you. I thought you were made of better stuff than that. You knew perfectly well that what I was asking you to take to New York were not pills, that that word was only used as a cover, and that I was only offering you the large sum I did--you and Mr. Beckwith--because there was something very funny about the whole transaction. Now, frankly, isn't that the case?"

"I have already said I admit it; it is."

"That's better. Now you're getting to the point. You trusted me and I trusted you; although I'd never seen you in my life before I had implicit faith in your word. So much did you impress me that I should have been willing to stake a very large sum and in fact did stake a very large sum on my belief that in every respect you would be as good as your word and would not play me false. And in spite of those beauties and the lies they told I still do not believe that you propose to play me false. I am beginning dimly to understand that there's something behind the attitude which you seem to be taking up. Now what is it? Let's have it out. I'm sure it's nothing you need to be ashamed of, and we shall know where we are."

There Was a considerable interval before the girl replied. She sat propped up by pillows, her hands, whiter perhaps than they were wont to be, crossed on the coverlet, her eyes looking steadily in front of her, on her face a wistful something which a keen sympathetic observer might have found pathetic. In her plain words, when they came, there was a curious sincerity.

"I will try to make you understand. I did know from the beginning that there was a mysterious something about the whole business into which I had better not inquire. That was one reason why I did not look at what you called those 'pills.' I didn't want to discover what they were; I just wanted to take them for you to America. Hugh told me how you became possessed of them, they having been hidden in the pony-skin coat which they made him wear. I knew you would not be willing to pay the large sum you offered me, and Hugh, and go out of your way to take such elaborate precautions, if about the whole business there was not something which was not all that it might be. Though I knew all this and own that you warned me against the risk I was running I should have had nothing to do with the business if it had not been for Hugh."

She paused; they watched her. She again went on. There could be no doubt that she was trying her best to speak the truth.

"I don't quite know how to say it. It's rather difficult." She paused again. "I did want to see the world, and you offered me a chance I might never have again I own it. But I wanted first of all to make money for Hugh, and you offered five hundred pounds; that's a sum of which we have always dreamed it's an immense sum to us. Hugh and I have been engaged nearly four years. We had hoped to marry before this, but have never dared. I had just heard that he had lost his situation with Hunter & Barnett. Then your offer came along. If we could get five hundred pounds we might marry at once; we should be rich."

She stopped, as if to give careful consideration to what she had to say; clasping and unclasping her hands as if labouring under a nervous strain.

"I did have some idea what was the sort of thing you wanted, and of the risk I should have to run. I own it. I thought I should have a better chance of succeeding than Hugh would have; somehow he doesn't seem to be made for that sort of thing. Really I was sorry, though I did not like to say so, when you gave him the chance of going also. I was afraid that something would happen to him; and it did; then I was done for."

"How do you mean you were done for?"

For the first time she turned and looked at Mr. Stewart an expression on her face which transfigured her.

"Isn't it plain? If anything happened to Hugh what was I to gain? I wanted to be married to Hugh that was the only thing I cared for. The prospect was the only reason which had induced me to accept your offer marriage with Hugh."

She lifted her hand with a little grotesque gesture which almost suggested that all hope was lost.

"Well, I won't go on you wouldn't understand; you'd probably think I was silly a romantic fool half off her head. But I tell you this, Mr. Stewart. You say that what you told me were pills were really pearls. I dare say they were worth a great deal of money."

"They are so much that they are priceless. You see I am frank."

"Then I'll be frank with you--you'll never get your priceless pearls until I've seen Hugh and know he's well again."

The man and the woman eyed each other as if, though startled, they were reassured.

"You do know where they are?"

"It's no use your asking me questions, because I won't answer them. I won't talk to you on the subject till I've seen Hugh and know he's well. I suspect you both; I believe you're keeping something from me. Where is Hugh? Why can't I go and see him? What is there wrong with him? You won't see your pearls again until I'm satisfied about Hugh."

"And then?"

"I tell you I won't talk about them you satisfy me about Hugh."

Mr. Stewart addressed Miss Galstin.

"This is a very obstinate young woman. Is there any reason why she should not see Mr. Beckwith?"

"None whatever that I'm aware of, if the doctor will let her."

"My doctor will let me, I promise you that. You tell me where Hugh Beckwith is to be found and I'll see him just as soon as I can get to him, so the quicker you tell me the better perhaps it will be for you."

"You will tell us where those pearls are as soon as you learn for yourself that Mr. Hugh Beckwith is getting on as well as can be expected?"

"I promise nothing. Let me see Hugh Beckwith."

Mr. Stewart, who had been sitting on the edge of the bed, stood up and sighed.

"For the Lord's sake let her see him. It beats me what some women can see in a man but it's her funeral, not mine."

"There's nothing in this world a woman wants to see except her man. You may laugh, but that's so. With Hugh the world's all right; without him it's less than nothing. I perhaps wouldn't say it to him if we were face to face--it isn't good for a man to be too puffed up--but I say it to you, and don't you forget it!"

"I'm not likely to, Miss Fraser. I never heard a more remarkable sentiment in my life. However, let's quit talking. When is the earliest possible moment at which this young woman can see her young man? Hullo, here's Rasselton, let's ask him."

At that moment the doctor entered the room followed by the nurse.

"So you two are here," was his greeting. "What do you think of the patient? Isn't she getting on just fine? She'll soon be better than ever she was."

"Rasselton, when did you last see Mr. Beckwith?"

"I saw him this morning."

"Miss Fraser wants to see him."

"Does she? Well, she can if she has a little patience."

"She doesn't want to have any patience." He stopped the doctor just as he was opening his lips. "All right, Rasselton, I know the usual medical formula. Come outside for a moment, I want to speak to you."

As the two men were leaving the room the girl in the bed asked the girl on the chair:

"What are they going outside for? I want to hear what they say."

Miss Galstin smiled.

"My dear, you'll hear soon enough. I don't suppose they're talking secrets. I expect Mr. Stewart wants to induce the doctor to let you have your own way, and he thinks that the shortest way of doing that is to talk to him in private."

In the little anteroom without Mr. Stewart said to the doctor:

"Rasselton, how is this fellow Beckwith?"

"He's pretty bad."

"How bad? See here, I'm in a hole. That young woman, I am persuaded, has information in her possession which it is very essential that I should have at once, and which she won't pass on to me until she's what she calls 'satisfied' about Hugh Beckwith. So she's got to be satisfied quick I and don't you make any mistake about it."

"What does she call satisfied?"

"For one thing she wants to be sure that he's alive; she's got an idea into her head that he isn't. She wants the ocular proof, that's what she wants. And if you can use any particular art with which you are acquainted to what you may call 'ready' the young man so as to make him seem tolerably fit, all the better for me and, in the long run, also for you. When can she go and see him?"

"She may go and see him to-morrow, if there's all that hurry."

"There is, and more you bet!"

"He's not getting on so well as she is; he's not yet out of the wood they made an awful mess of him! But he is getting on, and I dare say by tomorrow he can be made presentable enough to pass muster with her." NEW PAGE

CHAPTER XXVIII
NURSE ADA

The room was not well lighted; the day was dull, there was only one window, and the blind was drawn. Catherine had come up on the elevator. The prospect of seeing Hugh and at least satisfying certain doubts had acted on her as a tonic; her health seemed to have given a great stride forward even since yesterday. It was a nursing home to which she had come. The door was opened apparently by a member of the staff, who stared at the sight of her, and even more at the sound. The visitor held herself very straight, and spoke in a clear, resonant voice which was not in the least like that of an invalid.

"I am Catherine Fraser, and I have come to see Hugh Beckwith."

"Come in, Miss Fraser; Mr. Beckwith is expecting you. But I gathered from Dr. Rasselton that you were rising from a sick bed to come here. You must allow me to say that you don't look it."

"I dare say; I don't feel it. I stopped in bed as long as I did just because there was nothing to get up for. Directly there was I got up, feeling as fit as ever I did, and here I am. Who are you, and where is Hugh Beckwith?"

The person who had opened the door smiled; the visitor's manner seemed to tickle her.

"I'm Nurse Ada. I hope you are not expecting to find Mr. Beckwith as well as you seem to be, He's mending, slowly, but his is a difficult case, and recovery takes time."

"I'm expecting nothing. You take me to him."

Miss Fraser was taken. When she got into the room she was a little startled.

"How dark it is in here; how can anyone see?"

"Mr. Beck with cannot bear light."

"I can see nothing. Where is his bed? Where is he?"

"His bed is in the corner."

Miss Fraser was conducted to what, as her eyes became accustomed to the dimness, she recognised as a bed of an unusual kind.

"Hugh," she whispered. A voice came back to her.

"Catherine--is it Catherine? Thank God."

"My dear love! Wherever are you?" She turned to the attendant. "I must have more light than this--I can't see."

"He won't be able to see you in any case. There's been great trouble with his sight, but it is gradually improving."

"Do you mean that he is blind? You must pull that blind up anyhow; I'm not going to be satisfied with a light like this. I can't even see that it is Hugh."

Crossing to the window she drew up the blind for herself. It was of a dark green material whose absence made all the difference. The bed became visible. She returned to it. The bedclothes were drawn up over a figure which was outlined beneath. Only a head was above them, which was so covered with bandages of various kinds that there was very little to be seen of that. Something happened to her throat so that her breath seemed hampered. When, however, she did speak, it was quietly, cheerily, a smile on her lips if there were tears in her eyes.

"My dearest dear, how careful they seem to be of you! They've not been as careful of me; they never bothered to cover me up. Can you hear me?"

A faint voice came from the bed.

"Rather; I've been hearing you all the time."

"Sweetheart, what do you mean?"

"They thought I was dead, but I wasn't. I couldn't speak, I couldn't move, I couldn't see, I was deaf; but I could hear you. I did not know where you were, but you seemed to be speaking to me from a distance, and sometimes you kissed me."

"I'll kiss you now." Bending forward, laughing through her tears, she sought his lips. "There doesn't seem to be much of you to kiss. Did you feel that?"

"All over me. They told me you were ill. I wondered if you were dead."

"I've been wondering the same thing about you, but it seems that we are still both of us alive and kicking."

"There's not much kick about me, but I'm still alive, and, thank goodness, I can also hear and speak. And I can see--not very well, but I can; only they won't let me. They keep bandages on my eyes. Nurse Ada--is Nurse Ada there?"

"Yes, Mr. Beckwith, I'm here all right."

"She's a despot, Nurse Ada is. She and the doctor between them make me do just what they like. My sight is getting better; I've a prickly pain which they say means that it is. Soon the bandages are coming off--then I shall see you. Oh, Catherine, if you only knew how much I want to see you."

"When you do you'll be disappointed. I'm nothing to look at, that's sure. I'm just she who loves you -- that's all."

"Has anything happened to your face?" There was a new note of anxiety in the whispering voice.

It was Nurse Ada who took it upon herself to answer him.

"No, Mr. Beckwith, indeed there hasn't. Miss Fraser looks to me as if she'd never had a day's illness in her life. She's a picture, she is, a picture of health and happiness. I suppose that is because she's so happy at seeing you. And there'll be nothing the matter with your face before long. Dr. Rasselton told me only the other day that there may be a scar or two left, which will fade in time, but you'll just be as good-looking as ever you were before very long, too."

"You hear that's how she talks! Good-looking! did you ever see me when I was good-looking, Catherine?"

"I never saw you when you weren't. You've always been the best-looking man in the world to me, and though it may make you conceited I tell you so to your face."

"That's right, Miss Fraser; that's the way to talk to him. If you only knew how he's been worrying about you."

"If he only knew how I've been worrying about him."

"There you are a worrying pair, I call you! But never mind, the worrying time is past. I'm a great reader of fairy tales, I am."

"She's been reading them to me. My word, you should hear her!"

"I was reading to you only the other day about a girl who went about the world looking for a land where the sun was always shining. She found it at last, and so will you you worrying pair. You'll just walk through a little grove of trees, as the girl did in the story, and on the other side you'll find the land where the sun is always shining. You'll marry and stay there, and be happy ever after."

"There! that's how she talks. What do you think of our marrying, Catherine?"

"My dear Hugh, I seldom think of anything else I don't mind owning up. I came to America because I thought that it was a short cut to marriage. A short sea voyage, I told myself, some fresh air, a peep at the wonders of that wonderful land, a pleasant homeward trip, and almost as soon as we were back we would be married. It was in a kind of a sort of a way a case of putting the cart before the horse honeymoon first and marriage afterwards."

"So far there hasn't been much honeymoon for me."

"Or for me either but we'll make up for it. We'll be married when we do get back, and have a real proper honeymoon afterwards. You mark my words and see."

"That's a sensible way to look at it no make-believe the real thing. Then you'll be in the Land of Sunshine, and be happy ever afterwards."

This was Nurse Ada. Not long after that sapient remark Miss Fraser took her leave, being advised by the nurse that a further stay on the occasion of her first visit might be bad for the patient. So the worrying pair parted being left alone by the nurse for quite a minute to permit of their approaching as near as possible to a proper lover-like parting.

A few remarks were exchanged by the nurse and visitor as the latter was going. The visitor began; she was wiping her eyes.

"He does seem frightfully ill."

"He's been worse; as near dead as makes no difference. He's making a grand recovery."

"Grand, you call it! I wonder what you'd feel like if he belonged to you."

Nurse Ada considered a moment before she spoke.

"No man ever has belonged to me, or ever will. My work is my husband; we are joined till death us do part. But I think, if he did belong to me, and were on the road to a complete recovery complete recovery, mind! I should be grateful to God Almighty."

"Grateful!" Miss Fraser distinctly sniffed. "There's not much gratitude about me. If he were your property do you think five hundred pounds would pay you for what he's gone through, and has to go through yet?"

"Five hundred pounds? That's two thousand five hundred dollars. No, I don't think it would."

"And it won't pay me." Miss Fraser sniffed again. "I've been the most perfect gaby there ever was, but if they think I'm an utter fool they'll find themselves mistaken and that before very long."

With which cryptic utterance her head in the air Miss Fraser took her leave. When Nurse Ada got back to her patient her manner was a little curt.

"Well," he inquired, "what did you think of Catherine?"

"I think she worships the ground you stand upon, and I don't think you're worth it."

"Oh," he whispered, as if taken aback, "that's good." NEW PAGE

CHAPTER XXIX
PARKER VAN GROOT

A large apartment on the sixth floor of Paper Buildings. What purpose it was intended to serve it was not easy to decide. It might have been an office there was a large roll-top desk and other articles.of what one sees described as "office furniture," all of the most expensive and elaborate kind. It might have been a study; a bookcase ran along one side of the room, crammed with books, in bindings which suggested that they were intended rather for use than ornament. There was another smaller bookcase in one corner; there were books on tables, chairs, the floor everywhere. It might have been a reception room; there were two fine extra large Chesterfield couches, and at least a dozen easy-chairs in all sorts of coverings tapestries, chintz, even silk.

The room was very airy and light. Long windows were on one side, reaching almost from wall to wall, rising from the floor nearly to the ceiling. Pale blue curtains of some flimsy oriental silk served as decorations rather than screens.

Two of the windows were wide open; the roar of New York came continuously in. It would not have been easy even for an accustomed ear to decide what all the different noises were caused by. In some odd way, in spite of the occasional dissonant note of a hooter or a whistle, they seemed to blend into a harmonious whole.

Two persons were in the room. One, Paul R. Stewart, we already know; the other, the tenant of the apartment, Ezra George Bennington, we meet for the first time. His is a familiar type in New York; the streets are full of him. He belonged, after a fashion, to the middle path which we are told is that of safety; he was nothing in extreme; always unobtrusive; neither too young nor too old, too tall or too short, too much in the fashion or too much out of it. Somehow one felt when one met him first that one had seen his face before. The carefully brushed and parted hair, the clean-shaven, shrewd countenance, the quiet air of almost retiring self-possession, the well-made, perfectly fitting clothes attracting no attention; in externals he had all the characteristics of the New Yorker who knows his world and has no desire to admit it.

He was speaking clearly, crisply, without effort, in low, even tones for one ear alone. The ear on this occasion belonged to Mr. Stewart, who was fidgeting from chair to chair as if his feelings would not permit of his keeping still.

"You know, Stewart, this really will not do."

"You said that before."

"I say it again. Between you you've not treated me well."

"For the life of me I can't see how you make that out. It's not my fault if things have gone wrong; I've done my level best."

"I'm afraid I differ; you've none of you done your best. Here's a man, Parker Van Groot, who is probably at this moment the richest man in the world. He has a wife it is true she is his fourth whom, we will say, he adores."

"Adores? It's not so easy to adore four women in succession unless adoration becomes a habit."

"Perhaps in Parker Van Groot's case it does. He's somewhere in the fifties, she is in the early twenties. Her birthday is coming along. Mr. Van Groot wants to do something adequately to celebrate the occasion. An idea comes to him; he will give her something a birthday present which is unique. He consults her. She, also, has an idea a modest one. 'Parker,' she says, in her simple, child-like way, 'you might give me the finest pearl necklace in the world. I think I should like it.' It seems to him an inspiration. He remarks, 'You shall have it.' She is anxious not to be misunderstood. 'I do not want,' she says, in an explanatory way, 'a hundred thousand dollar affair, or any rubbish of that kind; I want the finest pearl necklace in the world. That will cost money.' 'You bet!' he observes, 'the one I shall give you will cost money.' Then he came to me."

"You mean he came to us."

123

"If you prefer it; though I would remind you that in the first instance he came to me. He explained what he wanted. 'Bennington,' he observed, 'I'm prepared to spend five million dollars on that necklace.'"

"You ought to get some pearls for that."

"He meant to. All the really great pearls on the market are known. I drew up a list. I consulted Rothenstein, I consulted you, I consulted others. The list was amended. It was admitted that if we procured all the pearls which were on it we should have the foundation of a really fine necklace. But at the same time it was felt and I think rightly felt that there was nothing, we will say sufficiently distinctive about it which would entitle Parker Van Groot to wave his wife's necklace in the face of American society, and of the society of the continental capitals, exclaiming l What do you think of that? Did you ever see anything like it?'"

"I rather think if he had done, a good many of the people in whose faces he waved it would have had to admit that they hadn't. It would have been some necklace even as it was originally planned."

"Granted; but it was not some necklace which Mr. Van Groot wanted he wanted one which would be hailed on all sides as unique, the finest in the world. Besides, all the pearls upon our list at anything like a fair price would not have cost five million dollars. . . . And Van Groot is not a man to over-pay; he knows there are a hundred cents in a dollar. At that point you came in."

"I wish I hadn't."

"You and your friends."

"Confound my friends!"

"The first suggestion came from you. You mentioned what I knew already that there were certain pearls in Russia which were admittedly the finest in the world. They were the property of the royal family. They were known as the Romanoff pearls, and they numbered twenty-two. 'What,' I inquired, 'is the use of talking? They're not on the market.' Then you began to talk business. 'If they were on the market,' you said, 'would you or would Van Groot, acting on your advice, be prepared to pay a million dollars for them?' You put it into English currency and said two hundred thousand pounds."

Mr. Bennington leaned back in his armchair, pressed the tips of his fingers together, smiling as if he were attracted by the humorous side of an abstract proposition.

"A million dollars--or two hundred thousand pounds call it which you will--is a considerable sum. Some men who have that amount of money consider themselves rich."

"Let them. They don't own the Romanoff pearls."

"That's a fact--that's what I felt. For the unique one has to pay."

"Through the nose. I've had to. We've all had to."

"You all seem to have been paying for nothing. Where are the Romanoff pearls?"

"Blamed if I know! There's a young woman who does know, but the problem which has given me sleepless nights and restless days is who's going to make her talk. Some feminine pets you can't stop talking; you can't start her. Hullo, here's someone who may give us some sort of a pointer as to the direction in which the cat is likely to jump, and when."

Miss Galstin came into the room just then the allusion was to her. Mr. Bennington, rising, greeted her with unobtrusive courtesy.

"How's Hugh?" asked Mr. Stewart.

The lady drew off her long white gloves as she replied:

"Improving--always improving. Not quite presentable yet: but give him time and Dr. Rasselton says that he'll be as beautiful as of yore."

"How much time? We've got to deliver those pearls in ten days. Hanging about entails a risk of which when I'm alone I don't care to think besides the doubt that all the while that girl may be playing the fool with us. I pointed out to her only this morning that the man was getting on like a house on fire, and there really was no reason, even from her own point of view, why she shouldn't open her mouth, and all she did was to smile as if she thought that I'd said something funny. Hang Hugh l"

"And so say all of us." This was Miss Galstin.

"And who is this Hugh in whom you seem to take so great an interest?"

The inquiry came from Mr. Bennington.

"He's a young ass with whom the young woman of whom I told you thinks herself in love. He's got himself into serious trouble, and she declares she won't drop so much as a hint as to the whereabouts of the pearls, which I--I, fool that I was!--entrusted to her keeping until her young sprig of a jackass is restored to perfect health. That mayn't be for some weeks, and we have to deliver the pearls in ten days."

"That's a fact that's what I wished to point out to you. Mr. Van Groot is getting restless. You're behind your contract as it is."

"Through no fault of mine." This was Mr. Stewart. Miss Galstin corroborated. She was smoothing out the gloves which she had taken off.

"I can bear testimony to that. We're the victims of misfortune, Mr. Bennington. The luck has been against us."

"I don't wish to appear unsympathetic, but whose the fault is, is not the point. As I remarked, Mr. Van Groot is getting fidgety. He wants the matter put in hand. He wants to decrease the time rather than extend it."

"Good gracious, Bennington, you mustn't let him do that!"

Before Mr. Bennington could answer Mr. Rothenstein came into the room, as usual all top-hat, hair, and frock-coat.

"So here you are, the three of you, always doing things behind my back. Good day to you, Mr. Bennington. Has Stewart given you any pearls?"

"He has not. I have asked you people here because Mr. Van Groot wishes me to inform you that if they are not delivered within seven days he will be inclined to call the bargain off. He's only paying a fancy price for them--"

"A million dollars is not a fancy price for the Romanoff pearls!"

"If that is so, Mr. Rothenstein, then you'll not suffer if Mr. Van Groot gives you an opportunity of disposing of them in the open market which he assuredly will do if they're not to hand in seven days."

"You hear what he says, Stewart? He talks of disposing of the Romanoff pearls in the open market! He might as well tell us to cut our own throats. So soon as it was known that we had put them on the market our lives would not be worth an hour's purchase that he knows."

Mr. Bennington's suavity was as marked as the old man's violence.

"Come, Mr. Rothenstein please. If you and Mr. Stewart share any secrets I must ask you not to discuss them in my presence. You say that the sum which Mr. Van Groot is willing, under certain circumstances, to pay for these jewels is not a fancy price I say it is. Presently you may be able to prove which of us is right and which of us is wrong. I thought you were all here. Who is it now? Come in!" There had been a knock at the door. A nondescript individual, who might have been a clerk, a servant, anything, entered. He handed Mr. Bennington a sheet of paper; that gentleman proceeded to read aloud what was on it. "'Princess Kitty Vronsky Konstantin Ivanovitch.' Who are these persons?" The question was addressed to Mr. Stewart. "What do they want?"

"They're friends of Rothenstein's you'd better ask him what they want. It is they who have messed things up."

Mr. Rothenstein began to indulge in his characteristic step dance.

"It is not true! They were also his friends once, but when he played us false, and robbed us, then they were his friends no longer. It is not they who have messed things up it is he!"

He might have been a hobgoblin pointing an accusing finger at Mr. Stewart. Mr. Bennington never seemed to lose his suavity.

"Gently, gentlemen please. You must not force your private differences on me." Then to the man, who was still waiting, "Show these people in."

There entered a beautiful lady, charmingly dressed, and a gentleman who might have stepped straight out of a melodrama; he seemed to have been endowed by nature with the traditional scowl which the actor sometimes wears only with a considerable effort. We have met them before as Cara Oudinoff and Mr. Yashvin. Mr. Bennington bowed to them and they did the same to him; but no notice was taken of their presence by the three other people in the room, and not a word was spoken. The lady looked sweetly at Mr. Rothenstein.

"Will you not introduce us to this gentleman?"

His manner was not sweet in return.

"What do you want here?" he asked. "Did I not tell you not to come!"

The melodramatic gentleman snarled at the speaker like some ill-tempered cat. Possibly his appearance belied him, but he looked as if he were incapable of anything more genial than a snarl.

"You tell us not to come? You'd tell us anything you! Do you conspire against us then? You would rob the teeth out of our heads!" He turned to the proprietor of the room. "You, sir, I think, are Mr. Bennington. Have they given you the Romanoff pearls?"

"May I inquire, with all possible courtesy, what business it is of yours what they have done?"

"It is I who got the pearls I and her, between us. I send them to him, as was agreed. He, the fool! lets them slip through his fingers. Stewart gets them. We did all the work, we ran all the risk, now they want to cheat us of our share."

Mr. Bennington was studying the sheet of paper which had been given him by his servant,

"You, sir, I presume are Mr. Ivanovitch. I must say to you what I said to the other gentlemen I must request you not to discuss your differences in my presence. With regard to the pearls of which you speak I know nothing and wish to know nothing; be so good, all of you, as distinctly to understand that I wish to know nothing beyond the fact that a contract was made to deliver them by a certain date which contract has been broken. But here is Mr. Van Groot, who will be able to give you his views on the subject himself."

There entered possibly the most famous man in the world.

Everybody knows Parker Van Groot, by name and reputation. Everyone knows him also by sight. There is probably not a journal in the world which has not presented his portrait for the admiration of its readers. There are a very large number of publications to which his portrait seems to be a sort of standing dish; when there is a lack of matter out comes the portrait of Parker Van Groot. "Parker Van Groot in Wall Street," "Parker Van Groot driving his new 50 h.p. automobile," "Parker Van Groot in command of his 10,000 ton yacht," "Parker Van Groot taking up a collection in All Souls' Church;" he can scarcely have breathed during several years without the fact being portrayed for universal admiration. He is, report says, the richest man who ever lived that fact constitutes his claim to continuous universal attention.

We all know what he looked like as he came into the room. A big man, bow windowed, with rolling gait, almost suggesting that at some period of his life he was a seaman; a large bald head; a huge nose, with a sort of blob at the end; pimples; a loose-lipped mouth; a double chin; a short, thick neck. The description does not sound inviting, yet there is about the man an air of strength, mental and physical, particularly mental, of genial good humour, of careless satisfaction with the world and all who are in it, which everyone with whom he has come in contact has found irresistible and that long before he was the great Parker Van Groot.

It would perhaps be scarcely correct to say that on that occasion he was a trifle overdressed, because one hardly knows how such a man ought to be dressed; but his attire certainly was on the florid side. He wore grey suede gloves, carried in one hand a silk hat very much turned up at the brim, and in the other a substantial gold-headed ebony cane on which he leaned as he walked. Distributing, as it were, a general nod as he moved across the room, he placed himself in a big armchair and plunged at once into the heart of the subject on which he had come.

"Well, Bennington, who are all these good people? Got those wonderful pearls?"

"No, Mr. Van Groot, I have not. It seems to be unlikely that we ever shall get them."

Mr. Stewart came a little forward.

"If you will allow me, Mr. Van Groot, to explain--"

Mr. Van Groot, twisting his cane round and round, like a huge nail in a socket, cut Mr. Stewart affably short while he looked at the Princess Kitty Vronsky; and, it may be added, she looked at him.

"Quite right, sir, perfectly right. I was promised certain pearls on a certain date for which I was to pay a fortune; the money was there but they weren't; if they're not there darned quick they needn't come at all. There may be ten thousand good reasons why they're not there, but I don't want to hear one of them. You've got my sympathy, but you won't get my dollars. That's all I want to say. Bennington thought I'd better come and say it myself, so I have." He addressed the Princess Kitty. "I have seen you before." She did not seem eager to claim the honour of having also seen him. "I don't remember where it was I've a bad memory for that kind of thing but what a small world it is. Bennington, Mrs. Van Groot would like to see you to-night."

He rose, as if the interview were ended. The quintette showed signs of disturbance. Rothenstein opened and shut his mouth, but nothing came out of it. Mr. Stewart spoke.

"How long can you give us, Mr. Van Groot?"

"Give those pearls to Bennington inside seven days ad it will be a million dollars in somebody's pocket. Not wanted and will not be accepted after that. Come with me to the door, Bennington; got two words I want to say to you."

Mr. Bennington crossed and held the door wide open; Mr. Van Groot waddled through it. Mr. Bennington followed. The moment the door was closed the five persons left behind metaphorically flew at each other and not so very metaphorically either! When Mr. Bennington returned there was something in the atmosphere which suggested that certain members of the party had been very near to blows.

"I'm sorry," he remarked, "if I seem abrupt, but I have certain engagements which I must keep, and I must therefore ask you to be so good as to leave me." He spoke to the nondescript person who was standing in the open doorway. "Derwentwater, show these ladies and gentlemen out."

Derwentwater showed them out. There was something which was scarcely dignified in their bearing as they went. Nor, so far as they were concerned, were matters improved by the parting remark which Mr. Bennington courteously addressed to them as they went straggling through the door.

"May I ask you, as a favour, not to continue your discussion in the elevator as you go down? Wait till you are in the street." NEW PAGE

CHAPTER XXX
AN UNEXPECTED VISITOR

Hugh Beckwith was sitting up in bed. He was not yet a desirable object for contemplation, but most of the bandages were removed from his head and face; the chief medical protection which remained being a deep green shade which ran across his eyes. He had raised this slightly to permit of his looking at Catherine, who was seated at his bedside. His voice was stronger than before, but there was still something the matter with his utterance.

"He was in the deuce of a stew," he said.

"Let Mr. Stewart be in the deuce of a stew!" the lady rejoined. Mr. Beckwith's right hand was lying outside the coverlet; she was holding it in both of hers.

"I never saw a man in such a state of mind."

The lady was unsympathetic although she stroked the hand she was holding very tenderly. "Serve him right!"

"But, Catherine," the patient persisted, "are you quite sure you're acting reasonably?"

"No, I'm not; no one ever can be quite sure about a thing like that. I've resolved on a certain course of action, and I'm going to stick to my resolution, that's all."

"Is it worth it?"

"Is what worth it?"

"We shall lose every penny if you don't look out. Stewart says that he'll be ruined if he can't deliver by a certain date; it isn't likely that he'll have anything left for us. Then where shall we be?"

"On velvet, my dear Hugh, that's where we shall be."

"I don't see how you make that out." Mr. Beckwith's tone was querulous; it suggested a grievance. The girl continued to stroke his hand very softly, as if she were seeking to soothe his injured feelings.

"I dare say you don't; I do. My dear Hugh, those twenty-two pills, which turn out to be pearls, are worth a hundred thousand pounds to Mr. Stewart. He told me so himself."

"Do you believe him? It's an incredible sum. Think how they have been practically thrown about as if they were nothing."

"There's an explanation of that; I think personally I'd rather not know it; but there is. I more than believe Mr. Stewart; I believe he understates the sum they are worth to him."

"Catherine! Gently does it! Worth more than a hundred thousand pounds! I say!"

"Our ideas of money are limited. We've never had any, we've never even seen any. I've a feeling that here in America a hundred thousand pounds doesn't seem as much as it does with us; but, anyhow, don't you think that we shall get five hundred or even a thousand pounds from someone for what Stewart admits are worth a hundred thousand to him?"

With his left hand Mr. Beckwith raised the green shade a little higher, as if to enable him to see her more plainly. He seemed startled.

"Catherine! You wouldn't sell what he entrusted to you to someone else?"

"Wouldn't I? You wait! They used me pretty badly; for that I've almost forgiven them; but I'm going to make them pay for what they did to you; pay in more ways than one. When Mr. Stewart informed me that he had not slept since he had set foot in New York I found the thought of the unpleasant nights he must have spent very comforting."

"Catherine, what have you got in that head of yours? I suppose you do know where those pearls really are?"

"My darling Hugh, you're not nearly cured even yet. I am. Worry will do you harm; it will do me good especially worry of this particular kind. I've got to be even somehow with certain persons, and I've got to come out on top. I've got to get something out of this trip across the Atlantic, and I'm going to get it. All you have to do is to lie still and keep on getting better, and wait and see. I'll do the rest; and I'll love to do it, Hugh dear, if you don't mind."

128

There was an interval of silence. The patient was eyeing her as if he thought she was something remarkable. Presently his words showed that he did. He spoke with something very like solemnity.

"Catherine, I won't say to you, 'Do be careful,' but I've always found that when you seem to care least what you say or do you've always had your head screwed on right. It's a very great thing in a woman."

What precisely the speaker meant was not quite clear; Miss Fraser smoothed his poor thin hand, and smiled, and looked at him with love in her eyes, as if she understood him perfectly well. Rather more than an hour afterwards she was back in her apartment in Raymond's Hotel. It was not a stately apartment, but it was a fair size, comfortably furnished, and seemed on the whole to serve her purpose tolerably well. There was a pile of sewing on a table. She was one of those young women, a little out of fashion nowadays, who seldom seem happy without a needle in their hand. To a male mind her skill with that small implement seemed uncanny. Her belief in her own powers was profound.

"It's not conceit," she had been heard to say, "but I do believe I can do almost anything with a needle I can work wonders. I've not only got the right sort of eye, I've got the right sort of head. If I had to make my own living I should turn milliner. I can make the same sort of hat which you can get in Regent Street for less than a quarter of the money they charge there I'd back myself to do it. People may laugh, but let them give me a trial they should have a five-guinea hat for twenty-five shillings. I'd cater for the lower middle class; they should have charming hats for practically nothing and I'd make a fortune."

She was engaged on an article of head-gear when the door opened and a resplendent negro announced, with the grand air of one who is conscious of the importance of what he is saying:

"Mrs. Parker Van Groot to see Miss Fraser."

There entered the most beautiful being Catherine had ever seen. She had already discovered that there were beautiful women in America, but never, she felt sure, had she seen one who could compare with her unlooked-for visitor. The way she wore her clothes! and the clothes she had to wear! and the lovely creature there was inside them! In the manner in which she moved towards her across the room Catherine saw something which she found enchanting.

"I don't know if you've heard of me, but just lately I've heard so much of you that I felt I had to come and see you so I've come. My, what a saucy little hat; are you making this? Why, I believe it would just suit me."

She had picked up the work of art on which Catherine was employed, and was twisting it round and round, eyeing it from different points of view, as some women will do when they come upon an unexpected hat.

"Do you know, Miss Fraser, men think themselves clever, but anyone can pick up dollars if they find out where they're lying. But I'm of opinion that it takes a genius to make a hat -that is a hat. Seems to me that is. I'd love you to make me a dozen."

"I'd love to make them."

"Would you, honest? Then you shall. I'm told, Miss Fraser, that you haven't been very well."

"I've been nearly murdered which is perhaps the reason."

"Murdered? No? I never heard that. You poor child. You know who I am?"

"I heard the waiter say that you were Mrs. Parker Van Groot."

"And Mrs. Parker Van Groot means nothing to you? Now that's odd. It's a change to meet someone to whom it doesn't a treat! Now I'll tell you Mrs. Parker Van Groot is she's a person who is going to have a birthday."

The girl smiled; it was a peculiarity of Catherine's that directly she smiled you thought how extraordinarily pleasant she was to look at.

"You're not the only person in the world who's going to have a birthday."

"That so? Excuse me, but would you mind smiling again."

Catherine did, on the spot, perhaps unintentionally.

"What ever for?" she asked.

"Because that smile of yours is like a lamp which lights the soul so that you can see right into it. Sounds funny, doesn't it? but it's true. Do you know this birthday of mine was going to be something rather special, but you're making it commonplace. I ought to hate you, but I don't, although you do look like spoiling my birthday."

"How am I going to do that? Since I don't know who you are and have never seen you before."

"It's this way." Mrs. Van Groot, seating herself on a chair beside the table, began to play tricks with the hat which was in course of manufacture. "I was going to have a birthday present. I've no use for birthday presents as a rule, because you never know what you want."

"Don't you? I do, or I should if I had a chance. I don't know if you are lucky or unlucky. It must be rather horrid to have everything you want. You see, I've nothing."

"You have your genius for hats, and you've your smile. But this birthday present was to be rather special the finest pearl necklace in the world!"

Catherine opened her eyes. "Isn't that rather a tall order?"

"Parker that's my husband likes superlatives; the largest or the best of everything always appeals to him. He said that that was rather a good idea of mine, and wondered if it could be managed. So he went to a man who sometimes acts for him in delicate matters and asked if the thing could be done. The man said, 'If you're prepared to spend five million dollars.'"

"What!" Catherine's eyes opened still wider. Her wonder as to who this beautiful person could be was growing.

"Parker told him that he didn't mind spending that much."

"But five million dollars; isn't that a million pounds?"

"A million pounds more or less is nothing to Parker; he made that much in one deal last year, and more."

Catherine, drawing herself up, observed the visitor with a suspicious eye. Her manner became a little frigid.

"I don't know why you're making fun of me. May I ask what you've come for?"

"I'm getting to it if you'll give me time. I know that education in England isn't worth much, that they only teach people to be ladies and gentlemen; but I didn't know there was anyone even there who was ignorant enough not to know that Parker Van Groot is the richest man in the world."

"I've always understood that Rothschild was the richest man in the world."

"He's not in it with Parker; Parker could buy him up with his loose change. Europe isn't in it where dollars are concerned. You'll be taught a thing or two if you're in America long. Anyhow, Parker said that he was willing to go to five million dollars for a pearl necklace for me. When he told me I was interested."

"I should think you were!"

"My dear, I find it difficult to be really interested in anything. It's so tiresome, by merely touching a button, to be able to get every material thing you can think of. I mentioned to Parker only the other day that I'd like to have the smallest griffon that could be got. He cabled to wherever griffons come from, and ten turned up the other morning, such wee, wee mites, with black faces and no noses. It's impossible for anyone to say which of them is the smallest, so I've had to keep the lot. It's too absurd! But about my birthday present; if you will keep interrupting me I shall never get on. All the finest pearls in the world were got together, but the feature of the whole thing was to be twenty-two pearls, which were to come from I'm not supposed to know from where, but I do know that they were to come from Russia." The listener pricked up her ears at this. "They were to be something altogether out of the common, gems in every sense of the word. I don't know how they were to be got, and I've been told not to inquire; but they were to be got, and they would make my birthday present beyond the slightest shadow of a shade of a doubt the finest pearl necklace in the world. Everyone would ask me everywhere just for the sake of having a peep at it. I dreamed of those twenty-two pearls. They must be something remarkable, because Parker was to pay a million dollars for them."

"A million dollars? That's two hundred thousand pounds. I thought--"

Yes you thought what?"

The girl stopped and showed no marked inclination to continue.

"Oh, nothing I just thought."

"Now you understand what I have come about. I'm told you have those twenty-two pearls."

"Mrs. Van Groot, who sent you here?"

"No one; I came on my own. And, between ourselves, if Parker knew I had come he might be rude. But when he calmly told me that I should have to go without those twenty-two pearls, and have my necklace spoilt, made commonplace, ruined, because you refused to hand them over, could I keep from making a personal appeal to you?"

"Mrs. Van Groot, do you know anything about the history of those twenty-two pearls?"

"No, I don't, and I don't want to know. I'm told that I ought not to know. But I daresay they are smeared with blood and reek of crime."

"I believe you'd be quite correct if you said they were."

"All famous jewels I'm given to understand are. Mrs. Milliard she is the wife of John P. Milliard, the packer told me that that famous ruby of hers had been the cause of dozens of people being murdered; she hardly likes to wear it lest she should see their ghosts. It lends it such an atmosphere of romance. Now, Miss Fraser, you can't want to spoil my birthday present. You don't look like that sort of person at all. Won't you let me have those pearls?"

"I didn't know they were your pearls."

"Strictly speaking, at present they're not; they will be when Parker has paid for them and the money's ready."

"You say that Mr. Van Groot is to pay two hundred thousand pounds for them? That is rather funny."

"It's not at all funny it's tragic pathetic. Why won't you give them up? I understand they're not your pearls."

"They're not. As you said just now, whose they are you'd better not inquire."

"I don't mean to. All I want is the pearls."

"Mrs. Van Groot, I'm what you call a pauper. My mother lets lodgings in a little house off the Fulham Palace Road in London. I'm engaged to our lodger--"

"How nice; this sounds like the beginning of a romance."

"He's himself a poor man, and has lately lost his situation. Someone offered him five hundred pounds to bring those pearls to New York. I thought he would run a great risk in doing so, and I offered to take them myself, feeling that we should be surer of that five hundred pounds if I did."

"You appear to be a remarkable person, Miss Fraser."

"I didn't know they were pearls; I was told they were twenty-two pills."

"That the Romanoff pearls were pills!"

"My offer was accepted. Hugh that's our lodger was to travel first class, and I second, on the same steamer. I was to have the pills, or, as they appear to be, pearls. We were each to receive five hundred pounds on their being safely delivered in New York. A thousand pounds was a magnificent sum for us. Hugh might never have another chance of getting hold of that amount of capital. On the passage over Hugh was almost worse than murdered; he was treated with incredible cruelty. Someone thought he had the pills or pearls and, like you, wanted them. I also was nearly murdered. I have recovered, but only the other day Hugh was still at death's door, and frightfully disfigured. I told them they might whistle for their pearls until Hugh was entirely recovered and so they can."

"What a romantic story! Fancy that sort of thing happening to-day! But isn't this gentleman on the road to a perfect recovery? I was told he was. And let me tell you something, Miss Fraser. Someone is going to make a big deal over those pearls. If I were you I would ask more than five thousand dollars to hand them over."

"I'm going to. I was offered twenty-five thousand dollars to betray my trust; I shall want that amount for having kept it."

"Twenty-five thousand dollars is nothing, especially after what you've gone through."

131

"It is something to me and to Hugh; if we get it we will be richer than we ever expected to be in all our lives."

"How delightful to be able to rejoice in such a prospect as that. I'm not certain I shouldn't like to be poorer; it would be a change. Parker is always talking about the millions he has made. When I told him the other day that I should sometimes like to hear about the millions he'd lost, he stared as if he thought there must be something the matter with my brain. Now, my dear Miss Fraser, entirely between ourselves, won't you tell me where those pearls are only me? Who is this at the door? just as we were getting to the most interesting part of our conversation." NEW PAGE

CHAPTER XXXI
EXERCISING PRESSURE

MR. Parker Van Groot came rolling into the room, his wide-brimmed silk hat on the side of his head, in his right hand the gold-headed ebony walking-stick, without a portrait of which a caricature of the great financier would be scarcely recognisable. Behind him Mr. Ezra Bennington, very dapper, very neutral tinted, very unobtrusive. Since no one had announced them, and they had not even condescended to tap at the door, their appearance took the ladies by surprise. Catherine, who was standing by the table, suddenly turned to stare. Mrs. Van Groot, seated, looked round with what might almost have been mistaken for an air of interest. Her pronunciation of his name suggested a note of exclamation. She let Catherine's work of art pass from her tiny hands on to the table.

"Parker! Whatever do you mean by coming here? I thought you were doing some horrid thing at the office."

Mr. Van Groot removed his beautiful silk hat as he addressed his companion.

"Bennington, Mrs. Parker Van Groot! She told me she was going shopping. Is this a store?"

"It is; and I've as good as bought in it ten new hats from the very latest word in milliners. Are you here to buy new hats?"

"No, Isobel; I am here on the same errand as you are. I've come to make inquiries about the Romanoff pearls."

"I don't think, Parker, that you're entitled to take it for granted that I have."

"Perhaps not; but the fact remains. Have you got them?"

"Parker, you may find it as easy to make millions as to shell peas, but you'll never make a diplomatist. What a pointed way of asking a delicate question! Miss Fraser, I must apologise for Mr. Van Groot."

"Miss Fraser if, young lady, that is your name where are the Romanoff pearls? If it's a question of price name it. When you deal with thieves you expect to be robbed."

"Parker, what a terrible what a tactless thing to say! In an ethical and potential sense every woman who wants to sell you a hat is out for plunder. What do you think the public think of you? I heard someone say only the other day that Parker Van Groot was the biggest thief in America."

"So I am. A man who wants another man's money is a thief. I want everyone's money; I get some of it. Isobel, don't chip in when the talk's about business. Well, Miss Fraser, what's your price for the Romanoff pearls?"

"Parker, Miss Fraser and I have arranged the question of terms. Her ideas on the subject are on a most modest scale. She will be willing to accept fifty thousand dollars."

Miss Fraser regarded the lady with not unjustifiable amazement.

"Fifty thousand dollars! that's ten thousand pounds. I told you--"

Mrs. Van Groot cut her short, her pretty cheeks dimpled by the sweetest little smile.

"Am I not correct, Miss Fraser, in saying that you would accept fifty thousand dollars?"

"I should be perfectly willing to accept fifty thousand dollars--"

"Isn't that what I told Mr. Van Groot?"

"But I couldn't give you the pearls."

"Couldn't give me the pearls!"

Mrs. Van Groot's large blue eyes seemed to open a wee bit wider. Her husband commented on Catherine's remark.

"You mean, Miss Fraser, that you'd like fifty thousand dollars for nothing? There are a good many about like you."

"I mean," explained Catherine, "that the pearls were placed in my charge by Mr. Stewart, and I can only hand them over to him. I've told Mr. Stewart, and he quite knows, that before I consider the question of handing them over, even to him, Mr. Hugh Beckwith must be perfectly recovered. And he's far from being that."

"Isn't Mr. Beckwith out of bed? The mistake is yours. Nurse, wheel Mr. Beckwith into Miss Fraser's room."

While Catherine was speaking, the fact that the door on to the landing was being quietly opened went unnoticed. She possibly spoke louder than she thought, since Mr. Stewart, who opened the door, apparently heard what she said. Uninvited he entered the room, as Mr. Van Groot and Mr. Bennington had previously done. Nurse Ada wheeling a Bath chair in which, propped up by cushions, was a man with a green silk shade across his eyes, and strips of what looked like white sticking-plaster ornamenting his countenance here and there, came close at his heels, and behind her was Mr. Isaac Rothenstein, his extraordinary hat seeming, as usual, glued to his head, his superabundant wealth of hair covering him as with a thatch. At the back was Dr. Rasselton. Although he came last, when the procession was all in the room, it was he who moved to the front. He pressed his rimless glasses a little closer, and his manner was beamingly bland.

"Good day, Mrs. Van Groot and Mr. Van Groot and you, Mr. Bennington. What truly delightful weather we're having. Miss Fraser, I called to see Mr. Beckwith soon after you had left him. He told me you had been, and said how anxious he was to get up, if he could without risk. I examined him most thoroughly, and found, to my satisfaction, that he was so far convalescent that he might not only get up but, observing proper precautions against chill, and so on, might even venture in a Bath chair, escorted by Nurse Ada, to return your call. Here, as you see, he is; not yet, as he will be shortly, as well as he ever was, but prepared, I believe, to assure you that he has not suffered any sort of inconvenience from his little journey."

Long before the physician had concluded his somewhat involved sentences, Catherine, kneeling beside the Bath chair, was treating its occupant to a display of affection which suggested perfect indifference to the presence of anybody else. After a certain period she dissolved into words, uttered in a voice which was more than tremulous.

"Hugh! my darling! did you want them to bring you here?"

The gentleman's voice as he replied was not so affectionate as querulous he, possibly, was more conscious than the lady of the presence of strangers. Men, as a rule, do not care to be kissed and hugged in public, even by the dearest woman in the world.

"Of course I wanted them to bring me here. Do you suppose they would have brought me if I hadn't? Catherine, don't be silly! When Mr. Stewart told me how serious the position was about those pearls I made up my mind that I'd show you how practically perfectly recovered I am. You know, my dear girl, we don't want to be landed high and dry without a penny piece just because you will persist in thinking I'm dying, when you can see for yourself I'm not."

The lady treated his little display of pettishness with a meekness which was fine: her manner was if anything more tender than before.

"I'm very glad, darling Hugh--" He cut her ruthlessly short.

"Don't call me darling in public; I don't like it."

Still she continued to show how closely a loving woman can approach to an ideal of perfect patience.

"I'm afraid, Hugh, that you are not yet so well as you think yourself, or you would hardly speak to me like that. I won't ask what it is you wish me to say, but I should like to know what you wish me to do."

"You know, Catherine, I don't want you to think I'm a beast or anything, but Mr. Stewart has been telling me all about Mrs. Van Groot's necklace, and it does seem to me that you might as well hand them over instead of keeping them until it is too late for them to be of any use. I understand that Mrs. Van Groot wants her necklace."

"You understand quite correctly Mrs. Van Groot does. I am very glad to see you, Mr. Beckwith I suppose you are Mr. Beckwith. I am Mrs. Van Groot. I have been hearing the most romantic stories of your heroic deeds in defence of my poor pearls."

Mrs. Van Groot had gone fluttering towards the Bath chair, and was leaning over its occupant with an air of sensitive solicitude. Mr. Beckwith raised his green shade to enable him to get a better view of the most beautiful being he had ever seen in all his life.

"Are you Mrs. Parker Van Groot?" he asked, speaking with what was very much like reverence.

"I am. The pearls are for me; they are to be a birthday present from my husband. My birthday is in a very few days. I cannot tell you how disappointed and desolate I shall be if I have to go without them."

There are occasions when a man is more tenderhearted than a woman. That was one of them. Hugh Beckwith seemed moved to the very depths of his being by the thought that this radiant vision might have to go desolate. His manner was emphatic, especially considering that he was still an invalid. He almost glared at Miss Fraser.

"Catherine, you're not going to make Mrs. Parker Van Groot go without those pearls? They're to be a birthday present."

"Mrs. Van Groot has so much, Hugh, that it will not hurt her very much to have to go without for once in her life. Still, if you'd rather she did not, she shan't. Since you say you are so nearly well--"

"I am! Don't you see I am? In a few days I shall be as right as a trivet, especially if the fear of getting nothing at all after all I've gone through after all we've both of us gone through and being left penniless in New York is off my mind."

"That fear certainly shall be off your mind. I didn't know you were worrying about that. Mr. Stewart, when would you like to have your twenty-two pills?"

Mr. Stewart referred to a big gold hunter watch which he took from his waistcoat pocket.

"It is now two forty-two," he announced, "eighteen minutes and a fraction to three. I should like those pills by two forty-five or a little earlier if it can be managed."

"You can't have them by two forty-five; according to you that's in less than three minutes."

"You asked me a question, Miss Fraser, to which I replied. Which is the earliest moment at which I can have them?"

"That depends."

"On what?"

"On how soon you can give me twenty-five thousand dollars."

"Twenty-five thousand dollars!" Mr. Stewart repeated the girl's words as if surprised. "What for?"

"For placing you in possession of those twenty-two pills."

Mr. Stewart looked as if he were not quite sure that he had understood what the lady said.

"The sum agreed upon between us was five hundred pounds for you and another five hundred pounds for Mr. Beckwith besides expenses, which have not been light."

"Circumstances have changed since then."

"In what respect have they changed?"

"The sum I understood you were willing to accept was fifty thousand dollars, Miss Fraser."

The interposition came from Mrs. Van Groot. She went over and stood by Catherine, laying her gloved fingers lightly on her arm, eyeing her with something significant in her smiling glance.

The girl observed, glancing back at her, "It was you who said fifty thousand dollars."

"You told me that you were willing to accept it." Still standing by Catherine's side she looked at Mr. Stewart. "I arrange--" she put an accent on the personal pronoun "--that Miss Fraser should receive fifty thousand dollars which is a trifling sum. She cannot accept one cent less."

Mr. Stewart seemed nonplussed. He muttered, "This is blackmail."

"I beg your pardon? What did you say?"

Nothing could have been suaver than Mrs. Van Groot's manner or, in its way, more ominous. Mr. Stewart, big man though he was, winced.

"I beg your pardon, but I arranged with Miss Fraser--"

"Never mind what you arranged with Miss Fraser, Mr. Stewart; you may consider that arrangement at an end." Still all smiles, the lady turned to her husband. "Parker, I must manage with the pearls you have got; they will make a beautiful bracelet without the addition of any others. Miss Fraser, would you mind asking these gentlemen to leave the room; there is something which I wish to say to you in private."

Again there was significance in her glance towards the girl. As if acting on the hint received, Catherine addressed Mr. Stewart.

"Do you hear what Mrs. Van Groot says? Would you mind going?"

Mr. Stewart seemed unhappy, as if there was something which distressed him. He spoke as one who was in pain.

"But, Miss Fraser Mrs. Van Groot I hope you won't jump too hastily to conclusions. I assure you, Mrs. Van Groot, I had no intention to offend nothing could have been farther from my thoughts."

Mr. Van Groot was distinctly acid.

"Your intention is your own affair. You were offensive."

"I beg ten thousand pardons if I seemed to be."

"If you seemed to be? Sir!"

"If I was! Do I understand that the position is that Miss Fraser wants fifty thousand dollars--ten thousand pounds before she hands me back the pearls?"

"The sum mentioned was fifty thousand dollars, but it will presently be higher. The market moves quickly. In about a minute it will be a hundred thousand."

"But how can I pay such a sum out of my own pocket?" Mr. Stewart turned wildly towards Mr. Rothenstein. "You will have to pay half."

The bare suggestion moved Mr. Rothenstein to indignation.

"Pay half me? What for? Because you robbed me."

Mrs. Van Groot was frigidly scornful.

"Miss Fraser, if these persons will not go we must. We do not wish to listen to their vulgar recriminations. Come with me to my house, I will talk to you there. Parker, you understand the Romanoff pearls are off. Miss Fraser, my auto is at the door; it's a limousine, and well heated. You need not stop to put on your hat. Come just as you are."

Mr. Stewart was moved to frenzy.

"Mrs. Van Groot," he exclaimed, "I implore you to give me just one moment. Rothenstein, do you propose to pay half that ten thousand pounds or do you prefer to lose the market?"

The little man, torn by conflicting emotions, could only stammer:

"No, no, no! I will not lose the market! I would rather pay five thousand pounds although I have not so much money in the world."

Mr. Stewart turned to the girl.

"Miss Fraser, if I give you ten thousand pounds, which will include any claim which Mr. Beckwith may have, can you produce the pearls inside five minutes?"

Catherine's calmness contrasted with Mr. Stewart's agitation.

"Ten thousand pounds would certainly include Mr. Beckwith's claim and our expenses--"

"I don't think, Miss Fraser, that that should include your expenses. They should be a matter for a separate account."

This was Mrs. Van Groot. Catherine, ignoring her, went quietly on:

"And our expenses." She paused as if awaiting comment; which presently came. As she spoke Mrs. Van Groot looked the girl straight in the face, as if she telegraphed a wireless message.

"Very well, Miss Fraser, let it include your expenses if you prefer it. You are rather obstinate."

The girl went on, leaving the rebuke unnoticed:

"In any event, Mr. Stewart, I do not see how you can get the pearls inside five minutes. How long does it take to get to the General Post Office?" NEW PAGE

CHAPTER XXXII
MR. BENNINGTON'S OPINION

The eight persons stood looking at the girl as if they were not sure that they had heard aright. Mr. Stewart put their doubt into words.

"How long does it take to get where?"

"I asked you how long it takes to get from here to the General Post Office?"

"What do you want to go to the General Post Office for now?"

"I'm afraid that that's a matter on which I am unable to inform you, Mr. Stewart." Catherine's manner was distinctly snubby. "Can anyone tell me how long it takes to get from here to the General Post Office?"

"In a taxi-cab you can do it well inside five minutes if you're not hung up by the traffic."

The information came from Mr. Bennington. It was supplemented by Mrs. Van Groot.

"If you want to go to the General Post Office, Miss Fraser, let me take you in my auto. I think I can promise that you shall get there in less than five minutes though the traffic does its worst."

"Isobel, I'd just as soon that you didn't have any fuss with the police just for fun."

This was Mr. Van Groot. His wife beamed at him.

"Dear Parker! when you know how I hate a fuss."

Three of them went in Mrs. Van Groot's auto she with Catherine inside she would go, treating the more than hints which dropped from her husband as if she were hard of hearing. Mr. Stewart was on the front seat beside the driver he also would go. Mr. Rothenstein would like to have gone. He seemed to be under the impression that there was something underhand about the proceeding; as if it were the germ of a conspiracy to get the better of him somehow.

"If you get those pearls," he anxiously inquired, "how am I to know it? Suppose you say there are only nineteen or twenty, how am I to prove it? I know that in some way you will cheat me."

Mr. Stewart looked at the excited little man as if he would have liked to say a few plain words to him; apparently it was only with an effort he refrained. He turned to Mrs. Van Groot.

"Do you object to taking Mr. Rothenstein in your auto? I can squeeze him in with me beside the driver."

The lady's manner was conclusive; her words could not have been plainer. She was moving towards the door as she was speaking.

"I do object. Miss Fraser, are you ready? How long does it take you to put a hat on?"

The girl gave her a demonstration on the subject then and there. Her hat was on the table which stood against a wall, where she had left it on her return from the nursing home. It was on her head, and being secured in its place, as she followed the lady across the room. Mr. Bennington opened the door. Mrs. Van Groot glanced round at Miss Fraser.

"Now, I do call that being quick and you've got it on just right. I suppose a person who has a genius for making hats has a special gift for putting them on. Parker, I am going." Then to Catherine, "How long will it be before we are back with the pearls?"

"If it takes less than five minutes to get there we ought to get back in a quarter of an hour I hope with the pearls; but that I cannot absolutely promise."

"Why can't you?" There was a shade of anxiety in the lady's tone more than a shade on the faces of some of her listeners.

Catherine's reply was not only short and dry, it was the reverse of illuminative.

"Because I can't for reasons."

Just as the girl was going there came a voice from the Bath chair.

"I say, Catherine, supposing you do get the pearls, where are those fifty thousand dollars? Isn't it to be a cash transaction?"

"Of course it will be a cash transaction. I'm obliged to you, Hugh, for reminding me."

"Mr. Stewart, where are those fifty thousand dollars?"

The question came from Mrs. Van Groot. It seemed to take the gentleman a little aback. "The money will be forthcoming."

Mrs. Van Groot looked at Catherine.

"Forthcoming? It's a good word? Will it suit you?"

"No, it won't. I want to see the money before I leave the room."

"You hear?" This was Mrs. Van Groot to Mr. Stewart. "Miss Fraser quite properly wants to see the money before she leaves the room."

The gentleman was almost plaintive.

"Fifty thousand dollars may be a small sum to you, Mrs. Van Groot, but many of us are not so fortunate. It means a very great deal to me. I doubt if Mr. Rothenstein and I have so much money between us. Rothenstein, can you produce five thousand pounds if I produce the other five?"

Mr. Rothenstein began to lament.

"It's all the money I have in the world five thousand pounds! It is the savings of a lifetime. If I am robbed of so large a sum as that nothing will be left to me nothing at all."

Mrs. Van Groot cut him short by addressing Catherine.

"Really, Miss Fraser, I wish you would turn these people out of your room. They are so stupid! They seem to think that time is of no value. Mr. Van Groot cannot stay here for ever can you, Parker?"

"I am waiting to get off" just as soon as ever I can. When I thought of giving you a little birthday present, Isobel, I'd have found it easier to buy Niagara. What I say is let them keep their Romanoff pearls."

"That, also, Parker, is what I say; I dare say they're only silly old things anyhow. This is not my room, Mr. Stewart, and you, old gentleman" this was to Mr. Rothenstein "or I'd have had you out of it long ago. You'll be so good as to leave it now, at once; or, Mr. Bennington, will you be so good as to ring the bell and have them put out?" The autocratic lady turned to Catherine. "When they've gone you and I, and Parker, and Mr. Bennington will talk matters over between us; we'll soon square things up trust me!" She turned again to Mr. Stewart. "Are you going?"

While Mrs. Van Groot had been speaking there had been a short confab between Mr. Rothenstein and Mr. Stewart carried on in a foreign tongue. Mr. Rothenstein had dug out a pocket-book from some mysterious hiding-place in the inside of his waistcoat. Mr. Stewart, on his part, had produced another. From these pocket-books they had taken certain slips of paper with which Mr. Stewart advanced towards the table on which lay the work of art which Catherine was creating. He laid them down, counting them with deft fingers as he spoke.

"Miss Fraser, you will find here the fifty thousand dollars in return for which you are to hand over the Romanoff pearls. Will you count them, please?"

He held the bank-notes out to the lady.

"No, thank you; at least not now. I will take your word that they are correct. If I find out afterwards that they are not you will hear of it."

"To me this is a very large sum of money I believe also to you."

"To me it is a fortune." The girl's eyes were shining.

"Do you promise, if I give you this money now, that you will place me in possession of the pearls inside a quarter of an hour?"

"I cannot promise. I may never be able to place you in possession of them at all; I hope I shall, but beyond that I cannot go?"

"Then what am I to do?" Mr. Stewart spoke to Mrs. Van Groot. "Am I to hand such a sum of money as this to Miss Fraser when she can't even promise to produce the pearls?"

Mrs. Van Groot proffered a suggestion.

"Give your money to Mr. Bennington, he will act as stake-holder. When, in his presence, she produces the pearls Mr. Bennington will give her the notes."

"Bennington, you will know the Romanoff pearls when you see them?"

The question came from Mr. Parker Van Groot. Mr. Bennington, who had remained a silent spectator of all that had taken place, thought for a moment before he replied.

"I shall. I've seen the Romanoff pearls on at least two occasions."

"So you've seen them, have you? I didn't know that. Where did you see them?"

Mr. Bennington hesitated again.

"That is a point about which, if you'll permit me to say so, Mr. Van Groot, you had better hot inquire. I think that, having seen a really remarkable pearl clearly once, I should always know it again. I could not make a mistake about the Romanoff pearls."

"Good. Then, Mr. Stewart, if Bennington approves of what this young lady is about to show us, and guarantees them to be genuine, he will take charge of them on my behalf and will hand you a million dollars."

"In cash or in the form of a cheque."

"The agreement was that you should be paid in cash, and you will be. Now, sir, will you be so good as to go with this young lady? She undertakes to be back inside fifteen minutes. I will wait twenty. I don't see, Isobel, why it is necessary that you should go. You don't know what you may be letting yourself in for."

"I don't that's why I'm going. Come along, Miss Fraser."

When the trio had gone, Mr. Van Groot said to Mr. Bennington:

"Do you think they'll come back with the pearls?"

As seemed to be his habit, Mr. Bennington considered before he replied.

"The situation is rather beyond me; I should not care to commit myself. If they do, Miss Fraser must be an extremely clever woman."

"She is!" exclaimed Mr. Beckwith from his Bath chair. NEW PAGE

CHAPTER XXXIII
POSTE RESTANTE

Mrs. Parker Van Groot's limousine was, as might be expected, one of the biggest, most powerful, most luxurious which could be bought for money. Usually, besides the chauffeur, there was a footman in front in gorgeous livery. On that occasion he had been left behind in the vestibule of Raymond's Hotel to make room for Mr. Stewart. The two ladies were inside. Mrs. Van Groot was disposed to be conversational.

"I'm actually excited!" The words came from her with a little burst. "Isn't it extraordinary? I've not felt that way since before I don't know when. Aren't you excited? You look as cool and calm as if you were going out to some silly tea. What are you thinking about?"

There was a far-off look in Catherine's eyes, and a far-off tone in her voice as she replied.

"I'm thinking of those ten thousand pounds, of all that Hugh and I can do with them. If you'd had your fortune made all of a sudden you'd know what I was thinking about."

"Do you mean to say that you're not thinking at all about those pearls, with all their wonderful history?"

Catherine's manner was judicial.

"I suppose I am thinking about them a little. But, you see, they are of so much more interest to you than to me. You're going to wear them; I'm not."

"That's true. I've got some nice jewels, but I' got nothing unique. To own, and to wear, the finest pearl necklace in the world the mere idea sends a thrill through me. And I thought I was beyond thrills."

"I hope you'll excuse my saying so, but I fancy that you're younger than you think. I believe you're full of what I saw called somewhere 'the joy of life.'"

"Really? Miss Fraser, you're delightful. It's so nice of you to think that I'm full of what you call 'the joy of life.' Parker will be tickled to death." The car was slowing. "Here's your old office. What are you going to do?"

"I'm going in, of course."

"May I come with you?"

"I shall be very glad if you will. You'll at least be able to tell the people, if they want corroboration, that I am Catherine Fraser."

"I suppose there won't be any fuss? Parker is so afraid of what he calls a fuss."

"I've never been in an American post-office in my life, so I can't say how they manage things; but I shouldn't think there would be any fuss."

The ladies were standing on the pavement, Mr. Stewart having held the door open io permit of their descending. Mrs. Van Groot checked him when he showed signs of going with them into the building.

"You needn't come. Do you want Mr. Stewart, Miss Fraser?"

"I don't think so. If I do, I'll let him know." She looked the gentleman rather oddly in the face. "I think it's possible that he may do more harm than good."

His glance was as curious as hers.

"How long do you think you'll be?"

"I've not the least idea. I tell you I don't know how they manage this sort of thing in America."

"Send for me if I am wanted."

The girl made a remark which was full of sinister significance.

"If I were you I don't think I should wait to be sent for. If I'm not back soon, perhaps the best thing you can do is to go."

Mrs. Van Groot stood still just as they were about to pass through the great entrance.

"I'm not sure, after all, that I ought to come in." She spoke almost in a whisper: "Do you really think there's likely to be trouble?"

"I tell you that I have no notion of what will happen. If we were at home there wouldn't be trouble. That's the last thing I can tell you. Don't come in if you have any doubts."

"Let there be trouble!" Mrs. Van Groot passed into the building almost with the air of a martyr who is moving to the stake. "They can't do more than flay us alive."

"They," if by the pronoun she meant the officials, did not do so much; they did nothing. Catherine picked her way through the crowd, every individual of which seemed to be in a hurry, towards the nearest counter, addressing a worried person who was on the other side of it.

"I expect there's a letter here addressed to me from England; where shall I find it?"

The official courteously directed her to the proper place; having arrived at which, she repeated her inquiry. In less than a minute the clerk she had addressed produced a brown paper parcel, perhaps ten inches long, six or seven wide, and an inch thick. He read the address aloud

"' Miss Catherine Fraser, Poste Restante, New York, U.S.A. To be left till called for.' Are you Miss Catherine Fraser?"

"I am, and that's my parcel. I recognise my mother's writing."

"Anything dutiable in this parcel, Miss Fraser?"

"I believe it contains a photograph. Doesn't it say so on the wrapper? Shall I open it and let you see?"

"Thank you, Miss Fraser, I won't trouble you. I should like to look at your photograph, especially if it is one of you; but we're too busy at this time of day to permit of our looking at photographs."

What the clerk meant was not quite clear, but he was possibly under the impression that he was paying a compliment. With the parcel held loosely, Mrs. Van Groot and Catherine returned to the street to be greeted by Mr. Stewart.

"You haven't been long. Have you got them?"

Catherine's manner was frigid.

"You will learn in good time. Would you mind opening the door of the motor-car?"

Mr. Stewart did as he was told; perhaps there was nothing else he could do. The ladies, being seated, and the car again in motion, Mrs. Van Groot rushed out with a question.

"Do you mean to say the Romanoff pearls are in that?"

She pointed to the brown paper parcel. Catherine's remark was scarcely a reply. Her manner was primness itself.

"I can only tell you what I told Mr. Stewart you will see in good time."

Mrs. Van Groot apparently regarded the girl's conduct as outrageous.

"Miss Fraser, you're unspeakable! Do you mean to say that I've to wait, having come all this way with you so that I might be the first to know. Open your silly parcel now."

"I'm afraid I can't. It ought to be opened, for all our sakes, in front of the others; then whatever may be inside they'll have no ground for suspicion that the contents have been tampered with."

"Do you dare to suggest that anyone would suspect me of what you call tampering with the contents?"

"I can't say anything about that, but I'm quite sure that under certain circumstances they would be quite capable of suspecting me. Anyhow I think, if you don't mind, we won't open it till we get to the hotel." She added soothingly, "We haven't far to go."

"I never heard anything so--so--so--" The lady seemed unable to find a word which adequately described her feelings; so she rounded off her sentence a little lamely, "I really never did!" She adopted what she perhaps meant to be a tone of injured dignity. "I really never thought you'd behave to me like this, Miss Fraser. Think of the Romanoff pearls being in that silly parcel and you won't show them to me. It's incredible!" NEW PAGE

CHAPTER XXXIV
HUGH'S PORTRAIT

There was an addition to the number of persons they had left in the sitting-room at the hotel; Miss Galstin had arrived during their absence. She was seated by the Bath chair talking to its occupant. She stood up as Catherine and her companions entered, and was the first to greet them. "Good news?" she asked.

Mr. Stewart treated the question as addressed to himself.

"That's more than I can say. I'll tell you what I've been told wait and see. Apparently Miss Fraser is of opinion that waiting does one good." The speaker's tone was a little peevish. Something in it seemed to alarm Mr. Beckwith.

"Catherine!" he cried, "what does he mean? Haven't you got them?"

Miss Fraser, crossing to the Bath chair, kneeling beside it, laid the brown paper parcel on the apron. Primness had gone from her; there was feeling in her voice and glance. Her heart was in her words.

"Sweetheart, I think I've got them; I'm not quite certain. How can I be? Goodness only knows how long it is since I've seen them. I believe they're in this parcel. Will you open it and look?"

The suggestion put Hugh Beckwith in a state of flutter.

"Has anybody got a knife, or a pair of scissors, or anything that will cut?"

The proffer of a penknife came from Dr. Rasselton.

"Here's something that will cut, but wouldn't it be better if Miss Fraser were to conduct her own investigations. You must be careful not to overexcite yourself."

"Over-excite myself!" exclaimed the patient. "It won't over-excite me to cut a piece of string, will it? You wouldn't talk like that if you only knew how anxious I've been. This is a sharp pen-knife of yours."

Four touches and the string was severed in four places. The paper wrapping was removed with tremulous fingers. Within was a grey, rather broken cardboard box.

"Why," inquired Mr. Beckwith, "where have I seen that old box before?" He raised it to read something which was on the lid. "'Hugh Beckwith, Esq., 12 Grove Gardens.' Why, if it isn't!" Leaving the sentence unfinished he began hurriedly to remove the lid from the cardboard box, exclaiming the moment it was off, "It is! What on earth is the meaning of this?"

By now all the other persons in the room were gathered round the Bath chair. Mrs. Van Groot, who was behind him on the right, leaning over his shoulder announced:

"Why, if it isn't a photograph--just a silly old photograph."

Mr. Beckwith glanced round at her as if with resentment.

"It's my photograph. Pray, why is it silly?"

"But," went on the lady, "who wants anyone's photograph? Where are the pearls?"

"That does seem to be rather a question."

In the cardboard case was a photograph of a gentleman framed. Catherine, taking it from him, regarded it attentively. She harped on Mrs. Van Groot's uncomplimentary epithet.

"It's not a silly photograph! Hugh, it's an excellent likeness of you; I defy anyone to say it isn't. As for the pearls--"

She was taking the framed photograph from the cardboard box and was turning it over. Her leisurely movements tried the patience of the spectators. Mr. Van Groot struck in:

"Come, young lady, time means money what about the pearls?"

"If you'll exercise a little self-control, Mr. Van Groot, in less than thirty seconds you will probably know."

Catherine was unruffled. The frame was face downwards; she was removing the back. It came away in one piece. Within was a lining of what looked like cotton-wool.

"There, Mr. Stewart," she observed, "are your twenty-two pills."

Everyone, bending forward, stared eagerly.

"Where?" inquired Mr. Beckwith. "Catherine, what do you mean?"

Mrs. Van Groot followed with a question in the same strain.

"Pills? What does she mean? Who wants to have anything to do with pills? Besides, I see nothing anyhow."

Plainly the lady was irritated. Catherine's manner was not only cool, but it was soothing.

"You will in a second." She was feeling for something in the cotton-wool which served as a lining to the frame; finding what she sought, she held it up between her finger and her thumb. "There, Mr. Stewart, is one of your pills."

Mr. Rothenstein was quicker than the man addressed; he snatched what the girl was holding.

"My goodness!" he exclaimed, "what is this dirty-looking thing?"

Mr. Stewart took the speaker by surprise; with a hasty movement he relieved him of what he was holding.

"Can someone let us have a basin of hot water? I'll show you your dirty-looking thing."

Without waiting to be told, Nurse Ada sailed off to Catherine's bedroom, which adjoined; almost instantly returning with a wash-hand basin half-full of steaming hot water. She placed it on a table. In the meanwhile Catherine had produced from the cotton-wool other objects similar to the first, giving them all to Mr. Stewart.

"How many have you got?" she asked. Mr. Rothenstein answered.

"You have given him eighteen. I have been counting."

Mr. Stewart endorsed the statement.

"Rothenstein's right--eighteen--four more wanted."

"I expect they're here." She was still feeling with her finger-tips in the cotton-wool. Her words seemed to trouble Mr. Stewart.

"You expect? Please don't talk like that; they must be there."

"I'll bring the frame to the table and turn the wadding out. I shall find them. I packed them myself. Ah, here's another and another and here are the two others got together in a corner. So there, Mr. Stewart, are all your twenty-two."

Mr. Stewart had dropped what Catherine had given to him into the basin. From a waistcoat-pocket he took a small leather case; from this a small pair of tweezers and a tiny brush. On the table he laid out a piece of chamois leather, placing on it a little box containing some kind of whitish powder. He said to the people who had crowded round to observe his proceedings:

"Will you be so good, ladies and gentlemen, as to stand a little farther back? You will see me take these, one after the other, out of the water and lay them on that piece of chamois leather. It will be just as well that everyone should stand clear of the table until the whole twenty-two are before you."

He took each minute object from the water, held it in his tweezers, dipped his tiny brush in the whitish powder, and gently brushed the "pill"; they observing him almost with bated breath, as if he were working a miracle before their eyes. Indeed, it almost seemed a miracle. Each small globe as it came from the water was still brown; when it was deposited on the piece of chamois leather, it was of a peculiar translucent whiteness. At last he pointed towards them with a dramatic gesture.

"There, Mr. Van Groot, are the Romanoff pearls."

"Bennington," said Mr. Van Groot, "do you identify them as such?"

"May I look at them?" Mr. Bennington put the question to Mr. Stewart, who was affable in reply. Since Catherine had produced her charges, his manner, which had before been overcast, had entirely changed; now there did not seem to be a cloud upon his countenance.

"Certainly, Mr. Bennington, of course you may see them. Why do you suppose they've gone through all these strange and perilous adventures, by land and sea, except for the express purpose of letting you see them? Look at them, sir; examine them carefully. Tell Mr. Van Groot if, to the best of your knowledge and belief, they are not the Romanoff pearls."

Mr. Bennington crossed to the piece of chamois leather; produced what might have been a reading glass, with the assistance of which he subjected the shining array to a general scrutiny;

then fitted a jeweller's glass in his eye, through which he examined them one by one. The spectators watched him, no one speaking a word; fortunately for them the examination did not last as long as it might have done. Presently Mr. Bennington announced his decision.

"These, Mr. Van Groot, are undoubtedly the Romanoff pearls."

"In that case," directed Mr. Van Groot, "to begin with, hand over the dollars to the young lady. Close that deal first."

Mr. Bennington counted out a number of flimsy pieces of crinkly paper and passed them to Catherine.

"I think you will find those in order, Miss Fraser," he said, "but in case any mistake should have crept in, you had better count them."

Catherine smiled that rare and wonderful smile which transfigured her. She picked up the pieces of paper.

"I'm not afraid of any mistake. I saw you count them, and that's good enough for me." She addressed Mr. Stewart. "I suppose no receipt is wanted? I'll give you one if you like."

"No receipt is wanted." Mr. Stewart's tone was dry. The smile which wrinkled the corners of his lips was of quite a different type from hers. "You needn't trouble."

"Hugh!" she exclaimed, turning to the Bath chair, "just look at these! What won't they mean to us! My darling!"

That time the invalid allowed the endearing epithet to go unrebuked. The girl placed the notes on the apron in front of him. He touched one or two of them, then turned to Catherine. She was kneeling quite close to his chair. She whispered something which he alone could hear, leaning forward so that he should hear her better. With an awkward, stiff movement, as if the hinges were rusty, he placed one arm around her neck and drew her closer still.

At the table Mr. Van Groot was continuing his directions.

"Now if everything's perfectly all right, the next thing to be done is to pay over the agreed-upon sum for the pearls."

Mr. Bennington took from some mysterious receptacle what looked like an oil-skin letter-case.

"I arranged with you, Mr. Stewart, that payment should be made by means of twenty drafts, ten on London, ten on Paris, payable to bearer. If you look those over I think you will find that they are in order."

Mr. Stewart untied the letter-case; it also contained pieces of paper. Mr. Rothenstein made a snatch at them. He seemed tremulous with agitation almost inarticulate.

"Give me my share now!" he exclaimed.

"Don't be an ass!" returned his associate, withdrawing the letter-case from his reach. "Haven't I first got to count them to see if they are right? I'll settle with you afterwards. You need fear nothing."

Mr. Rothenstein seemed to be of a different opinion.

"But I do fear," he exclaimed; "I do!" He turned to Mr. Bennington. "Why did you not pay my share to me? He is not to be trusted."

Mr. Van Groot interposed.

"Bennington, allow these gentlemen to continue their own little discussions at their leisure. I presume that now we can take possession of the pearls. My dear, would you like to have a look at them?"

This was spoken to Mrs. Van Groot. She evidently did like. Bending over the piece of chamois leather she feasted her eyes on the sparkling gems.

"Oh, you darlings! You really are quite beautiful." She added in what for her were tones of awe, "And these are the Romanoff pearls!"

Before she could continue her sentence she seemed on the verge of what might have been an eloquent apostrophe the door was thrown open and two persons came in who were in evident haste: one was the lady hitherto known to us as Cara Oudinoff; the other, a gentleman Mr.

Yashvin. The gentleman was in a state of what seemed extraordinary excitement. He cried as if he were making an announcement of the first importance:

"The Suvarov is in the harbour!"

Mr. Van Groot stared at the speaker with what was perhaps meant to be an air of dignified surprise.

"Miss Fraser, people use your room in a very casual fashion, as if ignoring what may be going on they are at liberty to go in and out how and when they please. And pray, sir, who are you, and what may the Suvarov be?"

"The Suvarov?" Mr. Yashvin stared at the multi-millionaire as if he wondered who he might be. "The Suvarov is a Russian ship of war. It is in the harbour--that means trouble."

"And pray, sir," continued Mr. Van Groot, "why should the presence in the harbour of a Russian ship of war mean trouble?"

Mr. Yashvin laughed, as if the question struck him as uncomfortably ridiculous.

"You will see! We all of us shall see! It is all up with us!"

Mr. Van Groot stared as if he thought the speaker was a lunatic. Before he could ask the question which seemed shaping on his lips, the door opened again and someone else came into the room, someone who moved to the table on which was the piece of chamois leather with its glittering ornaments.

"I have come," he announced, "for the Romanoff pearls." NEW PAGE

145

CHAPTER XXXV
THE GREAT TEMPTATION

The new-comer was a tall thin man who spoke with an air of authority which had a curious effect upon those who listened. They stared as if he were a supernatural being. Catherine, still leaning, glancing round, seemed to see in him some shadowy reminiscence.

"Where," she said in an undertone, as if unconscious that she was speaking aloud, "have I seen him before?"

"Some of you," the stranger continued, "know who I am." He had on a long black overcoat, which he unbuttoned and threw wide open, revealing on a coat beneath a little silver star attached to a broad strip of curious-coloured braid. Beneath this was what looked like a gold button on which was engraved a hieroglyphic figure. "You see?" He turned so that everyone could see.

Some of them evidently saw only too well. Messrs. Stewart, Rothenstein, and Yashvin, and Mesdames Galstin and Oudinoff shrank back as if from the fall of a suspended whip. As the stranger drew attention to the insignia on the breast of his coat, they seemed all at once to become different people; as if he were an executioner who might, if he chose, mete out to them instant death.

To Catherine, with a slight inclination of his head, he addressed words which clearly took her by surprise.

"Miss Fraser, it gives me pleasure to meet you again."

The girl scrambled to her feet. "Why," she exclaimed, "if it isn't Mr. Abednego P. Thompson! What have you done to yourself? You look quite different. You've got different coloured hair and your moustache has gone, and you're different altogether."

The stranger smiled. "Not different altogether, at least to you, Miss Fraser. You at least have a different name; when I met you last you were Miss Forester. It's odd what a difference small things make in a man's appearance."

Catherine was staring at him with eyes open at their widest.

"You call them little things I don't! You're different altogether, and yet I should have known you."

"Of course you would; you're not a person from whom it would be easy to conceal one's identity." He addressed Mr. Van Groot, moving his head with a contemptuous gesture towards the cowering five. "Miss Fraser knows me, and these people know me. It's no use any of you sneaking towards the door. There are people waiting for you outside and below; you'd only be passing from the frying-pan into the fire. And I believe Mr. Bennington knows me is that not so?"

The retiring Mr. Bennington wore his most unobtrusive air.

"It's very good of you, sir, to do me the honour to remember me."

"Sir, you are too modest. One in my position can hardly help remembering a man like you. You are one by yourself, Mr. Bennington. You, I believe, are Mr. Parker Van Groot and have I the honour of meeting Mrs. Parker Van Groot? My own name in this distinguished company is of no consequence. I think I may say, with great humility, that at this moment I represent Russia. These are my credentials."

Again he pointed to the emblems on his breast. One could with difficulty recognise in this courtly gentleman the uncouth Mr. Abednego P. Thompson of the s.s. Columbia.

"Mrs. Van Groot, it is a very serious thing for a lady of your importance to have a birthday."

"It is a pretty serious thing for anyone to have a birthday. You're a very mysterious person. As I used to say when I was a small child you do seem to have knocked the stuffing out of some of them. But what has the fact of my having a birthday got to do with you?"

"It's not so much the fact of your having a birthday, Mrs. Van Groot, as the form of present which you thought you would like. When you told your excellent husband that you thought you'd like to have a pearl necklace, you said something which was heard all over the world."

146

"And pray how so? Can't a woman tell her husband that she'd like to have a pearl necklace for a birthday present without making a fuss?"

"If you had just said a pearl necklace yes; but when you said that you wanted the finest pearl necklace in the world that made the fuss. No one knows better than you what a devoted husband Mr. Van Groot is; and, having once taken a matter in hand, with what thoroughness he sees it through. Thoroughness is a great American attribute; in the case of Mr. Van Groot you find it in a superlative degree. You can't get the finest pearl necklace in the world by merely ordering it at a jeweller's shop, or by means of an ordinary commercial transaction with the most renowned dealers in precious stones. Mr. Van Groot knew that, so he went to Mr. Bennington who is a truly remarkable man."

The speaker emphasised the compliment with a courteous inclination of his head; which the recipient of the compliment returned as if he were quite willing that his merits should go unnoticed.

"You, Mr. Van Groot," continued the new-comer, "entrusted the task of assembling the pearls for the finest necklace in the world to Mr. Bennington. You could hardly have entrusted it to surer hands. Mr. Bennington's knowledge of precious stones is peculiar especially of pearls. He probably has somewhere a record of the present whereabouts of all the most famous examples. When Mr. Van Groot said to him, 'Bennington, get the finest necklace in the world, and spare no cost,' Mr. Bennington probably instantly referred to his record. He ascertained that there were certain exceptionally fine stones on the market; those he immediately acquired. When he had them, however, he had merely started. If he had to fulfil his commission he had to obtain stones which, in the ordinary sense, were not on the market. I don't wish to enter into matters which are no personal concern of mine; I will merely observe that some of these he did procure by what means I will leave Mr. Bennington to settle with his principal. It is permissible, perhaps, to remark that some of the means he employed were we will say peculiar. Is it not allowable to say so much, Mr. Bennington?"

Mr. Bennington glanced at the speaker as if he wondered who he was. His reply, when it came, was scarcely an answer to the question.

"I believe, sir, you were so good as to point out that you wished to confine yourself to matters which concerned you personally."

"That is perfectly true I did; so we'll leave the question of how you obtained possession of certain of those pearls unanswered. Mr. Bennington, going about the matter in the right way, had, in the first instance, drawn up a list of the pearls he proposed to assemble. This list he submitted to his client. The accident that certain of the gems upon that list were the property of persons who, under no conceivable circumstances and on no conceivable terms, could be induced to part with them did not seem to have troubled either the principal or his agent. Mr. Van Groot, like the English king who was above grammar, is above all ordinary rules of men and title; when he wants a thing, he does not worry himself about such an insignificant fact as that it belongs to someone else he has it. Mr. Bennington proposed carrying out his principal's bidding by incorporating in that necklace twenty-two of the finest pearls the world ever has seen and probably ever will see. Mr. Van Groot was quite alive to the fact that with those twenty-two pearls he would have a truly unique string to offer as a birthday present to his enchanting wife. You begin to perceive, Mrs. Van Groot, how the fact that your having a birthday was likely to lead to what you call a 'fuss.'"

Mrs. Van Groot beamed, as if she felt that the speaker was distinctly amusing. She put her finger up to her lips like a child.

"I really don't see why, if you want S. Peter's cathedral in Rome, you shouldn't get it if you can. I have a lady friend who wants the Great Pyramid to decorate some new golf links her husband has made. She says it would make such an excellent bunker, and you may bet that she'll get it if she can. I don't see why there should be anything which money won't buy."

The stranger bowed to her; he in his turn appeared amused.

"Such are the natural sentiments of the wife of an American millionaire. Alexander, and others, conquered the world with their armed cohorts so they came to own the earth. The billionaire proposes to do it with his billions. Who is he who is to say him nay? Possibly some beggarly fellow with some paltry few thousands a year. Probably when the principal and his agent put their distinguished heads together that idea was in both of them. Said they, We've got the money, and we'll have the pearls particularly those twenty-two. So they set about getting them. And that, Mrs. Van Groot, was really where the fuss began."

"I still don't see why it need have done. Why couldn't they have said, 'Here are so many millions of dollars; sell us your silly old pearls.'"

The stranger shook his head; he seemed to find the lady more and more amusing. Judging by his manner, he might have been endeavouring to explain a knotty problem to a simple-minded child.

"The matter was not so simple both of these gentlemen knew that. If any action of theirs had caused the owners of the twenty-two even to suspect that they wanted them, they would immediately have taken precautions which would have prevented their getting them, at any rate until some time after your birthday was past."

"I don't pretend to be a business woman, but it does seem to me to be an unbusiness-like way of doing things."

"You should understand, madam, that these were not business men; they understood nothing about business methods; they were merely royalties. The twenty-two pearls in question belonged to the royal family of Russia. They have taken centuries to collect, and are their glory and their pride. They have been passed on from generation to generation. On state occasions, when royal personages vie with each other in splendour, they are the admired of all admirers. You could hardly expect them to dispose of them for money."

"Why not? They're not sacred. I don't suppose there's a royal family in the world which hasn't sold its jewels at some time or other, and glad to get a good price for them. Why shouldn't these Russian people be glad to get a good price for theirs?"

The stranger slightly raised his hand, as if recognising that argument was useless.

"Madam, I can only point out to you that Mr. Van Groot and Mr. Bennington, who do know something of business, were perfectly well aware that it would be useless to offer what you call a 'good price' so they tried another way."

"If I wanted the Great Pyramid, and they wouldn't sell it, do you think I wouldn't ship it over to America in spite of them if I got the chance? Rather! They'd got to try another way."

"They did hence the fuss. If Mr. Bennington's knowledge of pearls is peculiar, so also is his knowledge in other directions. Probably no one knows better how to deal with such a difficult problem as the one with which he was confronted. My desire, sir, is always to give credit where credit is due."

Another inclination of the head towards Mr. Bennington, who, though he returned it, one felt sure would rather not.

"You do me more than justice, sir," he courteously murmured.

"Impossible, sir. In a matter of this sort it is difficult to exaggerate your qualifications. You probably know as much about Europe's shady characters as any other man now living. You wanted the Romanoff pearls; you knew the man who was the most likely to get them for you. You went to him with a proposition I will hardly call it that, I will say a suggestion. 'Mr. Stewart,' you probably said--I was not present at the interview; I draw on my imagination, but I am inclined to believe that I'm not very far wrong--'I want the twenty-two Romanoff pearls; I have a list and description of them here. You know them?' 'Yes,' said Mr. Stewart, 'I do. But how do you suppose you're going to get them?' 'I don't suppose; I want them, that's all. Bring them to me at my offices in New York on or before a given date, and I will hand you a million dollars in return.' Mr. Stewart--the gentleman is present, and can contradict me if he likes--is also a remarkable man. He calls himself, I believe, a dealer in precious stones; but he deals in other things besides precious stones nor does he always buy or sell in the open market. Mr.

Stewart, I say, cocked up his ears at the mention of that million dollars; although I did not see him, I am convinced he did. He looked at Mr. Bennington, and Mr. Bennington looked at him. He remarked still I am only imagining 'A million dollars I think you said? Delivery to be by such and such a date? I'll see what can be done.' And he saw. I doubt if many more words were exchanged between them; these gentlemen understood each other so well that a wink was as good as a volume. And so, Mrs. Van Groot, to provide you with a fitting present for your birthday was then and there planned one of the greatest crimes of recent years."

"And now are you going to hint that I am responsible for the crime?"

"I'm going to do more than hint--I'm going to say right out that you were the direct cause of the crime."

"This is delightful! Parker, do you hear? And pray, Mr. Mysterious Stranger, how do you make that out?"

"Easily--it was the great temptation that did it."

"And what do you call the great temptation?"

"Consider. You and your esteemed husband deal in such inflated figures--inflated even for America--that you do not realise what to a European money means. You offered a million dollars--"

"I offered what next?"

"Your husband offered on your behalf, which comes to the same thing. I wish to ask no inconvenient questions, but I've no doubt that you had a general idea of what was going on. You wanted the finest pearl necklace in the world. To begin with you knew what that meant!; you had at least a vague notion that certain gems, which were not accessible to the ordinary buyer, had been corporated in it; you were willing, so far as you were concerned, to pay any amount of money to get them. Mr. Van Groot, realising this, to please you offered a million dollars. What I don't think you perhaps realised is what such a sum means to a person in Mr. Stewart's position.

Mrs. Van Groot, I can assure you of my own knowledge that there are people in Russia where the pearls were who would commit murder for half a dollar. Read Maxim Gorki's novels--he knows what he's writing about--and you'll see what I mean. To Mr. Stewart a million dollars meant a big fortune. Miss Fraser here told me with her own lips that to her five hundred pounds--two thousand five hundred dollars--meant a fortune. For that sum she was prepared to embark on a desperate venture, of whose details she knew nothing except that it involved risking her life. When Mr. Stewart was offered a million dollars for property which it was well known he could not get by open, honest means, it was direct incitement to robbery and murder. It was, as I have said, a great temptation."

The speaker turned towards Mr. Stewart, who, on his side, stood with his back towards him. It was extraordinary what a striking change there was in his demeanour. The tall, well-set, up-standing man had all at once assumed the hang-dog air of the discovered criminal who goes in mortal terror of the threatening punishment.

"Mr. Stewart knew other persons to whom even a fraction of a million dollars meant a fortune. Before the matter was through a large number of persons had become more or less involved, but the leading spirits were five: Mr. Stewart we will call him Stewart Mr. Rothenstein, Mr. Yashvin who is a cadet of one of the greatest families in Russia; the lady who at present calls herself Darya Galstin, whose relations are at this moment distinguished members of Russian society; and the other lady whose real name not even the police have been able to determine we will call her, for present purposes, the Princess Kitty Vronsky. Mr. Stewart was aware that if these four persons could be induced to associate themselves with him the impossible might be achieved. What was the nature of the bargain I am unable to tell you, but these persons had less cash even than morals which is saying a great deal and I have no doubt that twenty-five thousand dollars would buy any one of them body, soul, and spirit. If I have said anything which is libellous, I am willing to account for it."

The speaker paused as if to wait for something which did not come. Catherine, however, had a remark to make.

"Mr. Yashvin offered me twenty-five thousand dollars if I would betray my trust so he must have had some money."

"It is possible, Miss Fraser, that you might only have got hooked with that as a bait. But no doubt cash was found when the scheme really got going; such an enterprise could not have been carried on without it. Mr. Rothenstein here is not a pauper; he is merely a scamp. Ill-fortune has made him the inmate of a prison more than once."

"It is not true!" ejaculated the old gentleman referred to. "You take my character! I will not have you take my character."

"Don't pretend you have a character to take it is too thin. There is an individual downstairs who has your dossier, your entire history from your cradle until now. I will have him up; the dossier shall be produced, if you wish it. Do you wish it, Mr. Rothenstein?"

"No, I do not wish it; the world has always been so hard on me."

"Quite so. You also at times have been hard upon the world. I am sorry to have to tell you, Mrs. Van Groot, that my story now becomes a little scandalous. There is a certain laxity in Russia which I am given to understand is not to be paralleled here in America. Especially is this the case in circles of the most distinguished eminence. I will avoid names as far as possible; I will merely give you a plain, unvarnished narrative, as nearly exact as possible, of what occurred."

The speaker paused as if for the purpose of getting his thoughts in order. It was noticeable that each member of the five glanced furtively at him as if fearful of what was coming.

"At the moment when the wheels began to turn the Romanoff pearls were in the keeping of a distinguished lady we will call her the Grand Duchess X. I may premise by observing that in the Russian royal family the Romanoff pearls are, or were, regarded as a sort of joint possession. When one or other lady of the family had special reasons for wanting to wear them, she asked permission, and generally got it. There is a strong bond of affection in the Russian royal family, at least theoretically; one member is always ready to do a service for another, if it may be done without trouble or expense. So when the Grand Duchess X., who is young but not beautiful, wanted to borrow the pearls for some function which does not concern us, she had only to ask and she had."

"But it must have been a very remarkable function at which she could have wanted to wear such pearls as those. Parker said that I might not be able to wear them more than half a dozen times in my life; at an ordinary house they would seem too ridiculous."

"Probably. But did you propose, Mrs. Van Groot, to wear them only half a dozen times in your life?"

"Not much! I told Parker that I'd wear them in the street and in shops, and just everywhere. I'm not selfish, I'm not; I meant to let everyone see the finest pearl necklace in the world."

"I doubt if the function at which the Grand Duchess X. was to wear them was of much account, because here the scandal begins at that function they were stolen from her by a gentleman."

"What kind of a gentleman was it who stole them?"

"He was the Grand Duchess's own first cousin. There were some little passages between them; when those passages were over and the cousin had gone, so also had the pearls! The Grand Duchess did not discover her loss till she had returned to her own apartments, and then then she did not dare to mention it. Wicked tongues have stated I accept no responsibility for them that the cousin kissed the Grand Duchess, and in the act of kissing her removed the pearls which she wore as a star in her hair."

"A nice sort of gentleman he must have been!"

"Mrs. Van Groot, in this world there are some curious gentlemen. What amount of truth there is in the story I cannot say. The Grand Duchess was so afraid of what might happen to her, that she concealed her loss while she made frantic efforts to recover the pearls. Had she proclaimed her loss at once they would never have had such startling adventures till at last they found their way to that table. It is to be feared that the cousin, besides being a curious gentleman, was also not a very truthful one. He denied that he knew anything about the pearls, which was a painfully impudent falsehood, because nothing is more certain than that the very following night he lent them to a lady who was not the Grand Duchess X."

Stopping, the speaker partly turned, and in a very pointed way regarded Miss Galstin. Miss Galstin was a strikingly beautiful young woman. Most persons having looked at her once would have been willing to look at her again, especially if those persons were of the male persuasion. One could easily believe what the stranger said that her relations were distinguished members of Russian high society. There is an indefinable something which the world agrees to call "aristocratic"; Miss Galstin had that something in a very marked degree. Not only was she beautiful, but in voice, manner, bearing, in all externals, she was the true "great lady." She had something else which is supposed to be an aristocratic attribute self-possession. An ordinary person might have winced when the stranger said what he did. Not so Miss Galstin; she favoured him with a courteous and slightly condescending smile.

"Who told you that?" she said. "You policemen must do a great deal of peeping through keyholes."

"I'm not," rejoined the other, "ashamed of being a policeman; but I would remind you there are other ways of acquiring information besides peeping through key-holes. I believe it to be a fact the lady may contradict me if I am wrong that the remarkable cousin came to her apartment in an intoxicated condition, and that within three minutes of his arrival the Romanoff pearls, of whose whereabouts he has denied all knowledge, were in her hands and, I may add, within a very few minutes more they were out of them again. And this is where the humorous point of my story begins to come in."

This time he glanced towards the second lady, whom we have known as Cara Oudinoff, and who had all at once assumed what appeared to be a hostile demeanour.

"I perceive," he remarked, "that the Princess Kitty Vronsky appreciates in advance what is coming."

The lady referred to looked at him in what could hardly be called an appreciative manner.

"You had better," she exclaimed, "be careful what you are saying."

"I'll take the greatest possible care; my hearers shall be the witnesses." NEW PAGE

CHAPTER XXXVI
PRINCESS KITTY

"Let us, then," continued the mysterious individual, who seemed to have tumbled from the skies for the express purpose of upsetting all the calculations of those who were gathered together in that apartment, listening to his words with an intentness which in more than one instance was distinctly strained, "call for the sake of courtesy this lady the Princess Kitty Vronsky. It is not her name; she has had so many that possibly she has forgotten if she ever had a real one and no one else seems to know. Let us, therefore, I say, call her the Princess Kitty Vronsky, by which name and title she is known to quite a number of persons. The Princess Kitty Vronsky is quite a famous personage in more than one Russian city and even in cities out of Russia. She was never a friend of Miss Galstin's, who is a member of a family well known to all the world, while the Princess Kitty never had a family; but on the occasion to which I am coming these two ladies had to join forces. That remarkable cousin was to pay a visit to Miss Galstin in her apartment, and the Princess Kitty was to drop in while he was there; between them they were to relieve him of the Romanoff pearls. That, ladies, I believe, was the official programme."

None of the ladies, towards whom he inclined his head, gave any sort of answer.

"It so happened, however, that by the time the Princess Kitty arrived it was already too late the pearls had gone. Who Mr. Stewart is I cannot tell you. By birth he may be English, he may be Russian, he may be Danish. In the eyes of the law he is an English citizen that is sure. By profession he is a dealer, not only in precious stones, but in pictures, curios, works of art, old furniture, china anything which requires special expert knowledge and appeals to a restricted and very special market. He has many customers in America. There has been I hardly know what to call it an association between Miss Galstin and him for several years. He seems to have had relations with members of her family when she was quite a child when he made her acquaintance. The acquaintance has continued. Miss Galstin, as I have hinted, has had an adventurous career; in some of the most striking episodes Mr. Stewart figures largely. In commercial matters they have become, in a curious sense, partners. As I have told you, Mr. Bennington broached the question of the Romanoff pearls to Mr. Stewart, realising that he was the person who would be most likely to get them for Mrs. Van Groot's birthday present. Mr. Stewart went to Miss Galstin. She at once perceived that a considerable sum in ready money might be needed; so the pair of them approached Mr. Rothenstein. He produced the money. He approached the Princess Kitty, who is possibly a distant relation of his. She, in her turn, introduced the business to the man Miss Fraser knows as Yashvin." The speaker's tone changed, passing from suavity to sternness. "This man is a blackguard of the first water; a cool-blooded, cruel dastard, who cares for nothing and no one except his own foul instincts."

The gentleman referred to in such uncomplimentary terms did his best to meet the speaker's glance, but there was a quality in the other's eyes before which he quailed. As if conscious of how wholly he was at this man's mercy, wheeling round he made a strategic movement towards the door. The stranger's voice rang out like the crack of a whip.

"Stop!" The effect upon the man addressed was as if the lash of some peculiarly deadly whip had struck him across the shoulders. Instantly stopping, he hunched his shoulders up as if he expected the whip to fall again. "Remain in this room until you have orders to leave it. You need be in no haste to pass from here into the hands of those who await you."

The stranger pointed to the shrinking man as though he were some unspeakable thing.

"This cowardly hound can play the bully when opportunity offers. Princess Kitty, who knows him well, has allowed him to use her as his tool for goodness knows how long. She told him what Rothenstein had told her; the serviceable Mr. Yashvin promised to lend a hand in the acquisition of the Romanoff pearls for Mrs. Van Groot's birthday present. The business was to be arranged at Miss Galstin's apartment. The remarkable cousin, having procured the pearls from the fatuous Grand Duchess, was to visit Miss Galstin. Presently, as I have said, the Princess Kitty was to drop in; and later, at a given signal, Mr. Yashvin. He was, as usual, to play the part of the common bully. The cousin was to be primed with drink; cajoled and wheedled by the two women: then if he proved intractable, Yashvin was to force the pearls from him by methods of his own."

"I do not admit for one moment that a word of what you say is true."

This was the Princess Kitty. The stranger laughed at her.

"No admission from you is required. It so happened that this elaborate plan came to nothing. I have been informed that the cousin had drunk three bottles of champagne at dinner, before he paid his call. Three bottles were more than he could carry. In such a state of generous tenderness was he when he arrived that, as I have told you, almost immediately, of his own accord, he handed the Romanoff pearls to his hostess as a slight token of esteem. At that moment an idea seems to have occurred to Miss Galstin, which was, in a sense, the cause of all the trouble."

"The idea had occurred to me before then." This was Miss Galstin. "Since you know as much as you do I don't mind telling you exactly how it was. It was rather droll. Shall I tell you?"

The stranger was the soul of urbanity.

"Such a communication from you will be treasured for all time."

"Shall I tell him?" Miss Galstin turned to Mr. Stewart.

"Tell him if you please." Mr. Stewart spoke a little savagely. "What does it matter, now that everything is over?"

"I'm not prepared to admit that everything is over. However, no harm will be done and it is so droll. So I will tell you. Nikol--"

The stranger checked the lady at the very commencement of her story. He held up a reproving hand. "If you please no names."

"Well, if you prefer it, I will say the cousin. He thought he was in love with me."

"According to my advices there was no question of thought he loved you to distraction."

"Perhaps." The lady shrugged her high-bred shoulders. "What in the case of such a man does love mean? He was a fool a perfect fool. It is no secret, it is known to all the world. I told him, 'You say you love me prove it!' 'How can I prove it?' he demanded. 'There's nothing in the world I would not do to prove it.' 'All I ask is a trifle show me the Romanoff pearls.' He started. 'What do you mean?' he cried. 'Show you the Romanoff pearls? How can it be done?' 'That is for you to say,' I told him. 'You are a clever man, bring the Romanoff pearls here for me to look at just for me to look at! I shall then know you love me.' Quite how he managed it I did not know until you told us, but he did manage it. There came a note one morning to say that he had obtained the pearls and would bring them with him that evening for me to look at; but he could not stay long because he ran a great risk in having them in his possession at all, and they would have to be returned that night. It occurred to me, when I thought the matter over, that perhaps after all I might be able to manage without these two. So I sent for my foster-brother--"

"That is the gentleman," interposed the stranger, addressing the invalid in the Bath chair, "whom I believe you met outside that curious house in London, for whom the bag was intended when it was dropped from the upper window."

"Do you mean," asked Mr. Beckwith, "the thin, white-faced fellow, who ran at me across the street, and then, before I could speak to him, bolted for his life?"

"I believe that is the very individual. You will perhaps understand why he bolted before this lady has finished. Ten thousand apologies for my interruption."

"My foster-brother," went on Miss Galstin, treating the interruption as if it were nothing at all, "has his good points; he also has his bad ones from which I was to surfer. I told him to be outside my apartment that night at a certain time, when perhaps I would give him a little parcel with which he was to start to London that same night, by a route which I would explain to him, and deliver to a certain person whose name and address he should also have. He had been to London twice before, so he knew something about the way. I bought his tickets, I looked into the matter of his passport, I made everything ready; then the evening came, and with it Nikol--"

"Hush, hush!" The reproof came again from the stranger. "No names."

"What does a name like that matter? No one here knows who I mean. He had dined very well surprisingly well. He was sillier than ever. Without my saying a word he took out the pearls from I know not where. At sight of them my eyes sparkled, my mouth watered. He not only showed, he gave them to me. He said, 'You can have them to keep for ever. They are a present from me.' I had no reason to suppose that they were his to give, but that he did give them to me I swear. I had a bottle of champagne opened. I said, 'I will go and put them on; you shall see what they look like on me.' He sat down with the champagne, I went off with the pearls. I put them in a little box which I had ready, I made the box into a parcel, I gave the parcel to Alexis, my foster-brother. I said to him, 'Off you go to London now, at once. You have plenty of time to catch the train, but waste no time. You have all the directions, you have money go!' Alexis went, as I hoped and trusted, to London; I went back to my visitor. He was so engaged with the champagne that he had forgotten all about the pearls he did not even look to see if I had them on. I called on my servant; together we got him down to his auto, which was standing in the street outside the door we sent him home. Hardly had he gone than there came this person."

She designated the Princess Kitty with a little movement of her hand.

"Person!" exclaimed that lady. "And, after all, what are you?"

"She was most impertinent. I instructed my servant that I was not at home to any visitor. She affected not to believe it. She would not go away. She thrust herself into my apartment."

"And there I found you."

"None the less, I did not wish to see you. I was not at home to you."

"So soon as I saw you I suspected you of playing a trick. I had heard about you before; I knew your character; I never trusted you."

"You never trusted me! You! My character! What do you know of character?"

"I asked you politely where was the person I was to meet. You had the impudence to pretend you did not understand. I said to you, 'Where are the Romanoff pearls?' You had the assurance to tell me that it was no concern of mine. I knew then that we were to be cheated. When Konstantin came--"

Miss Galstin favoured Mr. Yashvin with another little movement of her hand; her manner suggested the sublimated essence of scorn.

"This is Konstantin this thing this scum of the street!"

"When Konstantin came we demanded of you to tell us what had become of the Romanoff pearls. We guessed, of course, that you had betrayed us; all the same we should have forced you to tell us what trick you had played if we had not been interrupted."

"Do not be so sure. Your 'Konstantin' would have had an uncomfortable half hour."

"No doubt you would not have confessed willingly; but for that we were prepared." NEW PAGE

CHAPTER XXXVII
MRS. VAN GROOT DISCLAIMS RESPONSIBILITY

"It must have been rather an amusing scene between these three persons." This was the stranger, who interposed with the apparent intention of playing the part of peacemaker. "But let us not recall it too intimately, or the amusement might begin all over again. Let it be enough to say that, as the Princess Kitty puts it, they were interrupted; let us also add that the pearls, which Miss Galstin had handled with such delicate diplomacy, did not leave that night for London. She has told you that her foster-brother has his weak points. One of them is that he suffers from an unquenchable thirst. She made a mistake when she told him that there was plenty of time for him to catch the train; to enable him to pass it to the best advantage he went to an establishment where they sold very bad drink to persons such as he, and in half an hour he was drunk so drunk that he chattered to a stranger who was sitting by him. He told him that that night he was taking to London something of the greatest value; he even showed him the brown paper parcel. When he was too drunk to know what was happening, his neighbour relieved him of the parcel. He went with it to another establishment of the same kind. He unfastened it to enable him to examine its contents, when he was interrupted by an agent of police. He was a notorious thief, and the agent, who was in disguise, knew him very well; he took him and his parcel to the station-house. It chanced this is n world of chance! that there had lately been appointed a new Prefect of Police, Stepan Korsunsky; that evening he was paying a visit to the officer in charge of that station. As he was passing through the outer office the thief was brought in by the agent. The Prefect stopped to inquire what was the matter; the agent showed what he had found in the possession of his prisoner. The Prefect was not as is sometimes the case a wholly ignorant man; at one time he had had something to do with the custody of the crown jewels. When he saw the star he no doubt started; it is possible that he recognised the pearls. He took them a I way with him no doubt intending to give the question of how they came into that man's possession careful consideration."

The speaker paused as if he also were considering.

"The proper course to be pursued by a person in his position is not always so plain as it might be; certain of the crown jewels had had we will say curious adventures before. Korsunsky had got himself into serious trouble before, on an occasion when, chancing on certain rings which he knew to be crown property, he had rushed off with them to what he had supposed to be the proper authorities. The proper authorities had not been grateful. The rings had been associated with certain incidents which made them desirous that their very existence should be blotted from the world. Their reappearance was the last thing they desired. Before the incident was closed Korsunsky had had reason to know it. He remembered that experience when he was so unexpectedly confronted by the pearl star. He did not know what to do, nor where to go. A whisper had reached him that one of the Grand Duchesses was suspected of improper dealings with certain of the family jewels. If there was anything in the report it might cost him his post if he produced that pearl star. In Russia an unwritten law obtains in all matters where the royal family is concerned; it is expressed in one word Silence. No royal person can do wrong; it is the rule that if any official discovers that wrong has been done it is his duty to say nothing about it. Korsunsky carried that pearl star about with him all night and the day following."

Again the speaker paused, as if in search of the most appropriate words in which to clothe his meaning.

"There are spies in all the countries of the world; in Russia everyone is a spy. That statement is not taken literally, but it is a fact that the government is conducted on the principle that everyone is spying upon everyone else. Look at me! I spy on the world the world spies on me; it is only a question of who spies best. It is certainly the case that there are probably dozens of persons spying on a Prefect of Police. He does nothing which is not reported unofficially. Although not a word had been said, in the morning many persons knew that overnight he had come into possession of a remarkable pearl star. Yashvin here is an example of the spy who is to the manner born. A spy himself, he is in communication with spies who spy for him. It seems that someone came along and told him about that star. He jumped at a conclusion in a moment, that it was possible that somehow the Prefect had got hold of the star the Romanoff pearls. He caused certain inquiries to be made which convinced him that he was right. He went with his story to the Princess Kitty. In the evening of the following day the Prefect was murdered in the open street. It is not for us, at this moment, to attempt to apportion the blame; it was said that the crime was the work of Nihilists. Where Russia is concerned, 'Nihilist' is a word which covers a multitude of things. It may be mentioned that on the previous night a burglary had been committed at the Prefect's apartments. It was not stated what the burglars were looking for, but it was generally understood that they went empty-handed away. Some of the persons who had been connected with that burglary were in some way associated with the murder. When the Prefect fell, a person in uniform was standing close by. He came to the Prefect's assistance, unbuttoning his tunic to learn where the wound was. Whether he did learn is not known. When inquiries came to be made later, this individual seemed to have vanished off the face of the earth; his identity has never been discovered and no pearl star was found on the Prefect's person or in his apartment. This may be said to be the point at which I first came upon the scene; but before passing to my personal association with the matter, I will pause to ask Mrs. Van Groot seriously to consider if at least a certain part of the responsibility for this long catalogue of crime, and even bloodshed, may not be placed on her."

If Mrs. Van Groot seemed for a moment to be slightly ruffled the inclination passed and she gaily continued to beam. She took up the work of art in the millinery line on which Catherine was engaged and she held it up to the general view.

"Miss Fraser, it's a very fine hat you're making, but be careful! If any lone lorn woman sees this hat when it is made, and mentions to her young man that she'd like it, and he breaks in to steal it, and spills a box of matches in striking a light to see where it is, and the room catches fire, and the house burns down, and the whole block, and ninety-seven people, and fifteen dogs, and thirteen cats are burnt with it, the fault will be yours. This gentleman, who tells a very good tale very well, will explain to you how that is I can't. You should not make such a hat, you really shouldn't, because I shall feel like breaking in myself to get it." She held up the hat still higher. "Isn't that the great temptation, Mr. Man?" NEW PAGE

CHAPTER XXXVIII
HIS FIRST APPEARANCE

The stranger regarded Mrs. Van Groot, a little satiric something on his face which was not quite a smile and not quite a sneer. Catherine, as she glanced his way, thought what a difference there was between him and the Abednego P. Thompson she had known on the boat; she could hardly believe that the two persons were the same. Thompson, so crude, so uncouth, so angular; this man such an excellent example of the cosmopolitan man of the world.

"Mrs. Van Groot," he said, "hardly presents the case as it actually is. The person who naturally desires Miss Fraser's beautiful hat can scarcely be compared to the multi-millionaire who incites impecunious creatures to gain possession of private property, well knowing that it can only be obtained by crime. To pass on to my part in the drama."

The speaker indulged in another of the pauses which punctuated his narrative.

"It should be stated," he went on, "that I am not prepared to vouch for the literal accuracy of all I am about to say; that, however, it presents the truth as a whole I do guarantee. I was officially informed of the loss of the Romanoff pearls on the afternoon of the day on which Stepan Korsunsky was murdered. I was at the same time furnished with a variety of details which made me think. Certain instructions were given me. In less than an hour afterwards I learned that there were certain persons in America who would like to have those pearls, and, indeed, were prepared to pay an enormous sum of money to get them. The service to which I belong has innumerable channels of information. Mr. Bennington should have known that."

Mr. Bennington did not allow the innuendo that he was ignorant to pass unchallenged. He quietly remarked:

"I did know; I even knew that you knew; but I was of opinion that if the matter was properly handled we might beat you. The service to which you belong has been beaten before."

"Of that I was conscious; the consciousness acted as a spur. When I learned that a market for the pearls existed on this side, I was almost as certain that they would be recovered as if I already had them in my hand; but at the same time I was aware that the would-be buyers in New York might prove more difficult to deal with than an ordinary criminal. Your amateur thief with brains and money is apt to beat the professional every time. I knew, because I had had dealings with Mr. Bennington before and he had beaten me."

The two men eyed each other for some moments in silence. In appearance they presented a striking contrast. The one so unpretending, so unobtrusive, so likely to pass unnoticed in a crowd; the other so striking, so unusual, so sure to attract attention anywhere.

"The first thing I had to do was to obtain at least some vague idea of what had become of the pearls. That Korsunsky had been killed for the sake of them, that they had been taken from his inanimate body, was obvious. Inquiries I set on foot made me practically certain that the person in uniform who had been near at hand at the time of the crime was the individual we know as Yashvin."

Mr. Yashvin started and vehemently protested.

"It's a lie! How dare you to say such a thing? You cannot prove it!"

"Be not so sure; be careful before you say positively that such a thing cannot be proved. However, that is by the way. Mr. Yashvin is a clever man. That night he appeared at a fashionable restaurant appeared, mind you, within a very few minutes of the murder where he made merry the whole night long. In his absence the rooms in which he lived were searched without result. The apartments occupied by the Princess Kitty were also searched there were no pearls there. I, however, ascertained that Yashvin had been driven from his quarters to the restaurant in a public conveyance which we in Russia call a drosky, whose driver had rather an unfortunate record, besides having been associated with Yashvin in more than one curious episode. It was not my wish to call Mr. Yashvin's attention to the fact that the pursuers were closer than he perhaps thought; my instructions were at all costs to avoid a scandal. The driver of the drosky was asked no questions; but it was learnt from a friend of his that at a certain point he had been met by his wife, who had brought him his evening meal. The fact that it was not his wife's usual custom to do anything of the kind was suspicious. The next day a visit was paid to his wife by a feminine friend. This person was so intimate a friend that she knew everything about her. Directly she came into the living-room she felt that something was missing. The wife had a brother who had also been a drosky driver, among other things. Circumstances had arisen which had made it advisable that he should remove himself to as great a distance as he conveniently could. He had left the sort of uniform he had worn as a driver behind him; it had always hung upon a certain peg. The visitor saw in an instant that it was no longer there. The wife noticed that she was struck by its absence, and volunteered the statement that she had sent it to her absent brother; she had packed it up and sent it, she said, the night before. When the report reached me I wondered if Yashvin had given the pearls to the driver, and the driver to his wife, and if his wife had got rid of them in the parcel in which she had despatched that costume. The visitor, not wishing to arouse suspicion, had not asked where the parcel had gone, and would probably not have been told the truth if she had. I have learnt, from another quarter, that certain persons had left the city in a hurry. No attempt was made to stop them though they quite easily might have been stopped. Their destination, it was understood, was London."

The speaker stopped as if to collect his thoughts.

"There are two cities in Europe which have caused the authorities in Russia a good deal of trouble. One is Geneva, which is the resort of a certain section of individuals who may be called intellectual revolutionaries, whose business seems to be to ferment the discontent which is bound to exist in a great country like Russia; again and again they have brought it to the danger point. The second city is London. London, in a sense, may be called a dust-bin. Disreputable characters of all sorts and kinds at some period of their careers have made it their residence.

We in Russia sometimes know a good deal about things of which we are supposed to know nothing. For instance, as a rule we are acquainted with the haunts frequented by fugitives from Russian justice, whose whereabouts are imagined to be an impenetrable secret. There are reasons why we often do not wish our knowledge of their existence to become known; frequently so long as such persons keep themselves out of Russia we are content. In a certain shabby street in London there is a house which has been the resort of such persons for quite a considerable space of time. There are reasons to believe that some of the wretches connected with the murder of Stepan Korsunsky were making for it as fast as they could. I had a code telegram one morning to inform me that the rascal suspected of being the actual murderer had already arrived there."

The speaker once more addressed himself in particular to Mrs. Van Groot, illustrating his words with movements of his hands.

"You drop a stone into a pool, a circle appears often two or three which continue to extend until the whole surface of the water has been covered. You dropped your stone into a pool when you instructed your husband to obtain for you that pearl necklace--"

"I never did instruct him fancy instructing Parker! I merely dropped a hint. Can't a woman drop a hint to her own husband?"

"The disturbance caused by your stone grew and grew until it reached two of the most innocent persons in the world in the first place, Mr. Hugh Beckwith through him, Miss Fraser. Mr. Beckwith will tell you if one day you care to question him how, half beside himself with chagrin at having lost his situation, he walked the streets of London until, passing a certain house, something thrown from an upper window fell on his head and all that came of it. The something which was thrown was a bag containing coins intended for Miss Galstin's foster-brother, who, half out of his mind because of the mess he had made of things, was waiting in the street, penniless and hungry. Afraid to tell his foster-sister that he had lost her parcel, he had taken advantage of the ticket and money she had given him to get to London where he had found himself the recipient of a very cold welcome. The inmates of the house were aware that he was out in the street, and when Mr. Beckwith knocked at the door to learn how the bag came to have tumbled on his head, rather hastily they took it for granted that it was he, and handled Mr. Beckwith rather roughly. When they discovered their mistake they dared not let him go.

Full of terror of avenging justice, they feared that if they did let him go he would certainly bring the police upon them. It seems that Korsunsky's actual assassin was present in the house. They were a penniless lot he had not the wherewithal to procure a change of clothing. At his instigation they stripped Mr. Beckwith of his clothes, of which the ruffian possessed himself in exchange for his own filthy rags."

Pausing, the speaker raised his hand, as if he desired to make a special demand upon their attention.

"How short-sighted is a criminal! These wretches were in actual possession of what they had sold their souls to obtain and did not know it. My suspicions had been correct the drosky driver's coat had been used as a cover for the pearls. A parcel had reached this house addressed to Isaac Rothenstein. In his absence it had been opened people of that sort do not stand much on ceremony. When it was found what it contained, the dirty old coat was thrown contemptuously aside, and, presumably, as a sort of joke, Mr. Hugh Beckwith was forced to put it on. In that coat he passed the night in a cellar; still wearing it, next morning he escaped from the house."

The speaker lowered his voice, as if, at this point, he was addressing them in the strictest confidence.

"A little bird who sings little songs to the department with which I am connected twittered this part of the story. He was present, I understand, at that house at the time. His report, for which he received a few shillings the price of treachery among these sort of people is very low reached me in New York. I found it amusing. It seems that Miss Galstin's trustworthy foster-brother had arranged to be at that house on a certain day, and she was to meet him in a street at the back. She was there. A man in a pony-skin coat came rushing towards her. Whether she mistook him for her foster-brother she will be able to inform you. Anyhow, she took him on board her motor car, and to the house in which Mr. Stewart was residing. Mr. Stewart's surprise, and her surprise, when they discovered who the person in the pony-skin coat really was, must have been worth seeing. But their kindness to a complete stranger, who happened at the moment to be very much in need of assistance, was not to go unrewarded. How they lighted on the Romanoff pearls I don't know, but between them they did sewn in the lining of the pony-skin coat intended for Mr. Rothenstein. Poor Isaac Rothenstein! I made my actual first personal appearance on the scene that same night. Miss Fraser will recall the occasion." He addressed himself to Catherine. "You remember our first encounter?"

Catherine's manner suggested the impression which the meeting had made upon her. There was conviction in her tone.

"I'm never likely to forget it."

"Nor, Miss Fraser, am I. It brought me into contact with one of the few women in the world I have learned to respect."

The stranger pressed his hand to his heart as he bowed low to Catherine.

"It was at Bedford Station. I was in the train which was taking me to the boat at Liverpool. By that time I had learnt about the great temptation."

"I would rather you did not use that phrase the great temptation."

This was Mrs. Parker Van Groot she seemed slightly annoyed. The stranger made a little gesture with his hands.

"Possibly, madam; but to me it appears that no other phrase describes the situation so well. I repeat that by that time I had heard of the great temptation with apologies to Mrs. Parker Van Groot. Information flowing through the usual underground channels had reached the department that on or about a certain date the pearls were to be delivered to a distinguished gentleman in New York. Whereabouts they were at that moment no one seemed to know, I felt that the best thing for me to do was to pay a personal visit to New York if possible incognito. The distinguished gentleman who was to receive the pearls would no doubt be delighted to return them to an accredited agent of their rightful owners. When Miss Fraser entered the compartment at Bedford in which I happened to be I was at once struck by three things. In the first place, I was struck by the lady herself if she will permit me to say so; she appealed to me in a fashion in which very few women have done. Her simplicity, her honesty, her courage I admire these qualities because I so seldom meet them I knew at once that I had met them in her. In the second place, information had just reached me that Mr. Stewart, the arch-plotter, was outside the station in a motor car and this innocent lady had just parted from him. This piece of information being so startling gave me furiously to think. In the third place, I had seen the Princess Kitty on the platform and she had seen Miss Fraser. She was taking stock of Miss Fraser in a fashion which, knowing the Princess as I did, made me think still more. It was all very droll."

The stranger smiled with an appreciation of the humorous side of the situation which was perhaps a little hidden from his friends.

"When, on the steamer, I found the lady of the train, and the Princess Kitty, and Mr. Yashvin, the plot thickened. There was a person, a young man, in a state-room, in whom these three persons took a most lively interest. It did not take me long to put two and two together, and to come to the conclusion that the Princess Kitty, and Mr. Yashvin, were of opinion that the missing pearls were in the possession of either the young man in the state-room or of Miss Fraser. I was not long in deciding that the young man had not got them."

"How did you find that out?" The question was Catherine's.

"My dear Miss Fraser, it is not difficult to draw deductions from unconsciously candid statements made by a gentleman of Mr. Beckwith's sociable habit of mind. Mr. Beckwith will tell you here he is that he did not breathe a word about the pearls to a soul on board that ship. Let me not suggest a contradiction; but shortly after we left England I knew he had not got them. About you I was not so certain. You have a curious knack of keeping your own counsel."

"Do you mean to say that you were trying to pump me all the time you were telling me those extraordinary stories about yourself?"

"The word 'pump' is perhaps misplaced."

"I thought you quite a nice man. After this I shall feel that you can't trust anyone."

"You can't, Miss Fraser, you can't. One conclusion I did arrive at that you knew where the pearls were."

"How on earth did you find that out?"

"Unless I made my remarks already too long much longer, it would not be easy to explain. What you had done with them, where they were on that point I failed to glean from you the slightest information as was the case with the Princess Kitty and Mr. Yashvin. But, unlike them, I recognised that I was beaten and resolved to await, with such patience as I could, my meeting with that distinguished gentleman."

Here the speaker slightly inclined his head towards Mr. Bennington.

"Before I reached New York I had a slight attack of illness, and Miss Fraser an adventure from which she barely escaped with her life. Miss Fraser, there were three persons who were trying to take advantage of the fact that you were alone on board that ship; you were more than a match for all three my felicitations!"

Catherine's manner did not suggest that she was gratified by the compliment which he apparently intended to pay her.

"Thank you, I would rather be without your congratulations. You may be satisfied with the part you played; I am dissatisfied with the part I played."

She gathered together the bank-notes, which had been lying on the hood of the Bath chair.

"Hugh," she said, "what am I to do with these?"

Hugh Beckwith's reply was succinct; it came instantly.

"Give them back to Mr. Stewart. We don't want money got like that."

"So I think." Catherine crossed with the notes in her hand to Mr. Stewart. "Here's your blood-money; keep it."

She thrust the notes into Mr. Stewart's astonished hand. Without another word, she returned to the Bath chair, where she stood with Hugh Beckwith's two hands held in both of hers. Crossing the room, the stranger rang the bell.

"What are you doing?" cried Mr. Stewart, seeming as startled as if the other had sounded a tocsin of alarm.

Before anyone had a chance even to attempt to reply to the inquiry the door opened and a short, plump, round-faced man came into the room. He was dressed in a suit of dark blue serge; he carried a hard felt hat in his right hand. When he was in he looked at the stranger as he stood at attention. The stranger had placed himself at the table, close to the piece of chamois leather.

"Come here," he said. The new-comer moved briskly towards him. "Do you recognise these?"

He motioned towards the objects which were lying on the piece of chamois leather.

The new-comer placed his hat on the table. He took a jeweller's glass out of his coat pocket. Picking up the objects gingerly with a tiny pair of padded tweezers, he examined each carefully through the lens which he had fitted in his eye. When he had examined them all.

"They are the Romanoff pearls," he said.

"You are sure of that?"

"Certain. I have known them intimately for more than twenty years."

"You hear?" The stranger spoke to Mr. Parker Van Groot. "This gentleman is one of the keepers of the Russian crown jewels. He recognises these pearls as the property of the Russian royal family. Will you give them up at once, or do you prefer that we take the matter into the courts?"

Mr. Van Groot took scarcely a moment to arrive at a decision. His reply was prompt.

"You can have them, right now. I wish I had never heard of the things! Only I should like to point out to you that I've paid for them a million dollars, which is certainly more than they would fetch in the open market."

"You cannot say that. I believe you are in error, but that is by the way. You have been guilty of a criminal action, Mr. Van Groot; you and Mrs. Van Groot and Mr. Bennington between you. You have incited to robbery. However, there are reasons, as you will have gathered, why we are as anxious to avoid scandal as you are. Where are your million dollars?"

"He has them." Mr. Van Groot pointed to Stewart.

The stranger turned to the gentleman at whom the other pointed.

"Hand over that money."

Stewart made a feeble attempt at bluster.

"I don't see why I should! The bargain was--"

The stranger turned to the man in the blue serge suit.

"Ring the bell."

Before the order could be obeyed Stewart went rushing towards the table.

"Here's your money." He addressed the stranger. "You score!"

The stranger rejoined.

"The Suvarov is in the harbour. The intention was to put the lot of you on board I don't think there would be much objection raised by the authorities here and ship you to Russia, to be dealt with there. However, that intention has been altered. We are going to leave you here." He inclined his head towards Mrs. Van Groot. "Madam, your obedient servant."

The lady rejoined, "Sir, you have not behaved as if you were."

The stranger retorted, "Madam, I am a slave to duty. Miss Fraser, will you permit me to shake your hand?"

No," said Catherine, "I don't think I will."

Then she relented. "However, I don't mind. I liked you very much on board the ship; and I don't know that I altogether blame you for being so deceitful. You're rather a splendid sort of man. Goodbye."

"Good-bye. The world is small. It may be my good fortune to meet you again. There are some who tell me that it is a good thing to be married I hope you may find it so." He picked up the photograph which was lying on the table, glancing from it to the original. "Mr. Hugh Beckwith? It is a good likeness. So the pearls were here?"

Catherine explained on lines of her own.

"I saw the photograph standing on the sitting-room mantelpiece when Mr. Stewart was talking to Hugh. The instant I saw it an idea came into my mind. When Mr. Stewart agreed to entrust me with the twenty-two pills, I took the photograph out of the room with me. I opened the back, filled the space with wadding, packed the pills in the wadding. Then I told mother to put the phonograph into a cardboard box, and the box into brown paper, and send it just as it was, addressed to me at the General Post Office, New York to be left till called for. Mr. Stewart was afraid of what might happen to the pills if he sent them through the post; no doubt he had his own reasons for being afraid; I wasn't. I had no doubt that they would reach me safely. They did. As you say, it is an excellent likeness of Hugh."

"An excellent likeness. Miss Fraser, you are a woman of resource. Once more, not good-bye, but au revoir. I also feel sure of one thing; that is that we shall meet again. Until then."

Bowing in turn to Mr. Van Groot, Mr. Bennington,

Nurse Ada, Hugh Beckwith, and Dr. Rasselton, the stranger left the room; preceded by the man in the blue serge suit, who had the pearls in a leather case which he had placed in a pocket inside his waistcoat. NEW PAGE

CHAPTER XXXIX
"THE JOYOUS BRIDE"

The stranger had left the room. The letter-case which had originally come from Mr. Bennington lay on the table, where Mr. Stewart had tossed it. It was open. The string which had secured it had been untied, the drafts it contained peeped out.

Mr. Stewart and his friends looked at each other. There was this great sum waiting, so it seemed, for anyone who chose to pick up. Mr. Parker Van Groot stood a little way back from the table. Mr. Bennington, a little in front of him, looked as if he scarcely knew what to make of the situation. Mr. Yashvin, white-faced, wild-eyed, made a sudden movement towards the table, his attitude suggesting some predatory beast of prey. His hooked fingers were held in front of him like claws.

"As I live," he exclaimed, "I won't be robbed of everything! Give me some of that money. I have done what I undertook to do, I have earned it. Give me the money!"

As he was stretching out his claw-like fingers, again the door opened: someone else came in; a man in height about five feet eight or nine, squarely built, straight as a ramrod.

"What is that gentleman doing there?" he inquired as he came in.

All turned to look at him. He was in uniform; whether he was soldier or civilian was not clear; that he was somebody in authority was beyond a doubt. He was clean-shaven, broad-browed, square-jawed.

"I am sorry to trouble you." He glanced towards the table. "You, Mr. Van Groot, and you, Mr. Bennington, know who I am. I daresay some of you others do also. If you don't you may have all the information you require."

He held a pocket-book in his hand, which he opened and began to study.

"I don't know whether or not to read you certain notes which I have here; they are sort of studies for biographical notices. You are the person who calls himself Paul R. Stewart you are Isaac Rothenstein you are Konstantin Ivanovitch, known also as Vladimir Yashvin. This note-book of mine has memoranda about which would supply the papers with some of the best copy they have had for years. Cara Oudinoff, Darya Galstin those are the names, ladies, by which I understand you wish at present to be known. There are pretty little stories here about you, also, any one of which would sell an edition. Whether I shall have to read them aloud or worse cause them to be published, is rather for you than for me to decide. I think it would be as well, if possible, that anything of the kind should be avoided. A nod is as good as a wink to a blind horse."

With that oracular utterance the speaker shut his note-book with a little snap. With a twinkle in his eyes, and a glimmer of a smile about his lips, he continued to make a little speech.

"Ladies and gentlemen, there has recently quitted this room a gentleman who is not particularly anxious to enter into personal details about himself.

The same retiring modesty marks me. I want to go so slightly into family history that I am not even keen on giving you my name. You can call me Captain Blunderbuss if you like or just anything you darned well please. At the same time, if you feel that way, you can have enough personal details to fill you up to the neck; and you shall have my name, title, and profession thrown at you so hard that you would sooner it had been a gun."

To what extent the speaker was in jest or in earnest it would not have been easy to determine; but in his humorous manner of speech there was a sinister something which had an uncomfortable effect upon his hearers.

"I am going to make you a proposition which, mind you, I have no right whatever to make. If you feel that strongly you've only got to say so, and the irregularity shall go by the board, and you shall have the full majesty of the law in all its glory; in which case may the Lord have mercy upon your souls! Mercy is the thing you'll be most in want of."

The speaker, reopening his note-book, referred to it again, continuing with his eyes fixed on the page:

"I've come upon some poison in my time, but according to what's written here you do seem to be the most poisonous crowd I ever have struck. What I want to know is what is to be done with you. There's a squad of police outside; shall I have them in and have you jugged and extradited and sent in chains to Russia, where you'll be fried in boiling oil? Or would you rather we played the game another way? I'll tell you just what that other way is, then you'll be able to choose; the choice will be up to you."

Re-closing his note-book, his glance passed from one face to the other as if he found them quite amusing to look at.

"There's a nice little ship not so far away from this, with a nice captain and officers and crew, and all the necessary trimmings. It's going for a voyage round Cape Horn and back up the Golden Gate. If there are any among you five who would like to travel by that ship, you can. The intention of that trip will be to deport you; you are undesirable aliens you know you are. This country has no use for you it never had. We've got enough bad men of our own without importing them. That ship will make certain calls on its way to the Golden Gate, and at each call it will drop one of you; a good long way apart, so there will be no risk of your skipping over to pay each other an afternoon call. And before going on that ship you'll be required to sign certain papers which are waiting for me at the police station which I frequent. They will be in the nature of undertakings not to return to this land of the free; and, as I understand you all have money, you will be required to pay in advance for your passages on board that ship."

He bestowed upon the five collectively an affable little grin.

"Now, ladies and gentlemen, which is it to be? I regret to learn that you have been guilty of various offences against the law of this country; I won't go into them at this time and place, but you know you have. Will you be tried for them and punished, and, having served your sentences you know you will be sentenced be passed for extradition and returned to Russia, or will you pay for your passages on board that ship? The boat will be sailing before to-morrow morning; you'll have to be aboard in a couple of hours, so you haven't much time to make your choice."

He began to punctuate his words with his notebook.

"Mind you, I'm not here as an official, I'm here as a private individual to make you a little private proposition, strictly between ourselves. I don't mind telling you that, like the gentleman who has just quitted, we want this thing done quietly; we want to avoid fuss if we can. We don't want anyone to know that such poison ever reached these shores. If it so much as becomes suspected you are goners. That part of the remainder of your lives which you don't spend in gaol here you will in Russia. You know what awaits you there; they have their own way of dealing with such as you. In America we do everything by rule and compass; we countenance no irregular tampering with the established law; so again I tell you that if you want me to call in that squad of police and have you run off in the wagon to you know where you've only to say so, and the law shall be vindicated in the eyes of all men. And won't you be sorry! Now, say! quick! which is it to be? The ship or the law? Let's have it from you individually, starting with the ladies. Miss Galstin, how would you prefer to have it?"

Rapid glances were exchanged by Miss Galstin and Mr. Stewart. Her reply was prompt.

"I prefer the ship. Will Mr. Stewart and I go together?"

"How do you mean, will you go together? You'll all of you go together, all the five; but you won't be dumped together not much! Haven't I been telling you? You'll be shot ashore maybe at Pernambuco and the gentleman at Valparaiso that's how we're going to play this game. We're going to have you as far apart as can well be managed; we don't want to be too hard on those unfortunate lands. Now, Miss Oudinoff you say."

"I also choose the ship; but I deny your right to separate me from Mr. Yashvin."

"Deny! that's the way to do it. Wave the flag of your country and stand no fooling. But I may tell you that Mr. Yashvin, as you call him, who I am told is the worst poison in the crowd, will probably be dropped at Tierra del Fuego, the last place on earth, where he'll be all alone by himself, and you somewhere round Chile. I don't quite know how far those two places are apart, but they're quite a distance. It's about as difficult to get from one to the other as it is to get from here to the moon and it takes quite a while to do that. Now, Mr. Rothenstein, you next; how is it to be?"

The old gentleman addressed began to show emotion in his usual way, by treating them to a sort of ungainly, crab-like dance.

"I will not go on the ship. I have done nothing. I'm a good man; it is I who have been wronged! You shall not do with me as you please!"

"Good we won't; we'll do with you as you please yours is the way. You are arrested, Isaac Rothenstein, on the charge, to begin with, of inciting to robbery and murder. After you're through whatever you get if a man of your apparent age lives to get through it you shall be returned to Russia, the land which gave you birth. You won't live through what they're likely to give you there."

As the speaker began to raise a little whistle to his lips, Mr. Rothenstein redoubled his saltatory exertions.

"I will go on the ship," he screamed, "I will go on the ship!"

"I don't know if it isn't too late to change your mind. I was starting to make a note 'Rothenstein for the wagon.' I doubt if the note I was going to make won't have to stand."

Mr. Rothenstein began to stammer.

"You--you--you did not understand! You--you--you--you did not give me time. I--I--I was about to say from the first that that I would go on the ship!"

"Is that so? Well, we'll take it this once though it was very near a misunderstanding, for sure." He made an entry in his note-book. "Isaac Rothenstein the ship. Maybe they'll drop you at Rio."

"I do not want to be dropped at Rio! I do not want to!"

"Then perhaps they'll make it Buenaventura way up the other side, where the climate's bad. At certain seasons of the year people round there die like flies."

"Nor do I want to be dropped at Buenaventura!"

"Entirely between ourselves, Mr. Rothenstein, you won't be asked. Maybe they'll drop you into the sea, owing to their being dead sick of carrying you. Mr. Stewart, you next."

"I choose the ship."

"That's right--no palavering--just yea or nay. He knows his own mind; that's the sort I like."

"And you--you poisonous insect! how will you have it quick?"

This courteous inquiry was directed to Mr. Yashvin. He showed his teeth, knit his brows, looked like murder, uttered two words:

"The ship."

The other put his whistle to his lips and blew. The door opened. Six men marched into the room, two by two. He with the whistle addressed them curtly.

"Escort these ladies and gentlemen to my quarters. They have all booked passages on board the Joyous Bride. The Joyous Bride, ladies and gentlemen, is the name of the ship on which you are going to travel." NEW PAGE

CHAPTER XL
THE MOST EXPENSIVE HAT IN THE WORLD

There were left in the room Mr. and Mrs. Parker Van Groot, Mr. Bennington, Nurse Ada, Dr. Rasselton, Catherine, and Hugh Beckwith. There was a curious expression on their faces as they stared at the door through which the others had vanished. Mr. Van Groot put up his hand and felt his chin: his glance travelled from the door to Mr. Bennington.

"It's made me feel sort of shivery, that little interview. I'd like something comforting in a tall glass. The Joyous Bride! What a name for a ship with that lot of passengers on board! Bennington, let's take the hint."

Mr. Bennington, unobtrusive as ever, was retying his letter-case, having first glanced at the contents to learn that they were intact.

"We were beaten by Prince Serge Laminoff."

"And who in thunder is Prince Serge Laminoff?"

"He is the head of the Russian Secret Service; he has made of it an almost perfect weapon. He is one of the most remarkable men in Europe."

"Where did he come in? Would you mind explaining?"

"With pleasure. He was the man who appears to have travelled with Miss Fraser as Abednego P. Thompson."

"Was that rude man a prince? I thought his manners were unusual."

This was Mrs. Van Groot.

"In Russia a prince is not the high and mighty dignitary he is in England. His manners are not the only things about Prince Serge Laminoff which are unusual. Had I known that he was out against me I should have retired from the quest of the Romanoff pearls. -. I should have known that I was beaten from the start."

"Your Prince Serge Laminoff, if that was he, certainly does seem to be master of his job. Looks, Isobel, as if we'd have to go without your pearl necklace. It also looks, Miss Fraser, as if you'd had all your adventures for nothing."

Catherine was still standing by the Bath chair, Hugh Beckwith's hands still held in hers. Beckwith's head had dropped a little forward on his chest. Catherine held hers erect; but her eyes were troubled. Mrs. Van Groot interposed.

"Parker, you just don't know what you're talking about. I've had all the pearl necklace I want; I wouldn't put those Romanoff pearls round my neck, not if it was ever so. Mr. Bennington, out of the lot of money you've got in that wallet give me fifty thousand dollars."

"Isobel, what do you want with those fifty thousand dollars?"

"I just want them. They are going to be part of my present. I'm going to buy myself a hat. Did you hear what I said, Mr. Bennington? Hand those dollars over."

Mr. Bennington reopened his letter-case, extracted various slips of paper, and began carefully to count them. The process of counting appeared to strike the impetuous lady as a trifle leisurely.

"If you please, Mr. Bennington, would you think it unladylike of me to ask you to get a move on? Sorry, but I'd love it if you would. All I want's the dollars would you mind just passing them over?" He handed her various slips of paper. u Are there fifty thousand dollars here? It doesn't seem to be much of a pile."

"I think if you will examine those drafts, and add up the sums they stand for, you will find that they represent fifty thousand dollars."

"I don't want to waste time in examining and counting now; if you're wrong you'll hear of it afterwards." She turned to her husband. "Do you think he is right?"

"Shouldn't wonder; he generally is. No need to audit his figures, when it comes to a question of dollars and cents; I'm taking his totals every time."

"Then I will. Now, Miss Fraser, here's a hat. It isn't quite altogether finished, but it's going to be the hat I want. I understood from you that you were going to start in a millinery business; I'm going to be your first customer. I'll buy this hat and here are the dollars to pay for it."

She handed Catherine the bundle of drafts she had received from Mr. Bennington. Catherine gazed at them in amazement.

"Why, Mrs. Van Groot," she inquired, "whatever do you mean?"

"I've bought the hat and they're to pay for it."

"They're to pay for it?" Catherine gazed at the strips of paper.

"You hide them away in some old place, and don't you worry. This is a case when the customer fixes the price of the purchase made. I've fixed it--cash paid, account closed. Now, Miss Fraser, what I want you to do with this hat is just to give it a little twist which will make it seem just the cutest thing on earth. You catch what I mean?"

"No, Mrs. Van Groot, I do not; and you don't catch what I mean. I'm very much obliged, but I cannot take this money from you."

"You've taken it, my dear don't be silly. Now about this hat."

"I'm quite willing to sell you that hat for twelve shillings and sixpence--say three dollars. I'll be glad of cash for that. But I can't have anything to do with these."

"Miss Fraser, a little while ago I thought I was going to be ill. The doctor said that if I was agitated I might be so don't you do any agitating. Dr. Rasselton, you're a doctor; do you think agitation would do me good?"

The doctor, in accordance with what seemed to be his custom, settled his glasses on his nose.

"Agitation is good for no one. I imagine, having in view the peculiarities of your temperament, it might be particularly injurious to you."

"You hear that? Now, Miss Fraser, don't you attempt to force your property on to me, or I'll be agitated right away, and the responsibility will rest on you. Now, Parker, don't you let her! Just you tell her that that money is in payment for the hat. I was to have had the finest pearl necklace in the world; I'll have the most expensive hat instead. I'll trot it round everywhere you'll see them stare. Speak to her, Parker; she may assault me if she's not stopped."

Mr. Parker Van Groot obeyed orders received.

"Miss Fraser, would you be so good as not to assault my wife."

"Mr. Van Groot, I wasn't dreaming of doing anything of the kind."

"Then calm yourself and don't give Mrs. Van Groot a different impression. The money you have there is in payment for a hat. Mrs. Van Groot says she wants the most expensive hat in the world, and my thunder I it seems to me she's got it."

"That makes it seem so absurd; it is really too ridiculous. I will not have this money."

"Miss Fraser, I just have half a dozen words I want to say to you." Mrs. Van Groot's voice and manner had become suddenly curiously serious. "I did it all; I'm the temptress; mine was the great temptation. Every word Prince Serge Laminoff I like the name; I think more of what he did say now that I know that he's a prince said, I knew at the time was true. I do not want to take too large a share of the blame for all that happened upon myself or I'll never be able to stand up straight again; when I think of what you and Mr. Beckwith have suffered, just because I wanted those silly old pearls, I go goose-fleshy all over. I admire you, Miss Fraser I admire you more than I can say; to think that you could do a thing like that just for the love of a man--"

"Just for the love of a man? I'd like to know what there is better worth doing things for. Why, there's nothing I wouldn't do for love of Hugh; and nothing he wouldn't do just for the love of me. Is there, Hugh?"

Mr. Beckwith's reply was brief and sufficiently to the point.

"No, nothing that I'm aware of."

"Which means," interpolated Catherine, "that there is nothing. We were going to do what we did do for five hundred pounds apiece, enough for us to get married on--"

"Preposterous, ridiculous, senseless, idiotic nonsense! You can't get married on two thousand five hundred dollars, or on twice two thousand five hundred dollars. Miss Fraser, I'm a disappointed woman; what's worse, I'm an agitated woman. If my agitation continues to increase as it is doing I won't be answerable for the consequences. I might have a weak heart Parker knows I might have a weak heart--"

"Anyone might have a weak heart," interposed the speaker's husband.

"You hear? Now you understand the risk you're forcing me to run. I've set my heart on having something unique as a birthday present, and I've got it a fifty thousand dollar hat. Maybe my portrait, and the portrait of the hat, will be in all the papers to-morrow, and I'll again be the most famous woman in America until some scheming creature goes one better, and flaunts herself in one at sixty thousand. If there's a competition started in high-class hats there's no knowing where it will get to but it won't get past me, because I'll be the one who started it. I've been the most famous woman in America several times already; I want to fill that niche in the gallery of honour we'll call it a gallery of honour, though the last most famous woman in America has had seven husbands, and killed three of them in five years still once more. Do you really think I'll allow you to thwart my ambition? You're in error. Parker, don't you think that my idea about the most expensive hat in the world is great?"

Mr. Van Groot was cautious.

"I won't say what I think, because my thoughts in matters of this kind don't count. I can only observe generally that your thoughts are mine."

The lady again appealed to Catherine.

"You hear? What did I tell you? Now will you let me buy this hat at my own price? What have I done to you that you should wish to do this thing to me?"

Catherine did not seem to be sure whether to laugh or cry she said so.

"Mrs. Van Groot, I do not know whether you're in jest or earnest. The whole thing is too outrageous. The idea of paying fifty thousand dollars for a hat--"

"What are fifty thousand dollars to me? Think of the circumstances under which they are paid. Dr. Rasselton, are fifty thousand dollars anything to me?"

"I should imagine they're not much to Mr. Parker Van Groot."

"It's the same thing. That's what I said. Once more, you hear? Dr. Rasselton, it's your business to give advice. What do you advise Miss Fraser? '

"I do not know that I'm entitled to meddle in Miss Fraser's private affairs, but, in face of your appeal to me, I think that, on the whole, I should advise her to take the money."

A possibly unexpected endorsement of these views came from Nurse Ada. She came bustling forward, speaking as if in a glow of excitement.

"I should certainly take the money if I were in your place, Miss Fraser. If it means nothing to her, it means all the world to you."

"What an excellent nurse this lady is," observed Mrs. Van Groot. "I shall certainly have her next time I'm ill."

Catherine's comment conveyed that she was considering Nurse Ada's words.

"It certainly would mean all the world to us."

"Then there you are!" cried Mrs. Van Groot. "Whatever else can you want? Why pretend you can't see the right thing you ought to do when you can?"

Nurse Ada laid her hand softly on Catherine's arm, as if to her the situation was full of weighty meaning.

"I should accept it if I were you."

Catherine looked from the nurse to Hugh.

"Would you accept?"

Mr. Beckwith's reply made it evident that, at any rate, he knew his own mind. It consisted of two words only.

"I should."

Catherine knelt down beside the Bath chair, placed the slips of paper in Hugh's hands, bowed her head, and positively cried. Through her tears she managed to say something.

"Thank you, Mrs. Van Groot."

Mrs. Van Groot put her arm round Catherine's neck, lifted her head, and kissed her. NEW PAGE

CHAPTER XLI
THE "MAISON CATHERINE"

Two years afterwards Mrs. Van Groot and Mrs. Beckwith were in a small room, reserved for the use of the more important customers, in the "Maison Catherine," the hat-shop which, although only in its first youth, was already doing so well in a street off Hanover Square. Hats were everywhere; in particular there were a large number spread out upon a table.

"That, I think, makes fifteen," observed Mrs. Van Groot, regarding the hats on the table with dancing eyes.

"It does."

"Then mind you send them round to my hotel this afternoon."

"I will though, if you'll excuse me, I don't see what you can possibly want with fifteen hats."

"Want with fifteen hats! One of the reasons why I've come to Europe is to wear hats; I always wear two, and sometimes three a day. Since I became known as the purchaser of the most expensive hat in the world, I've had to keep up my reputation. Parker buys works of art, and I buy hats; everybody knows it." The lady knitted her pretty brows. "Sometimes it's rather a nuisance. The hats one buys aren't always becoming. Sometimes I make a point of buying hats which don't become me. Once I thought of starting a craze for wearing hats which made one look hideous; but, when people started asking me every time if I was ill, I changed my mind. How's business? On the up grade?"

"Indeed; mounting by leaps and bounds. Do you remember my telling you that I'd like to be the owner of the biggest hat-shop in London? If things go on as they are doing, I shouldn't wonder if one day I was."

"Then I shall be your best client. To be the biggest customer of the biggest hat-shop in the world is just the kind of thing which appeals to me. Besides, now and then, it amuses me to drop a hint that it was I who started you because I did, didn't I?"

"You certainly did; I owe everything to you."

"You don't know how it pleases me to hear you say that; it is so sweet to feel that one has done someone a good turn. You're a dear; if ever I do go into business I'll become your partner. How is Mr. Beckwith?"

"He's all right; he's my managing man. You know he never has quite recovered from what they did to him on that horrible ship, so he gave up the dried fruit trade, and as my manager he's simply invaluable. I tell him that "most of the success of the establishment is owing to the way in which he handles the accounts."

"And how's the family?"

"The family?" One of her rare smiles illumined and transformed Catherine's countenance. "The family is in the next room. I can't do without my baby boy all day and every day, so I have him brought here every afternoon, and he sleeps nearly all the time."

"Goodness! Catherine! Let's go and have a look at him."

So they stole softly into the next room and tiptoed towards the cradle. Mrs. Van Groot bent over it.

"Why, he's awake! Let me take him out and kiss him."

And she did while Catherine smiled.

THE END